GW00722480

HOW
THE WAR CAME

BY

THE EARL LOREBURN

NEW YORK
ALFRED A. KNOPF
1920

CONTENTS

HOW THE WAR CAME

THE Dispatches referred to in this Volume will be found in the "Collected Diplomatic Documents relating to the Outbreak of the European War, printed in 1915 under the Authority of His Majesty's Stationery Office," which contain—

The British White Book or Paper
The French Yellow Book
The Russian Orange Book
The Belgian Grey Book
The Serbian Blue Book
The German White Book
The Austro-Hungarian Red Book

and other documents.

HOW THE WAR CAME

CHAPTER I

INTRODUCTORY

THIS volume has been written in the hope that it may help toward the avoidance of war in future by showing how we came to be suddenly brought into the Great War of 1914. Many volumes would be required and, no doubt, will hereafter be written to recount details. At the present moment our pressing necessity is to escape being overwhelmed by a mass of auxiliary detail and grasp the salient features which are really material. We stand in danger of not being able to see the wood for the trees.

There is a good deal of leeway to make up. From the moment when the war broke out, a sure instinct taught the community as a whole that discussion at such a time about its origin would lead to recrimination, whereas patriotism required that we should stand together in the hour of imminent danger and say only what we might think suited to diminish that danger. So that the public at large held its breath almost in silence. Ministers, however, or some of them, together with a large portion of the Press which was at their back, did not remain silent. They assured us that this war had been for some time inevitable, without explaining why, if that were so, adequate precautions had not been taken to encounter so grave a certainty. And various versions, not always consistent the one with the other, of the diplomatic negotiations that preceded the war, have obtained currency. Few people had the time or opportunity for studying the story as a whole. In the critical days these and other things passed practically without challenge. The mass of documents is so great that it was easy to confuse them.

While the war lasted no criticism of what had gone before or even of what was passing at the time would have met with public approval, except such as might be necessary to prevent blunders being made, or to prevent blunderers from being sheltered by secrecy. But it is to be deplored that outspoken and effective discussion after the war is ended should have been prejudiced in advance by the course things have taken. Nearly all those whose public utterances would most command attention have been in one way or another drawn into positions which disable them from criticizing with effect. Before giving to France on 2nd August 1914 that definite promise of armed naval support against Germany which irrevocably pledged us to war, Mr. Asquith received an undertaking from Lord Lansdowne and Mr. Bonar Law that they would assist him in Parliament. When the war broke out, all the Cabinet Ministers then in office, except two, were persuaded to remain, though some of them did not conceal their dislike of the Ministerial policy.

Their tongues are tied. Nine or ten months later, when naval and diplomatic and military mishaps had reduced the Cabinet to acknowledgment of its own inability to carry on any longer without fresh support, Ministers who had consented to remain against their own judgment were ejected, and room thus made for Conservative recruits. In theory the newly arrived Ministers would not be responsible for errors committed before the Coalition came into being. In practice their acceptance of office may, however unjustly, be construed as an endorsement of the past. This is only one of the unfortunate consequences of a Coalition. Each party to the Coalition possessed or was possessed by an organization of its own, with its central offices in London and an attendant train of newspapers and a network of agents all over the country. Both the Caucuses and all their retinues are committed to the dissemination of whatever views their respective employers may entertain. It is as difficult to catch up an erroneous point of view, when once it has got a start, as it is to overtake an actual falsehood. The point of view presented in these pages is that of a Liberal who has always thought the infusion of Imperialism a source of danger, and who believes that the tragedy of this war would not have come upon us if the Ministers of 1914 had been true to our traditional principles, and outspoken in regard to what they were doing.

One outstanding feature in the whole of this war has certainly been the unprecedented violence of the German Government, and, it must be added, of the Austro-Hungarian Government. Germany could easily have averted war even up to the last,

And after it came, the true character of German warfare has been written in letters of blood all over the face of Europe. With such a background it is easy to paint a picture in which every impression might be lost except that of overpowering horror. If the mind is allowed to dwell only on the terrible side of what has happened it will soon be unable to see anything else. The most serious thing of all is that ever since the war began the expression of honest and reasonable criticism and the publication of accurate news has been made very difficult by the stupid and ill-conceived pressure of the Censorship. Facts have been suppressed or ignored, and untrue conclusions have been fostered in the supposed interest of the nation. If we omit to note disastrous errors of method and policy from which we have suffered in the past, we may suffer from them again. The best course will be to begin by stating in a compendious form the view which is to be presented in this book. Then to make it good. When that is done it will be possible to make practical suggestions for the future. At present when anyone speaks of the secretiveness and consequent weakness of our Ministers the " good party man " and the " good party Press " explode in well-deserved indignation at the guilt of our enemies, as if that disposed of every criticism automatically and left nothing more to be said.ˑ There is a great deal more to be said. Unless the people of this country are prepared to examine these things and take them into their own hands, the same methods of secrecy, the same restlessness and irresolution in policy, the same blindness alike to foreign conditions and to our own true interests that preceded this war may herald us into another.

* * *

The German militarists are never tired of saying that Great Britain planned this war. No man who will honestly consider the available materials can doubt that, when the crisis actually came upon us, Sir Edward Grey exhausted every effort he could think of to convince all the nations concerned of the danger that was at hand. He repeatedly urged concessions and compromises and expedients, almost any one of which would in all probability have succeeded had his advice been generally accepted. There must be a great number of documents relating to this crucial time which will not see the light for years to come ; but those which have been published are obviously genuine, and their tenor is unequivocal. It is impossible to doubt Sir Edward's sincerity in this respect, or his efforts to prevent war. In adopting this course he was acting in accordance with the wishes of practically every inhabitant of the United Kingdom. There had been, it is true, for some years in this country a growing dislike for the peremptory methods of German diplomacy and a growing uneasiness at successive increases of the German Fleet. It was absolutely necessary for the security of these Islands that we should retain our Naval superiority. There had also been a growing distaste of German commercial methods. No one thought of making these grievances a ground for war. When Lord Roberts pressed upon us the necessity of compulsory training, he and his friends carefully pointed out that compulsory service was to be for home defence and not for service abroad. This shows how remote from all men's thoughts was any project of attacking Germany at that time. There were some who thought that Germany would attack us or put us in peril by attacking Belgium. But during the two or three years preceding August 1914, those who knew all, and whose special duty it was to keep in close touch with foreign affairs, frequently assured us that we had no unpublished engagements which bound us to take up arms in a foreign quarrel, and, in particular, that our relations with Germany were excellent. Mr. Haldane, their close confidant, enlarged upon the lofty ideals of the Kaiser, and people took these Ministers at their word. Very likely they believed all they said, and certainly they could never have spoken as they did speak if there had been any sort of intention to quarrel with the Germans. It is needless to enforce this on any Englishman. We all know here how averse this country was from any disturbance of the peace in any quarter of the globe. Any reflection upon Sir Edward Grey, or his colleagues, or the British public, that they desired this war must be dismissed absolutely by anyone who knows the men or the House of Commons of that day or the public opinion of that day.

Nor have our enemies any ground for complaint that Great Britain drew the sword against them. Their military chiefs had reckoned the chances, and come to the conclusion that, as in 1908 so in 1914 Russia would not risk a war. They knew that France would not break the peace unless compelled by her alliance with Russia, and thought that Great Britain would stand aside. Of all this there is abundant proof.

The German military leaders expected that they would be able to repeat with success the "Shining Armour" episode of 1908, and so, without risking a collision, re-establish their diplomatic credit in the Councils of Europe, which had been, as they thought, somewhat tarnished in 1911. Austria expected that by a bloodless victory she could become predominant in the Balkans, and punish the delinquencies of the Servian Government. When these Powers began to realize the truth, their Ministers did indeed make an effort late in the day to procure an understanding with Russia. That would have prevented war. But it was too late. The feeling and the forces created in a protracted worship of false gods, seconded by a panic alarm lest they should be anticipated by a sudden attack on their own frontiers, gave to the Military Party in Germany a fatal opportunity, and the irrevocable step was taken at Berlin. This is the most probable explanation of the German ultimatum. The other version is that their Civil Government had from the beginning decided and worked purely and simply for war. Whichever was the true motive, nothing can entitle our enemies to complain that their action led to resistance. Any Power in the world must expect to meet with resistance which treats its neighbours in such a spirit.

* * *

What the British Ministry of 1914 have to explain is something quite different, and the answer is due not to our enemies but to our countrymen. For generations the fixed practice of this country had been a watchful abstention from the periodical wars and quarrels that broke out on the Continent of Europe.

No one stated this more clearly than Mr. Disraeli. No one acted upon it more constantly than Lord Salisbury and Mr. Gladstone. They avoided all embarrassing exclusive friendships on the Continent. They knew how many deadly animosities and conflicts of interest still survived among European Powers, and they aimed at maintaining good relations with all our neighbours. In this way we might exert a friendly influence in composing differences abroad, for our interests lay wholly in the direction of peace, and in this way we avoided commitments which might compel us to take part in foreign wars and deprive us of an independent control of our own policy.

The reasons which inspired this policy of non-intervention lie upon the surface. We are a settled country, with no unsatisfied ambitions in Europe, or, for that matter, in any part of the world. We have no severed community of our own race to redeem from oppression. We had not, until the advent of this war, any disastrous legacies of national hatred which could preclude relations of complete goodwill with any nation upon earth. We are separated by the sea from all other countries. And in the few instances beyond the sea where the British Empire is coterminous with the possessions of other Great Powers, as in Canada or Africa, the risks of collision had become almost negligible, either by reason of our neighbours' pacific attitude, as in America, or by reason of distance and our command of the sea. On the other hand the Continent of Europe was not a settled continent at all. It was, and for years had been, in constant and most dangerous agitation. A little more must be said presently on this subject. For the moment it may suffice to point out that during the sixty years preceding 1914, every single Great Power on the Continent was repeatedly engaged in Continental War. Not once, but repeatedly; France thrice, Germany thrice, Russia twice, Austria three times, and Italy four times, counting in her case the recent war with Turkey. Great Britain had only once been engaged in a Continental War during those sixty years, namely, the Crimean enterprise of 1854. But Europe was a volcano, in which the fire broke out first at one crater and then at another. You could never be sure how the Powers would group themselves even for a few years ahead. During the sixty years already specified, Russia had been the ally of Germany, and then formed an alliance against her. France had made war against Russia, and then become her ally. Austria had fought Germany and had fought Italy, and then became the ally of both. Further illustration would be superfluous. Was there not immense danger in this country becoming, by alliances or their equivalent, a part of an European system such as that? This was no doubt a reason, the main reason, for the policy of Disraeli, Gladstone, and Salisbury.

* * *

There was another reason for continuing this policy. All the Great Powers on the Continent had adopted universal compulsory service. They could not do otherwise. If once one of them began it, the others had to follow. We, on the other hand, had always made it a cardinal principle to rely upon overwhelming superiority at sea. If we entered upon Continental Alliances, whether formal or in the infinitely more

dangerous guise of " understandings," it was clearly
necessary that we also should have, if not compulsory
service, at all events a population trained to arms.
Rightly or wrongly, however, the advocacy of compulsory military service in England during the few
recent years in which alone it had been advocated at
all, has always been associated with apprehensions of
invasion. If we were fighting single-handed on our
natural element, the sea, a million trained men would
be ample to defend us against any force that could be
landed here, unless the Navy were so destroyed that
the enemy could do what he pleased at sea. We had
no need for a larger land force than that, so far as
home defence goes. But if we were to contemplate
taking part in war on the Continent against great
military powers, we need not one but five or six
millions. And for this reason. Should our Continental Ally be defeated on land, our sea power could
not save him from destruction. All that he possessed,
territory, colonies, money, would be held as a pledge
in pawn to the conqueror, and we, though triumphant
on the sea, would be squeezed by the necessity of
loyally supporting our Ally into making concessions
and surrenders as though we had ourselves been overcome. No alternative would remain. We should
have either to accept the consequences of defeat,
though ourselves undefeated, or we must expect that
our Ally would throw up our friendship in disgust,
and very likely purchase better terms from his conqueror by becoming our enemy. Our Ally would
say—Send armies to help us or make territorial sacrifices to help us. If we did neither, he would consider
himself betrayed and deserted. Any judicious con-

queror would then say to him—You see that England
is selfish and faithless. Abandon her `alliance ; we
offer you easy conditions of peace if you will become
our friend instead of our enemy, and in due time we
will together have a reckoning with England.

All these things lie on the surface. The statesmen
already named .could not have ignored them. Even
Lord Palmerston, the most adventurous of our Foreign
Ministers, did not tie our hands till the occasion arose.
In short, the keynote of our Foreign policy was to keep
our hands really free from any Continental entangle-
ment, so that we might be able to decide our own
policy for ourselves, and to regard our Fleet as our
main instrument in the event of war. Reliance on the
Fleet alone was an impossible course if we were to take
a hand in the quarrels of the Continent in these days of
universal Continental conscription. So our policy for
generations had been not to take a hand in the quarrels
of the Continent.

* * *

No doubt a completely different policy was quite
open to this country if it thought fit. We might have
resolved to depart from the old lines. We might have
resolved to take a real share in the damaging inheritance
of international hatreds and jealousies and afflictions
which have been bequeathed to our Continental
neighbours, the fruit of horrible wars and horrible
misgovernment in times past. Not that we could have
anything to gain thereby. The sole motive for such
a course, if we exclude the idea of a quixotic ambition
to redress the wrongs of mankind, would have been
the fear of injury to ourselves by the excessive growth
of some military power, in this instance Germany.

Assuming that this was the proper course, then certain obvious precautions became indispensable. In the first place, this country would have to be placed upon a military footing that should correspond with its new policy. This meant not an addition of twenty or fifty or even a hundred thousand men, or a hundred batteries of artillery, but such a wholesale levy as should enable us to place millions of soldiers on the Continent to face millions of adversaries. For armaments depend on policy. Suppose that this country had, with its eyes open, resolved to support France in arms against Germany. If we should be bound in honour to fight with France against Germany, having regard to the numerical disparity of their populations, it was pretty obvious that either we must fight alongside of her on land, or, if we refused, must accept her defeat as our defeat and pay a full share of the damages, together with the bitter cost of shame for having left our Ally to her own military resources, while she was being ruined and we were secure behind our Fleet in our own Island. Therefore an Army on the Continental scale would be needed if we should embark upon a new Foreign policy of this kind. In fact, however, no one—or if some passing suggestion of this sort can be disinterred from the mountains of forgotten oratory—then it is enough to say that no Minister of State, or ex-Minister, or man of recognized weight, either in Parliament or out of it, suggested that we ought to be prepared with an Army on such a scale, or anything like it, for service on the Continent. Those who were in favour of keeping this country free from Continental entanglements and wars had no occasion for such an Army. Those who favoured taking

part in such a war, and at that time really they were
not numerous, apparently had not realized the consequences. It is certain that Ministers had not entertained a project of sending millions of men abroad ;
for not only had they made no preparations for it,
but even after war had commenced, on 3rd August
1914, Sir Edward Grey stated that " we have taken
no engagement yet with regard to sending an expeditionary armed force out of the country."

* * *

An Army on the Continental scale, with artillery
and equipments of all kinds to match, was one of the
necessary precautions that undoubtedly would have
to be taken, if the new policy which has been indicated
were to be adopted. A second precaution was equally
necessary. Every man of business knows that, however honourable may be the person with whom he is
dealing, it is always desirable to have a definite bargain.
An understanding is very apt to become a misunderstanding. Dishonest people will of course take advantage of any ambiguity. Even the most honest
may easily misconstrue what has been said, or form
higher expectations than it was intended to raise,
unless the thing is made certain and the conditions
clear. In the relations between two States, precaution against this kind of error is in the highest degree
necessary. Ministers change. One set has to inter-
pret what has been said by or to their predecessors.
They are often under Parliamentary pressure. Certainly they are keen for the interests of their own
country. And even if the Minister does not exaggerate
the scope of what he or his predecessor was really led
to expect from a foreign Power, zealots in the Press

or in Parliament are sure to exaggerate or to minimize it according to the point of view which they espouse. And in this way arise imperceptibly general expectations, difficult to disavow openly before they become dangerous, yet which may create a very embarrassing atmosphere if a time of trial comes.

A definite alliance, if co-operation should be decided upon, would give this country and our Ally a clear reciprocal right to be heard and to carry weight in one another's counsels, in matters that might bear upon their joint obligations. It would make Germany realize the danger she ran and make her less disposed to take a high hand, and so diminish the chances of war. It would also specify and limit the purposes for which war was to be waged in common, if that contingency arose, and so prevent either Ally from being reproached with infidelity if he should desire a termination of hostilities when the limited purpose agreed upon had been accomplished.

These are some of the disadvantages attendant upon indefinite understandings as compared with definite engagements. They are still more pronounced if there is not even an expressed understanding, but only a condition of close military and naval and political intimacy in which secrets are exchanged and expectations raised, such that if they are disappointed they will expose the defaulter to the imputation of perfidy. In short, if we meant to join France in a Franco-German war, it ought to have been put in black and white, with the necessary conditions.

Adequate armaments, explicit agreements. These were necessary if it were decided to abandon the time-honoured policy of the past, and to make this

country a party to the European system, divided as
it was into two camps armed to the teeth by universal
conscription, with a number of smaller powers also
armed and awaiting events, and with such a multitude
and variety of traditional hatreds and racial aspirations and irreconcilable ambitions as infected the
Continent of Europe.

* * *

If Great Britain should decide to thrust her hand
into this wasp's nest and to make the necessary military
and political preparations, it involved the change of
policy being made public and the approval of the
country being secured. Money would be needed for
armaments. The reason would have to be given,
unless indeed a false reason were put forward, which
would have been difficult as well as dishonest. Quite
apart from money, the risk was very great. Few
would be found to justify the commitment of our
country by a secret understanding so momentous and
far-reaching as to place in jeopardy the very existence
of this Kingdom. The choice before this country
was between two courses, adherence to the old policy,
or the adoption of a new policy binding us to support
France in arms. Opinions may differ as to the choice,
but if the latter were adopted it involved the creation
of an army to be numbered by millions, the making
of a definite treaty of alliance, and procuring public
approval. The mischief is that Sir Edward Grey
slipped into a new policy, but without either Army,
or Treaty, or warrant of Parliamentary approval.
For this the only possible explanation is that the
Foreign Office did not realize what they were doing,
and that seems to be the truth. Slipped into a

new policy is a correct expression. For the intimacy with France grew by gradual stages from the Treaty of 1904, contracted by Lord Lansdowne, in which we mutually promised each other only diplomatic support in regard to divers foreign interests of the two nations, till of a sudden the dire prospect arose in 1914 of France being called upon to support Russia in a war against Germany in which France herself had no interest. And then Sir Edward Grey, who constantly asserted in public and no doubt believed in private that we were free and that Parliament was free to decide, must have felt, as indeed his own speech on 3rd August 1914 discloses, that he at least, who had been as our Minister a party to all our dealings with France, could not in honour refuse to stand beside her in arms. Upon this occurred the catastrophe.

* * *

It arose in the way we all know. Servia gave offence to the Austro-Hungarian Empire, cause of just offence, as our Ambassador frankly admits in the published despatches. We had no concern in that quarrel, as Sir Edward Grey says in terms. But Russia, the protectress of Servia, came forward to prevent her being utterly humiliated by Austria. We were not concerned in that quarrel either, as Sir Edward also says. And then Russia called upon France under their Treaty to help in the fight. France was not concerned in that quarrel any more than ourselves, as Sir Edward informs us. But France was bound by a Russian Treaty of which he did not know the terms, and then France called on us for help. We were tied by the relations which our Foreign Office had created, without apparently realizing that they had created them. It may be true to say that the cause of freedom and civilization in any case required us to intervene. But this country has a right to know its own obligations and prepare to meet them and to decide its own destinies. When the most momentous decision of our whole history had to be taken we were not free to decide. We entered upon a war to which we had been committed beforehand in the dark, and Parliament found itself at two hours' notice unable, had it desired, to extricate us from this fearful predicament. We went to war unprepared in a Russian quarrel because we were tied to France in the dark.

* * *

There is another aspect of this business to be considered. Assuming that we were bound to stand by France, if war should come, whether by ties of honour, or by a sense of self-interest, or by a duty to civilization, Ministers ought to have recognized it in time and acted accordingly. Difficult though the situation was, as soon as the arrogant obstinacy of Austria and the dangerous humour of Germany became apparent, there is real ground for believing that, even then, a war might have been altogether averted if our Government had seen the truth in time and had showed firmness. Both the French and the Russian Governments were convinced, and eagerly pressed upon Sir Edward Grey at the very beginning their conviction, that if we at once declared our resolution to stand beside them in the event of war Germany would not force matters to that extremity, and they added that Germany believed we would remain neutral. President Wilson said in America in March of 1919: " We know for a

2

certainty that if Germany had thought for a moment
that Great Britain would go in with France and
Russia, she would never have undertaken the enterprise." Now the truth was that in Sir Edward Grey's
opinion, fully expressed in the House of Commons
on 3rd August 1914, we could not safely or honourably remain neutral; but when the crisis came,
Ministers refused to see it or say it in plain terms and
at once. They thought that to make such a declaration would not tend to avert but rather to precipitate
war. A series of our despatches, however, show that
at this time the Government had not made up their
minds whether they would or would not espouse in
arms the cause of France or even the cause of Belgium
if that country were invaded. And in this irresolution
history will find the true reason for their refusing to
make an explicit declaration. If the Government
thought that neither our safety nor our honour required
us to intervene on behalf of France they ought to have
said so promptly, and in that case they ought not
to have intervened on behalf of France but to have
faced the House of Commons and told them their
opinion, leaving the House to procure other Ministers
if it desired a different course to be pursued. If the
Government thought that either our honour or our
safety did require us to intervene on behalf of France,
then they ought to have said so unequivocally before
the angry Powers on the Continent committed themselves to irrevocable steps in the belief that we should
remain neutral. Instead of saying either, they kept
on saying in the despatches that their hands were
perfectly free, and told the House of Commons the
same thing. The documents show conclusively that

till after Germany declared war our Ministers had not made up their minds on either of the two questions, whether or not they would fight for France, and whether or not they would fight for Belgium. Of course Belgium was simply a corridor into France, and unless France were attacked Belgium was in no danger.

* * *

In a preliminary statement like this it would be out of place to dwell upon an argument often used, that a conflict between this country and Germany could not in the long run have been averted and must have come sooner or later. This is an important contention, which requires and will receive full attention. It is the outcome of an interested fatalism which will need higher authority than the support of those who took and acted upon a very different view for years. Upon the question, however, how we actually did come into this present war, which is the question now under consideration, it sheds only an indirect light.

* * *

Those then who impute to Mr. Asquith and Sir Edward Grey a desire for war or a wish to injure Germany, not only do them a great injustice, but also obscure the truth. Whatever lessons are to be learned for the future from this dreadful passage in our history can be derived only from an accurate estimate of what Ministers did. Their original fault lay in departing from the old policy in secret, and in allowing our Entente with France to develop imperceptibly till at last it was transformed into the equivalent of an Alliance, without the needful security and advantages that an open Alliance would bring with it. On that followed the grave mistake of concealing from themselves and others the true character of what was being done, and imparting to Parliament only their own sanguine conclusion that they had kept free from engagements, without imparting also the facts which would have awakened apprehension. Their duty was to warn Parliament of the danger, and prepare to meet it. They did neither, but drifted on. The final mistake was that when, on the actual crisis arising, a decision one way or the other might and, so far as can be judged, would have averted the Continental War altogether, Ministers could not make up their minds or take a firm resolution in time. They had conducted our foreign policy on the lines of their own choice, without reference to, almost without regard to Parliament, and therefore could not have any confidence that the resolutions they might arrive at would have the indispensable support of the nation. No doubt they hoped that they would be able by diplomatic adroitness to avert the war, but the hope was disappointed. Diplomacy at times needs plain speaking, and they could not speak plainly, because they had no assurance that what they said would be supported. In other words, secret diplomacy is weak and ineffective diplomacy. But the facts and documents will most certainly show that, whatever may be thought of their sagacity, or of their firmness, or of their candour, our Ministers were wholly free from the guilt of desiring war.

CHAPTER II

STORM CENTRE IN THE BALKANS

AT the beginning of 1914 there was a good deal of disquiet on the Continent, due to the memories of past defeats and the growth of new ambitions. France had not forgotten the loss of Alsace-Lorraine. Russia still aimed at Constantinople. Austria was alarmed at Pan-Slavonic agitation, and Germany had great schemes in Asia Minor together with Pan-German aspirations of which no one knew the precise limits. Italy, too, had her ambitions. According to a statement made on 2nd June 1915 by Signor Salandra, the Premier, the Italian Government, during the negotiations preceding the war in 1914, emphasized "in clear and unmistakable language to Berlin and Vienna the question of the cession of the Italian provinces subject to Austria, and declared that if Italy did not obtain adequate compensation the Triple Alliance would have been irreparably broken."

* * *

Before the war commenced there were, as there had been for years in the midst of this general unrest, two principal Storm Centres in Europe, from one or other of which a tempest might arise if the outbreak were not prevented by honest and firm statesmanship. One of the Storm Centres was Alsace-Lorraine, of which we must speak later. The other was the Balkan Peninsula, of which we must speak now. It is to the Balkans that the source of the Great War must be traced. Indeed, one may fairly say that if the quarrel which arose in 1914 between Austria and Servia could have been composed (and even after the storm had arisen it came within an ace of being composed), a new and tranquil period might have been secured for Europe. When the spectre came close, so terrible was the prospect of war seen to be by all the nations concerned (though unhappily far less terrible in their vision than the reality has proved), that an accommodation might have been reached. A clear view of the main conditions then existing in the Balkans is indispensable. All unnecessary detail must be omitted, but it may be possible to present in a small compass what is needed to explain the situation in the south-east of Europe which led to the greatest war of all history.

* * *

To begin with, examine the map of the Balkan Peninsula and the surrounding territory as it stood in 1914. It is a large area comprising five independent States of comparatively small dimensions flanked by the territories of three large Empires. The five States are Rumania, Servia, Montenegro, Bulgaria, and Greece. Observe how, with the exception of Greece, all of them were so confined by their great neighbours that they had little direct access to the Mediterranean and thence to the Atlantic and the outer world. Montenegro indeed had a small coast-line bordering on the Adriatic with a very insufficient port commanded by its neighbour Austria. The

other three had either no access at all, or most imperfect access, except to the Black Sea, and from that
they must pass to the Mediterranean through the
Dardanelles, which are in Turkish territory. When
those Straits are closed, as they were in 1914, access to
the Mediterranean is for them almost completely
stopped. They must then send and receive their
merchandise overland. A route through Russia is
not only inordinately long, but also leads only to
Baltic ports which in the winter are icebound. If the
Straits are closed, these three States can in a practical
point of view reach the Mediterranean only over
Austrian or Greek railways. In short, they were in a
blind alley, with a wholly insufficient and precarious
waterway to the ports of the world. This circumstance
has greatly affected their progress and their policy.
Their geographical position places them largely at
the mercy of their three great neighbours, and Austria,
for her own purposes, has in modern times constantly
made difficulties in allowing them ports on the
Adriatic.

Next consider the distribution of races in these five
States and in the adjoining districts. Race means
much in these days everywhere, and more perhaps
in this region than elsewhere. All over the Balkan
Peninsula there are many different races, Slavs,
Latins, Greeks, Turks, and Jews, with a Russian
and also a German admixture. And all these races
are dispersed in varying proportions throughout the
Peninsula. Accordingly each State in 1914 contained
districts which might more appropriately belong to
a neighbouring State. Ethnological research and
ethnological speculation are favourite pursuits in the

Peninsula, not because they satisfy philosophic
curiosity, but because they lead to very practical
conclusions.   Moreover, the Balkan Peninsula is
hemmed in by the Turkish and Austro-Hungarian
Empires.   There are multitudes under the Sultan
and under the Austro-Hungarian Crown who are in
blood and sympathy closely associated with one or
other of the Balkan States, and were at the same time
in a greater or less degree misgoverned by their
present rulers.   In this way a situation of almost
unprecedented difficulty had been created in the
Balkans.   Not only were the States in natural antagonism toward more powerful neighbours, but also
they were in conflict among themselves.   These were
the main causes of the bloodshed which has caused
so much misery to the populations of south-eastern
Europe in recent years.   A few words may usefully
be said about each of these States.

*   *   *

Rumania is inhabited chiefly by people of a Latin
race, descended, it is believed, from the old Roman
Colonists in the Dacian Province.   Alongside of them
and beyond the Eastern Carpathians lies Transylvania,
a part of Hungary, where some four million Rumanians
were to be found under alien and unsympathetic rule.
That is why Rumania aims at possessing Transylvania.   On the south-east the Rumanians in 1914
possessed the Dobrudscha, a district largely inhabited
by Bulgarians, and that is one reason for the animosity
between these two States.

In 1914 the population of Servia exceeded four
millions, of whom perhaps four-fifths are of Slavonic
origin.   There are altogether something like ninety

million Slavs in Europe. Sixty millions of them were in Russia, where they constituted the largest element in the European part of that Empire. They were separated from the Southern Slavonic Kingdoms by Austria-Hungary and Rumania, which extended from the Adriatic to the Black Sea and completely blocked the Northern from the Southern Slavonic States. About eighteen million more Slavs were under Austria-Hungary. But Servian national aspirations have, ever since their independence was secured in 1879, been directed toward an immense enlargement of their country and the restoration of a Slavonic Servian Empire such as was destroyed by the Turks some six hundred years ago. Quite recently M. Pasitch, the Prime Minister and the most conspicuous figure in Servian public life, declared that Servia was fighting for the Southern Slavs as a whole, a policy which could not possibly be fulfilled without the dismemberment of the Austro-Hungarian Empire, in which no less than 42 per cent of the population are said to be of Slavonic blood. Certainly these are very large pretensions for a people numerically so small as Servia. But it has long been the ambition of Servian statesmen that their country should act as a magnet to attract Slavonic populations on this unprecedented scale. No doubt the incentive has been twofold— resentment at the oppression to which many of their kinsmen have been subjected by the German and Hungarian elements in Austria-Hungary, and irritation at the short-sighted commercial policy adopted toward Servia by that Empire, in constantly preventing her from obtaining a port in the Adriatic. In these conditions it can easily be seen how an acute antagonism arose between Austria-Hungary and Servia. It was out of this antagonism that the Great War began.

Montenegro is peopled by the same race as Servia, and without sharing her pretensions is sure to share her destinies. But this is a very small State.

Coming to Bulgaria, it is less easy to determine the problem of race. The population numbered about four and a quarter millions, of whom more than 75 per cent are Bulgarians, some half-million are Turks, and the remainder are chiefly Rumanians, Greeks, Gipsies, and Jews. But what is the Bulgarian himself ? He is partly of Slavonic origin mixed with Finnish or Ugrian and Turkish blood, but with a pronounced nationality of his own. Nationality is to him a more powerful incentive than racial affinity. He has no considerable number of compatriots under foreign government in territories outside the Balkan Peninsula, and therefore is not brought so much into antagonism with the Austro-Hungarian. But he had in 1914 within the Peninsula a considerable number of compatriots under Servia and Greece, occupying territory adjoining to his own and forming a majority of the population there, and for that reason he coveted the districts they inhabit. This was so all the more that Bulgaria was stripped of her possessions in the Dobrudscha, and of that portion of Macedonia which was secured to her in a solemn Treaty with Greece and Servia, in the second Balkan War of 1913. It is not so much race as nationality and a sense of wrong that in 1914 made the Bulgarians hostile to Rumania, Servia, and Greece.

Last of all there is the Kingdom of Greece. It is commonly said that the true descendants of the old

Hellenic race, whose literature and artistic master-pieces are the most highly treasured of all that has been bequeathed to us by antiquity, may be found in the islands. Though this is an exaggeration, it is fairly certain that the Greek nation of to-day is of very mixed blood, chiefly Hellenic, but Turkish in some measure, and Slavonic in a still greater degree. The Greeks, however, are still a distinct race and a distinct nationality. They had great numbers of compatriots in Asia Minor and in the Greek Islands under Turkey. In their newly acquired dominions just to the south of Servia and Bulgaria they became masters of a population alien to their own, but their natural aspiration is to regather the Hellenic populations of the Turkish Empire. At one time in moments of exaltation they have dreamed of reconstituting a Greek Empire with Constantinople for capital. It is a task for which they are manifestly unfit, and it is probable that they now recognize their own un-fitness. The Turk has always been their enemy. Their real ambition is to possess the islands with part of the coast-line of Asia Minor, and their chief aversion in 1914 owing to recent events was the Bulgarian.

*　　*　　*

An understanding of the situation in the Balkan Peninsula when the war broke out, which indeed led to the war, will be more easily gained if in a brief epitome the salient features of its recent history are presented. Its earlier and mediaeval history may be dismissed by way of preface in a few sentences; not that it is uninteresting in itself, but because for the present purpose it is of minor importance.

The entire Peninsula and the whole adjoining territory was part of the Roman, or, as it may be more accurately called, the Greek Empire of the East, and when the Turkish conquest broke up that decrepit survival of ancient Rome, all this territory came under Turkish rule. Nearly all the population remained Christian. Their religion was contemptuously tolerated, but they were deprived of all rights, their lives and property were at the mercy of any village tyrant, ánd they were at all times exposed to the danger of outrage and massacre. In this servitude the Balkan Christians lay submerged for hundreds of years. The Christian powers of Europe, engrossed in their own external or internal struggles, took no heed of the Peninsula. In course of time the Turkish Government fell into the hands of a lower and yet lower type of foreigners, to whom duty and patriotism and even humanity were meaningless words. They ruled by cruelty and terror, with little thought beyond their own aggrandizement.

But the power of Russia began to be felt early in the eighteenth century. No one can maintain that the policy of Russia toward Turkey in those days was dictated purely by sympathy for fellow-Christians and fellow-Slavs under the pitiless dominion of the Moslem. It was originally a policy of conquest aiming at the possession of Constantinople. The eighteenth century, like most other centuries, was one of continual warfare in the supposed interest of rival dynasties, and most of the sovereigns, together with most of the so-called statesmen who assisted them, thought that the chief glory of a State lay in obtaining victories by land and sea, and in reducing as many other States as possible to their obedience. The Czars were like the rest. But the suffering of the Christian population in the Balkans did undoubtedly from the first attract the sympathies of the common people in Slavonic Russia, and the more they learnt about it, the warmer became the sympathy. Such a sentiment would be naturally encouraged by a Government which for other reasons, and ultimately for that reason also, began a series of wars against Turkey. Those wars did not prosper according to Russian expectations, and it was not till the time of Lord Byron that Greece, then in open and apparently hopeless insurrection against the Turks, succeeded in gaining attention from the Great European Powers. At last the fleets of Great Britain, France, and Russia destroyed the Turkish fleet at Navarino in 1827, and thus procured the complete emancipation of Greece. What we have to note in this place is that about ninety years ago the main practical result of Russian sympathy with the victims of Turkey was the complete liberation of Greece.

Since then Russia, with her eyes no doubt still steadily fixed upon Constantinople, espoused more and more warmly the cause of the Christians under Ottoman rule. She fought Turkey more than once, and either extorted by treaty or assumed without authority a title to act as protectress of the Christians. But these hapless populations did not for many years derive much advantage from the patronage of the Czar. For Russian pretensions to Constantinople roused the opposition of the British Government. At what particular date and under the influence of what particular Minister the British Foreign Office definitely embraced the creed that our interests required the maintenance of " the integrity and independence of the Ottoman Empire " it would be superfluous to ascertain.   The formula had obtained ministerial and parliamentary benediction before the Crimean War, and once a formula or rule of policy had been accepted in the Foreign Office, it too often continued to be applied automatically without regard to change of circumstances.   This unhappy devotion to what Burke once called " the hateful and disgusting Empire " of the Turk has been pursued by successive British Governments up to very recent years, and we must admit that the antagonism thereby created between Russia and this country greatly retarded the cause of freedom and good government in the Balkan Peninsula.   Elderly men among us will recall how persistently our Governments adhered to the axiom that, deplorable as the effects of Turkish rule have been on the Christian populations of the Near East, we were bound in the national interest to uphold Turkey lest by acquiring Constantinople Russia should be enabled to dominate Europe.

The course of events in the Near East for sixty years before the Great War broke out may be very succinctly grouped round four historic occurrences of the first importance, namely, the Crimean War of 1854, the Russo-Turkish War of 1877, the Austrian annexation of Bosnia and Herzegovina in 1908, and the Balkan Wars of 1912–13.   During this period the Eastern Question became gradually transformed, and the principal factors in that transformation were the liberation of the Balkan States, the outbreak of quarrels among themselves, and the entry of Germany

into the field with great ambitions for the establishment of German dominion in Asia Minor. In the
following brief narrative nothing is said of many
serious incidents, including minor wars, insurrections, and massacres. Only what helps to throw
light on the relations of the Great Powers is recorded
here.

In 1854 the Crimean War broke out because Russia
desired to establish a protectorate over the Christians
in Turkey. France joined us, not because she had
any serious interest in the Near Eastern Question,
but because Napoleon III, who had recently usurped
the throne of France, desired to consolidate his
ill-omened dynasty by some military triumph. The
Sardinian Government joined us because Cavour
aimed at the establishment of an Italian Kingdom,
and thought, with justice, that he would in this way
secure the assistance of Great Britain and France in
his great object. No one ever supposed that any part
of Italy had any special interest in the quarrel between
the Russian and the Turk. The Crimean War would
never have come if the Russians had acted with
moderation, but its results unhappily left the Turks
free to continue their misgovernment in the Peninsula.
For example, in 1861 and again in 1864 they expelled
Bulgarian peasants from their lands without compensation, and settled on them no less than 12,000 Crimean
Tartars and a still larger number of Circassians, lawless
mountaineers who proved a scourge to the population
in their neighbourhood. Again in 1875 hopelessly incompetent and brutal administration produced an
insurrection in Bosnia and Herzegovina which greatly
excited the whole Peninsula and aroused the fanaticism

of the Moslems. The Bulgarians, fearing with too much reason a general massacre, organized a revolt which broke out prematurely in 1876. Upon this the Turkish Government let loose a horde of Bashi-bazouks and Circassians upon the people. Tens of thousands were massacred. The Great Powers remained inactive for a time and then summoned a conference. It made benevolent recommendations to secure better government which were practically set aside by the Porte. This was the time when Mr. Gladstone wrote his famous pamphlet on Bulgarian Atrocities, and put his whole strength in a political campaign against Turkish rule. The instances given are merely illustrations of the inhuman barbarity to which the Balkan people were from time to time exposed. But in truth chronic oppression caused much more misery than occasional massacres.

At last the appalling atrocities perpetrated in Bulgaria roused the sympathy of the whole world, and drove Russia to take up arms. It became apparent that nothing would be done by the European Concert. Russia declared war on Turkey in 1877. Her avowed object was to rescue the Christian inhabitants of the Balkan Peninsula. In the desperate struggle which followed (1877-8) the victorious Russian troops marched to Constantinople and outside its walls dictated the Treaty of San Stefano. That Treaty secured to Bulgaria nearly all the territory in the Peninsula in which the Bulgarian population predominated. But at this point the Great Powers, notably Great Britain, intervened, and asserted their right to revise the terms, fearing that so extensive a territory would make Bulgaria too powerful, though it contained only four million inhabitants, and that Bulgaria would become a vassal of Russia. A Congress was summoned at Berlin under the presidency of Prince Bismarck, with the result that Russia to a considerable extent gave way. In the Treaty of Berlin (13th July 1878) the projected limits of Bulgaria were greatly cut down and Eastern Rumelia turned into an autonomous principality. These two provinces received autonomy, not a release from Turkish sovereignty. Servia obtained some strips of territory and independence, but the remainder, including almost the whole of Macedonia, went back to Turkish rule. A solemn stipulation for reform in the Government of European Turkey finds a place in this Treaty. It proved quite valueless, for the Engagements of the Porte were never carried out. Nevertheless, the Treaty of Berlin secured the complete independence of both Servia and Rumania. Montenegro had always been independent. So the only one of the five Balkan States that now remained a vassal of Turkey after 1878, though an autonomous vassal, was Bulgaria. At the same time, Bosnia and Herzegovina were placed under the Protectorate of Austria-Hungary by the common consent of the Great Powers. Much good was done by the Treaty of Berlin, but still more remained unsettled. Slow indeed is the emancipation of oppressed peoples when it is in supposed conflict with the interest of powerful States.

In this way the greatest opportunity that had yet offered itself of settling for good the troubled affairs of the Balkan Peninsula was lost, mainly because of the antagonism between Russia and Great Britain. Our policy of supporting the Turk for fear of Russian

3

aggrandizement and aggression in India or elsewhere bore its natural fruits.

*   *   *

The next thirty years, from 1879 down to 1908, were by no means uneventful, but little notice need be taken here of the events. Eastern Rumelia joined Bulgaria and thenceforward formed one State. There was a war between Bulgaria and Servia, another war between Turkey and Greece, which, however lamentable, did not affect the course of history. During these thirty years the Treaty of Berlin, imperfect though it was, had some good effect. A large part of the Near Eastern Question had been disposed of. Four out of the five Balkan States had become independent, and the fifth, Bulgaria, was autonomous and practically independent. Thus the power of Turkey for mischief, that chief source of former trouble, was diminished. Still, some of her power remained, and fresh difficulties arose from other causes. Some attention must be paid to them, for they led directly up to the disputes which brought about the Great War of 1914 and have influenced its course. Put quite generally, the advantages derived from independence were balanced by the outbreak of hatred and jealousy between the Five States themselves, by the rivalry of Austria and Russia, and by the continued misgovernment of Macedonia by the Turks.

Macedonia, which had been destined almost wholly for the Bulgarians under the Treaty of San Stefano, was, as already said, restored to Turkey by the Treaty of Berlin. It remained under uncontrolled Turkish administration. Now civilization did not really exist under Turkish authority in the reign of Abdul Hamid.

An English writer recently described the sensations of a traveller in those regions who succeeded in escaping—and it was not easy to escape—from the Railway or Café or Club into the real life of the land. " His sensations were those sometimes felt in a bad dream. He found himself in a dreadful underworld—in a new moral dimension—where foulest vices were the only way to honours, where acts of the most noble virtue were punished worse than our gravest crimes, where the machinery of civilization—the railway, the telegraph, the police—were instruments for the destruction of all that makes for civilization, where the only hopes of progress lay in the success of dynamitards and banditti." The writer of those sentences had lived in those regions. Such was the government of Macedonia in the period under review. Massacre remained a recognized method of administration. Macedonia ran along the southern borders of Bulgaria and Servia, and also a part of it ran along the northern border of Greece. It contained a Bulgarian, a Servian, and a Greek population. The sympathy of all three States was assured for their neighbouring compatriots. The pity of it is that with this sympathy came to be associated a desire, more intense in Bulgaria than elsewhere, on the part of each of these States to possess themselves of as much of Macedonia as they could on ethnological or national grounds lay claim to. Races were mixed all over Macedonia. It was hard to say which nationality or race predominated in many parts of the country. This proved a fertile source of ill will. It was not in the Balkan Peninsula as it is in settled countries. These States had emerged from centuries of most cruel subjection. They had not learned the traditional sense

of responsibility which grows with the growth of freedom, and their conditions were still so uncertain that
no one felt sure what would be the boundaries of his
own State in a little time, with the break-up of Turkey
apparently imminent and with racial aspirations
undoubtedly on the increase in many provinces of
Austria-Hungary quite near to their frontiers. Macedonia became the scene of continuous violence and
anarchy. Servian, Bulgarian, and Greek bands invaded
it from time to time, sometimes with the purpose of
forcibly converting the inhabitants to their own religious faith, sometimes to pillage the inhabitants or
to fight one another, sometimes for a combination of
these purposes. Mussulmans from Albania had their
bands also, and filled Macedonia with terror. It seems
incredible that such a condition of things should have
existed in any part of Europe only ten years ago.

It was not to be expected that the Great Powers
interested in the Balkan Peninsula would view all this
with unconcern. Had they been able to agree,
nothing would have been easier than to end what had
for long been a scandal to Christendom and threatened
to become a grave danger to peace. But then the
agreement must have been sincere and unselfish if it
was to tranquillize the south-east of Europe. Unhappily, the Great Powers interested in that region
listened to ambitions of their own which could not be
reconciled. During the thirty years (1879–1908) now
under consideration it was becoming more and more
evident that the Turkish Empire in Europe was rapidly
approaching dissolution under the sanguinary rule of
Abdul Hamid. Who were to be its heirs? The
conflict of ambitions protracted the sufferings of

Macedonia. Servia had great ambitions. This of itself sufficed to alarm Austria, but Austria also desired to extend her territories and to gain access to the Ægean at Salonica, which could not be done without taking a slice of Macedonia. Also, her ally, Germany, had before 1908 come into the field, not as a direct claimant of territory in the Balkan Peninsula, but as a supporter of Austrian expansion, in order thereby to further her own schemes in Asia Minor. For Germany aspired to `the ·establishment of something like a Protectorate of the Sultan's dominions in Asia Minor, with a view no doubt to trade, but also with ulterior political designs which should enable her to hold in those regions a position analogous to that now held by the British Crown toward the independent Princes in India. Austria was to obtain an access to the Ægean and a dominant authority in the Balkan States so as to have a direct and safe route by railway from Vienna to Constantinople. Germany was to control Constantinople, thence dominating Asia Minor. At this time German diplomacy began to be very busy at Constantinople. In short, a new factor was introduced in the Near Eastern Question by the interposition of new German aspirations linked with the old aspirations of Austria-Hungary. Manifestly this fresh element would prove fatal to the hopes of Servia. Still more serious, it would prove fatal to the traditional policy of Russia. For the Russians have persistently aimed at Constantinople and at a commanding influence in the Peninsula which lay on their road to it. If a wedge were driven between them and Turkey by means of an Austrian predominance in the Peninsula and a German control of the Turkish

capital, farewell to their dreams. There seemed to
be some evil spirit perpetually at work to frustrate
every hope of pacification in the Balkans. When
Russia could have done the work in 1879 she was
foiled by the open resistance of Great Britain coupled
with the covert antagonism of Austria-Hungary.
When British enthusiasm for the Turk had been
dispelled by a better knowledge of that barbarian's
methods, all chance of an accommodation between
Russia and Austria-Hungary was defeated by the
introduction of a new factor—namely, the new world-
policy of Germany. Bismarck once said that the
Eastern Question was not worth to Germany the bones
of a single Pomeranian Grenadier. It has now cost
her millions of men, and instead of winning she has
been ruined.

*   *   *

To summarize the situation as it stood in 1908 on
the eve of the critical events of that year, Bulgaria
aimed at procuring complete independence and at
obtaining a large part of Macedonia. Servia too
desired a large part of Macedonia and also nourished
grandiose schemes of union with other Slavonic
populations then under the Austro-Hungarian Crown.
Rumania desired union with her compatriots in
Transylvania, also under the Austro-Hungarian
Crown. Greece desired to acquire the Greek Islands
and also that part of the coast of Asia Minor where
the Greek settlements were numerically very powerful.
Russia desired Constantinople and a predominant
influence in the Peninsula. However they might
differ among themselves, all these Powers were at
one in wishing for the downfall of the Turkish Empire,

and hoped out of its ruins to gain something for themselves. On the other hand, Austria-Hungary had at
heart not merely the maintenance of her own Empire
in the provinces which were inhabited by Slavs, but
also an expansion southward in the Peninsula, and
Germany now abetted her in order thereby to expand
in Asia Minor. Great Britain had no direct interest
in this conflict of ambitions. The policy of maintaining the independence and integrity of the Ottoman
Empire had been tacitly abandoned, for no one could
really defend that sanguinary despotism any longer
in this country. German projects in Asia Minor
were quite capable of adjustment, so far as we were
concerned, as appears by the fact that we did come to
an agreement with Germany about the Bagdad Railway
and its kindred problems in 1913 and 1914, not long
before the war, though the particulars have never been
published. Our chief tie with this great controversy
lay in the fact that we were on terms of friendship
with Russia and, as has since appeared, on terms of
something more than friendship with her ally, France.
We had also the common interest of all nations, the
interest of Peace. If our policy in these regions was
disinterested, it was also embarrassed by the interests
of our friends.

That was the situation at the beginning of 1908, an
exceedingly dangerous situation beyond all doubt,
though, so far as British interests were concerned, the
quarrels of the five small States did not concern us;
and if the three Great Powers—Russia, Austria, and
Germany—could have agreed among themselves, there
was no reason to doubt that we could have come
to satisfactory terms with them. Our danger was

simply that we might be drawn into a Balkan quarrel by our partnership in what is called the Triple Entente. So much for the situation in the Balkans up to the year 1908.

*　　*　　*

With 1908 began a new chapter of events which brought Austria and Russia face to face in a far more serious. antagonism than ever before. This time no artifice could conceal the fact that their respective ambitions in regard to the Balkans had become irreconcilable, and, this time too, a German alliance and partnership with Austria in a common Balkan policy encouraged Vienna to take up a more uncompromising attitude. Baron Aehrenthal had become the Minister in charge of Austro-Hungarian foreign policy. This aspiring statesman, who hoped to be another Bismarck, had no mind to continue the tranquil, inactive policy which satisfied his predecessors. He believed that the time had come for a forward policy with an Austrian advance to Salonica as its objective. The possession of another good port in southern waters would be of great advantage both to Austria and Germany, whose access to the Mediterranean was undoubtedly inadequate. With this in view, Aehrenthal inaugurated in 1908 a scheme for the construction of a railway through Novi-Bazar on the road to Salonica. Before long this was abandoned. Mr. Seton Watson, a great authority on these subjects, thinks that it was abandoned because of financial and engineering difficulties. But the scheme roused suspicions in Russia and in the Peninsula, probably also in Constantinople, as a step that indicated some aggressive designs. An Austrian port at Salonica, however useful to the Central

Powers, would help to make Austria the predominant power in the Balkans. However, though the project of a railway through Novi-Bazar soon fell through, the ambition to reach Salonica did not fall through, nor did Baron Aehrenthal's resolution to adopt a forward policy fall through.

At this juncture came what was least expected, a Revolution in Turkey in June 1908. Palace Revolutions have been common enough in that country, but this was in the nature of a popular Revolution, led by the "Young Turks." Nothing could be more commendable than their professions. They deplored the gradual dismemberment of Turkey by the blundering of an effete Government under the blind rule of Abdul Hamid. They said they were for complete reform, good government, justice, and toleration. All were to be brothers and all to be Ottomans in a regenerated Turkey. How far these professions were genuine may well be doubted. In a short time the Young Turks proved themselves to be quite as unscrupulous and brutal as their predecessors. However, at the moment it was supposed that this movement might before long lead to a strengthening of Turkey and a revival of her title to real power in the Peninsula, while it was certain that in the interval the actual strength of Turkey would be weakened by internal dissension. Baron Aehrenthal no doubt noted these things, if he did not secretly procure the Revolution, and was also well aware that Russia was weak, because she had not recovered from the effects of the Japanese War. Alarm at the prospective revival of Turkey and a sense of her temporary weakness served also to stimulate activity among the Balkan States. Turkey was the common enemy of them all. They had all secured their independence except Bulgaria, and the Turkish Revolution appeared to them as well as to Aehrenthal an excellent opportunity of inaugurating a forward policy on their own account, very different from his.

Bulgaria was the first to move. In October 1908 Prince Ferdinand assumed the title of King, and proclaimed the complete independence of that country. This was a plain violation of the Treaty of Berlin, signed twenty-nine years previously; but, as that Treaty had kept the Bulgarians, against their vehement protest, still under the odious suzerainty of the Sultan, very few sensible people were found to condemn what was in fact a legitimate act of rebellion. Only two days later a still more significant step was taken by the Austro-Hungarian Government. The Emperor Francis Joseph proclaimed the definite annexation of Bosnia and Herzegovina. These Provinces, with a Slavonic population of nearly two million, had been handed over to be administered as a Protectorate by Austria-Hungary under the Treaty of Berlin at the desire of the Great Powers. For practical purposes Bosnia and Herzegovina were already governed by Austria-Hungary, and on the whole had prospered greatly under that administration. Unquestionably the consent of the Great Powers ought to have been obtained before this change of status could be brought about, unless Treaties are to be treated as waste paper. But Baron Aehrenthal did not consult or even inform the Signatory Powers. No doubt he consulted Germany, but the assent of neither Russia nor France nor Great Britain was asked. Toward these Powers, all of whom were parties to the

Treaty of Berlin, the arbitrary annexation was a direct
affront. Toward Turkey, little as that Government
deserved consideration, it was an act of unqualified
spoliation. In public law it could not fail to shake
all confidence as indicating a contempt for solemn
Treaty obligations, such as the Treaty of Berlin.

Whether or not this annexation would have been
sanctioned on suitable conditions by the other Great
Powers, had they been consulted, it certainly provoked great resentment when carried out with a high
hand. Aehrenthal and his supporters declared that
annexation had been made necessary by the persist-
ency of the Servian agitation for a greater Servia,
which they alleged had been carried on in Austrian
Dominions among the Southern Slavs, in order to
undermine the Austro-Hungarian Empire. It is un-
questionable that bribery and forgery were employed
by Baron Aehrenthal's agents in supporting this charge
against Servia. But that ought not to make us ignore
the fact that Servia was in truth aiming at an expansion which could not be realized except at the expense
of Austria-Hungary. Servia, however, looked upon
herself as deeply wronged when her dream of obtaining
Bosnia and Herzegovina for herself was rudely dispelled by this Austrian annexation. At one time
there was a clamour at Belgrade for war, but common
sense prevailed, and the Servian Parliament decided
against that course. None the less did Servia continue to protest. Russia also took the strongest
objection—Austrian supremacy in the Balkans would
be fatal to Russia's designs on Constantinople. Had
Russia not been in a weakened condition at that time
there might have been war.

From October 1908, when the annexation was proclaimed, till the end of March 1909 the whole Peninsula was in a ferment. Aehrenthal proceeded ruthlessly as if his purpose had been to provoke a war, as indeed it may have been from the outset. He endeavoured to justify the annexation by establishing the existence of a pan-Servian conspiracy against the Hapsburg Monarchy. Domiciliary visits and arrests were followed by prosecution for High Treason, conducted in a spirit opposed to every maxim of justice or fair play. It would be outside the limits of such a treatise as this to enter upon more detail in regard to the protracted Bosnian crisis of 1908–9. The Servians nearly lost all self-control, and their Parliament, though not declaring war, voted a large sum for armaments. Early in 1909, to borrow Mr. Seton Watson's language, " the situation seemed to be going from bad to worse. On the part of Austria-Hungary a powerful and obstinate Minister, unwilling to admit his faulty tactics, an inspired press, suffering from a severe attack of jingo sentiment, a network of secret intrigues at Court (in Vienna), clerical, military, political, racial, personal ; on the part of Russia an irresponsible desire to score off a detested rival ; on the part of the Western Powers a doctrinaire outlook, combined with irresolution and *laissez-faire* ; on the part of Servia a complete lack of balance, a refusal to reckon with the facts of the situation, an inclination to stake the country's future upon a gambler's throw." Only one qualification is needed in this description. The Western Powers may have been irresolute, but their frame of mind was that they had no concern in a Balkan quarrel. They, in common with Russia, took their stand on the contention that annexation required the consent of the Signatory Powers to the Treaty of Berlin, while Aehrenthal contended that, though there might be a conference to give that consent, it could not be allowed to call in question an accomplished fact. The British Government, as Sir Edward Grey subsequently stated, desired to stand aloof from a struggle between Teuton and Slav, though sharing the view that the consent of Europe must be obtained at a conference. What they resented was not so much the annexation as the lawless and peremptory fashion in which it had been effected.

In the last ten days of March 1909 things had come to such a pass that war seemed probable. At this moment the German Government took a decisive step. The German Ambassador at St. Petersburg demanded that he should be informed of Russia's intentions. Such a demand at such a time could only mean that Russia must make a choice between acceptance of the annexation and war. Russia found herself in no position for a fight with the Central Powers. Her army had not yet recovered from the struggle with Japan. She yielded, and expressed her willingness to recognize the annexation of Bosnia and Herzegovina. Without Russian help, Servia could not prolong her opposition. Servia therefore submitted, disbanded her reserves, and recognized the annexation, at the same time promising to give up her attitude of protest and to resume neighbourly relations with Austria-Hungary. The Bosnian crisis thus came to an end in the triumph of Aehrenthal. The German Kaiser was not at fault when he said that the appearance of Germany " in shining armour " beside her ally had determined the controversy, but actions of that kind and phrases of that kind are not calculated to produce a lasting peace. Contempt for Treaties is among nations what the repudiation of a debt of honour is among individuals. It destroys all confidence. And when a Great Power shows an example of greed and faithlessness, smaller Powers will quickly follow suit.

* * *

An interval of three or four years elapsed between the " shining armour " episode of 1908 and the next upheaval in the Balkan Peninsula. During this period the evil fruits of Aehrenthal's policy became more and more visible. The Young Turks and their professions of fraternity among Ottomans of all races met with the failure that might have been expected. Civil war broke out in Turkey, insurrection in Albania and Arabia; the "bands" of Bulgarians, Servians, and Greeks appeared again in Macedonia, and attempts were made to destroy or expel the population and re-place them with Moslem immigrants. A commercial war broke out with Greece. Attempts were made by the new Turkish Government to arrive at an agree-ment with Bulgaria and with Servia, all to no purpose. It became manifest that no chance remained of attain-ing permanent peace or good government in Macedonia with either the Old Turk or the Young Turk. But it would be a profitless task to draw a picture of chaos. The Great Powers on the spot were obviously indifferent to the welfare of the Peninsula and merely playing for their own hand. The last blow fell when in October 1911 Italy, without either warning or ceremony, invaded Tripoli, an African province of Turkey, and avowed

her intention of annexing it simply because she chose
to do so.   Anyone who, after that imitation of Aehrenthal's enterprise in Bosnia and Herzegovina, pretended
that respect for Treaties governed the Great Powers
of Europe would require a considerable command
of countenance.   On all hands the final downfall of
Turkey was now expected, and the expectant successors
could not restrain their impatience to possess themselves of the spoil.   No doubt it was eminently in the
interests of civilization that Turkish tyranny should
disappear, but it was not in the interest of civilization
that the Powers, Great or Small, should play a game of
grab and scramble for that Potentate's dominions.

* * *

It is thought, and nothing could be more probable,
that the Italian descent upon Tripoli in 1911 finally confirmed Bulgaria, Servia, and Greece in the belief that
in the apprehended partition of European Turkey they
would forfeit their share unless they acted promptly.
What Italy had done the others would do unless their
action could be forestalled.   If Great Powers could
present one another with a *fait accompli*, why should
not Little Powers do the same ?   Accordingly, these
three small States, together with Montenegro, formed
a Coalition, and in October 1912 declared war on
Turkey, with the object of driving the Turks out of
all their European territories except Constantinople
and a small strip adjacent to it, which they knew they
would not be allowed to retain.   They agreed beforehand as to the partition of conquered lands among
themselves, and repelled with remarkable courage the
warnings of the Great Powers who told them that
they would not be allowed to retain any conquests.

There was no principle in these warnings. The Great
Powers simply dreaded the consequences of this
vigorous action upon their own schemes, and those of
them who had no schemes feared that as soon as war
began they might themselves be involved. In a very
few months the Turks had to confess defeat. They
had no choice but to surrender whatever territory
might be demanded, including an access for Servia
to the Adriatic. Thereupon Austria interposed. She
would not consent to Servia obtaining a slice of Albania
and thus gaining that access to the sea which has for
a long time been a great and indeed a necessary object
of Servian policy. Servia had to give way again,
and, for compensation, demanded a revision of the
partition Treaties made by the victorious States
before the war began, on the ground that they all
presupposed Servia's acquisition of an Adriatic port,
and ought to be amended now that this hope had
been frustrated. This meant that Bulgaria would
have to be content with less than had been promised
to her.

Bulgaria refused, claiming, with some reason, that
her troops had done the heaviest part of the fighting,
and that a bargain is a bargain. There never had been
any love lost between these States, and, while efforts
were being made to effect some compromise, Bulgaria
put herself fatally in the wrong by an unexpected
and perhaps treacherous attack on the Servian and
Greek forces. This at once led to what is called the
Second Balkan War of 1913. It would be a waste of
time to discuss the suspicions or conjectures which
find in the instigations of their powerful neighbours
the true source of this war. Mutual hatred, if it

did not primarily cause, at all events embittered beyond belief the deplorable quarrel. Servia, Montenegro, and Greece soon overwhelmed the Bulgarian armies. When the latter had been hopelessly defeated, the Rumanians, who had not taken any part at all in the war against Turkey, seized the opportunity of exacting from Bulgaria, by threats and indeed by actual invasion, some stretches of territory in the Dobrudscha. There is no affectation of chivalry in these regions. More stretches of territory which were owned by the Bulgarians, or had been promised to them as the price of their joining in the war against Turkey, were torn from them by Servia and Greece, including a part of Macedonia which was wholly Bulgarian in its sympathies. Then Turkey, smarting from the recent defeat, reappeared in arms, and Bulgaria was compelled to restore to the Sultan some of the gains, including Adrianople, which she had wrung from him a few months earlier at a fearful cost of life. These proceedings are perfect examples of the time-honoured methods prevalent in Europe, namely, secret conspiracies for a sudden attack by one or more States against another, followed by a distribution among the victors of the spoils of victory in which the populations were regarded as you would regard cattle at an auction.

It is understood that Russia blames Austria and Austria blames Russia for having brought about this confused fratricidal war of 1913. The inner history of it is obscure, but there can be no doubt as to the inhuman character of the war itself, and the whole conflict has never been outdone for horror in modern times—proportionately, that is, to the

4

area affected and the number of combatants. No
Great Power intervened in arms, though the danger
of it was at one time extreme. There were ambassa-
dorial conferences in London under the presidency
of Sir Edward Grey, who, working in complete
harmony with the German Government, contrived
to prevent either the Coalition war against Turkey
or the ensuing struggle between the victorious States
from disturbing the general peace of the Continent.
No one paid a more ample tribute to his services
on this occasion than the German Government, and
no one paid a more ample tribute to the co-operation
of the German Government than Sir Edward Grey.
It is right to add that Great Britain had no design
or interest throughout the whole affair beyond the
maintenance of peace.

*   *   *

The Treaty of Bucharest, which ended this fratricidal
war, was signed on 10th August 1913. It left Bulgaria
despoiled and disarmed, with a feeling of implacable
resentment against both Servians and Greeks, and
with no slight displeasure against the Russian Government, who were thought to have taken sides with
Servia. Thenceforth the main purpose of Bulgarian
policy might naturally be, and has been, the recovery
of what had been thus wrested from her in Macedonia
and in the Dobrudscha under hard conditions. Bulgarian ambitions did not extend to any territory
outside the Peninsula.

Within less than a year from the signature of the
Treaty of Bucharest the Great European War broke
out. It was the sequel, and in large measure the
consequence, of all that had happened in the Balkan

Peninsula, beginning with the annexation of Bosnia and Herzegovina in 1908 and ending with the Treaty of Bucharest in 1913. Servia, elated by her victory, by no means renounced her ambition of forming a greater Servia. Her Government did not, perhaps could not, repress the Secret Societies which sought to further that policy, though it is by no means established that there was any official intention to support the desperate methods adopted by those Societies or even their active propagandism in Austro-Hungarian territory. But, where there is a strong nationalist feeling, based upon motives so powerful as blood relationship and sympathy with kinsmen under oppression, excesses, especially in a country recently released from bondage, are difficult to restrain. It is probable that the apathy of some officials in a backward country prevented supervision from being so efficient as it should have been. It is certain that the Servian Government did not succeed in restraining these conspiracies, and doubtful that they made any adequate effort to do so.

The fruit of all this was that on 28th June 1914 the Crown Prince of Austria-Hungary and his Consort fell at Sarajevo at the hands of assassins who were members of a Servian Secret Society. The Crown Prince had been warned of his danger. His life had been already attempted. But he disregarded the warning with the high courage that became his lineage and the foul crime by which he perished has proved to be the death-knell of millions upon millions of brave men. Sir Edward Grey once said it would be detestable that any of the Great Powers should be dragged into war by Servia. All of them have been dragged into war by Servia. It is not irrelevant to remember that Servia suffered intolerably for many generations, and the Great Powers did little to help her. The sufferings of her peasants in the Great War entitle them to the sympathy of the whole world. We must learn to sympathize with peoples and to judge of their actions and interests on their own merits, without always identifying them as hitherto with their Governments.

CHAPTER III

STORM CENTRE IN ALSACE-LORRAINE

THE Balkans were one of the main Storm Centres of Europe; the other was Alsace-Lorraine—the Balkans in the East, Alsace-Lorraine in the West. From one or both of these centres would probably come any great convulsion that might overwhelm the Continent. To avert such an outbreak was the business of every responsible statesman in Europe. The storm came in the end from the East, but Great Britain would not have been involved, nor would France, had it not been for the Western trouble.

Old as the Eastern Question is, the question of Alsace-Lorraine is still older. We met with it at its original source in Cæsar's Commentaries in our schooldays, where it appears how two thousand years ago Ariovistus with his German hordes had crossed the Rhine and seized territory belonging to Gallic tribes. That territory lay approximately in Alsace-Lorraine, the greater portion of which, since those early days, some seventy years before the Christian era, has been inhabited by a people mainly of German origin. Here is to be found in its cradle the antagonism between French and German which has been perpetuated by profound differences of national temperament, intellectual characteristics, and language, and also by frequent hostilities throughout mediaeval and modern history.

But though the problem of Alsace-Lorraine is much older than that of the Balkans, it is also very much simpler. Only two Powers are directly concerned in it, France and Germany. There are no half-civilized populations to deal with, no little Powers to quarrel and fight, no States outside vying for a paramount influence or awaiting some sick man's inheritance. Whatever interest other nations may have in this bitter dispute was limited to the fear of a conflagration in which they may be brought in and suffer. Such is the interest especially of Belgium, whose dread, most cruelly realized in 1914, has always been that one or other of her powerful neighbours would insist upon violating her territory in order to attack his enemy.

Alsace-Lorraine were torn from Germany and annexed to France, roughly speaking, two hundred years ago. At that time Germany was disunited, under literally hundreds of Princes, nearly all practically despotic, and many of them indifferent to the national cause. This annexation was effected partly by force, partly by inheritance, partly by arrangement.

Nevertheless, France showed herself at her best after the annexation, and succeeded in wholly assimilating her new conquest. Germans, however, did not forget the grievance. After Napoleon I had been crushed, Prussia fought with great tenacity at the Congress of Vienna for a restoration of these Provinces. Ultimately she was compelled to give way, not without warning the Congress that their decision would hereafter lead to a frightful war. And so it proved. This was one of the thorns in the flesh which constantly reminded Germans of their need for union and facilitated Bismarck's task. The whole of Germany, except Austria proper, came to be included, after Sadowa in 1866, in a Military Alliance. Four years later the folly and weakness of Napoleon III and the insensate military vanity which he had encouraged gave Bismarck his opportunity. France lay at the feet of Germany in 1871. Bismarck, if he is to be believed, was averse to the reincorporation of Alsace-Lorraine in the German Empire, at all events to the reincorporation of parts of it, but military clamour prevailed and the Provinces became German territory. From that day to this there has never been a sense of real security in Western Europe. Gambetta expressed French feeling when he said, " Never speak of it and never forget it." Whoever might possess these Provinces, they seem destined to be a perpetual bone of contention. Sovereigns have quarrelled over them and Republics have quarrelled over them.

* * *

It could not, however, have been expected that a Great Nation, which has been for centuries in the forefront of civilization and has a record of military prowess unsurpassed in history, would easily acquiesce in so severe a humiliation. For a time France was disabled by the severity of her defeat, and for a time, whatever happened, she was sure to harbour the hope of recovering by force of arms what she had lost. Yet, as year followed year, it is more than likely that this feeling would have died down if the Germans had acted with tact and magnanimity. The idea of *La Revanche* lay dormant after a few years, and a dislike of war certainly spread very widely among the working classes of France. Under the Republic these feelings were likely to become predominant. And the inhabitants of the conquered Provinces, though at first deeply attached to France, became largely Germanized by emigration and immigration and intermarriage. Most of them, if the Provinces be taken as a whole, made the best of a bad business, and nearly all of them, whatever might be their predilections, deprecated a fresh change if it was to be at the cost of a great war waged, as it would be, within their own borders. This circumstance tended toward peace, for it is one thing to redeem your countrymen from bondage, and quite a different thing to reannex a population which wishes to be let alone.

Another consideration could not be absent from the mind of any Frenchman who looked facts in the face. The population of France is and for some time has been practically stationary. The population of Germany has been, up to 1914, very rapidly increasing. When the war of 1914 broke out, the relative numbers were—French nearly forty million, German nearly sixty-eight million. With such a fearful disparity in numbers, and such a perfect military organization as throughout existed in Germany, what hope was there of so crushing her in the field as to be able to extort from her Alsace-Lorraine ? In France the excess of deaths over births was annually about thirty-five thousand. In Germany the excess of births over deaths was about seven hundred and forty thousand.

There are good reasons for believing that if the rulers of Germany had been wise and generous, all

the thoughts of revenge would have been in time
dissipated. Unhappily the rulers of Germany were
not wise or generous. The Treaty which consum-
mated Germany's great victories in the Franco-
German War was signed in 1871, and, only four years
later, the victorious German Government was seriously
considering a new attack on France, not because of
any offence given—for France remained silent and
void of offence, though at no time submissive—but
because of the unexpected rapidity with which she
recovered from the blow and of her anxiety to redeem
her Army from the corruption and mismanagement
of the past. Was, then, France not to be allowed any
but an inefficient Army ? The meditated attack did
not take place. Other Powers remonstrated. That
it should have been even contemplated shows what
dangers follow upon a policy of conquest from a
powerful enemy. He thenceforth watches you and
you watch him, and, sooner or later, having taken his
coat you feel tempted to take his cloak also if you can,
lest he may still prosper and be troublesome. Macbeth has taught us that one murder is apt to lead to
another. This incident of 1875 also illustrates the
character of the German Government, or perhaps one
ought to say the Prussian Government. It believed
that force is the only real remedy, whereas in nine
cases out of ten force is not a remedy at all but merely
a means of creating fresh trouble. France was not
attacked in 1875, but on more than one occasion since
then it is believed that similar designs were entertained
at Berlin and checked, be it said to his credit, by
Kaiser Wilhelm.

Nor was consideration shown by the German

Government to the annexed Provinces. Unquestionably the administration was highly efficient, in-
corrupt, and coldly just in matters which did not
concern policy or military organization. German
government is never effusive, but in many ways it
possessed the respect, if not the sympathy, of Germans
who are accustomed to it, as it is to them. Toward
people of French nationality, conquered and smarting
under the recollection of defeat, yet obliged to obey
their new masters, good sense would have suggested
some kindliness. After all, the quarrels between
France and Germany have always been brought on
by their rulers, not by the peoples, as indeed may be
said of nearly all wars. Things might have been
made easier for the vanquished. Instead of that,
things were made more difficult. For the most part
it was the Prussian, not the more conciliatory Saxon
or Bavarian or Wurtemberger who appeared in these
Provinces as administrator, and, when there, he proved
himself even more of a martinet than elsewhere. And
the pretensions of the military, which have for many
years been carried in Prussia to a point which is to
other nations quite incomprehensible, were exaggerated in Alsace-Lorraine. The well-known Zabern
incident shortly before the war illustrates what it had
come to. Why should there not have been some
sympathy shown? The Alsatians and Lorrainers
were fully the equals of their new masters, though
the latter might not see it. And even if they were
not, do we confine our sympathy to our equals? All
men and women are far better managed by kindness.
The German people, or their rulers, gifted and educated as they are, do not seem to have learned the

lessons of history. In Prince Lichnowsky's famous Memorandum he tells us how an Austrian colleague of his, who had been long in Paris, once said to him : " If the French begin to forget *la revanche*, you (Germans) regularly remind them of it by a good hard kick or two."

The Kaiser has more than once declared that he had striven his utmost to come to some reconciliation with France, and that all his advances had been repulsed. Had his father, the short-lived Emperor Frederick, been spared he might have healed the wound without either loss or risk of loss. He was a great soldier and a great gentleman, in the true sense of that word. That is to say, he thought of others besides himself and could feel for others. Men of that stamp are, it is true, rarely found in great positions. When found, they can fight hard enough if need be, but they know that a touch of human nature will do more in a twelvemonth, whether with victor or vanquished, toward softening enmity than can be accomplished in a generation by the rough hand. Gordon in China, Lord Canning in India, General Botha and General Smuts in South Africa, in very different circumstances, proved themselves such men. Such men were found at Washington after the great American Civil War. Until success comes their methods are apt to be stigmatized as weakness, whereas they are the truest strength. It is not by civil phrases or meaningless flattery, but by a genuine understanding of other men and unpretentious efforts to meet them half-way, that the miracle has often been wrought of converting hatred into esteem. So long as a gallant nation of ancient renown was periodically made to feel afresh the bitterness of its defeat, the Kaiser's personal efforts were doomed to failure. Had there been a General Gordon in Berlin there would have been a General Botha in Paris. Instead of that there were toward Alsatians and Lorrainers alternations of kicks and elephantine caresses, accompanied by a menacing military attitude, which constantly alarmed the French people.

*   *   *

Allusion has been made to the legitimate apprehensions of France, aroused in 1875 and later, of an unprovoked attack merely to cripple her hopelessly. A similar spirit was manifested in regard to French Colonial aspirations. France has been building up a great Colonial Empire, chiefly in tropical or semi-tropical regions, West Africa, Tongking, Madagascar, Morocco. These are not sources of strength but of weakness. Only those Colonies where Europeans can live and bring up families are really sources of strength. Such was Canada, where the old French Monarchy built up a great edifice, and then lost it because, on the strength of a settlement with a few thousand inhabitants, Louis XV insanely founded a claim to almost the entire North American Continent, in defiance of the British Settlements incomparably more numerous on what is now the eastern coast of the United States. They were defeated and lost Canada. They had their revenge within a few years when by equal folly we lost everything on that Continent except Canada. Such are the colossal blunders of men who by birth or accident become the Rulers of Nations. We are seeing at this moment the greatest illustration in history of the havoc that can be caused by the crimes and incompetence of men in power.

But after their defeat in 1871 the French sought some compensation in insalubrious colonization. Bismarck was wise enough to encourage them. He was then averse to German expansion beyond the seas, and glad to see his neighbours busy on what to him seemed an embarrassing and harmless expenditure of energy that might be more dangerously employed. A very different attitude was adopted after Bismarck had been displaced. It is not intended in this place to present even a sketch of French Colonial enterprise or German interference with it, merely to give an illustration in a few sentences of the vexations the French had to endure. Morocco lies on the frontier of Algeria. It was a perfectly lawless Mohammedan State, and a source of much annoyance on the frontier. It may be very immoral to annex lawless and un-civilized States. We can hardly say so with a grave countenance, for we have done this very thing on a larger scale than even the Roman Empire did in the old days. Let it, however, be assumed that many very worthy people were right in preferring that Morocco should remain uncontrolled under its savage Sultan and be inaccessible to everyone except at the peril of their lives. France throught otherwise and desired to annex Morocco. For the official cant of maintaining the " independence and integrity " of Morocco, which appeared in various Treaties, signed by all the Powers, as the virtuous resolve of Europe, deceived no one. It is true that France had been exclusive in her tariff. Germany had been the same at all events in Europe. At all events, French ambition was directed to Morocco, where she undoubtedly had special interests by reason of her Algerian dominions. Germany set herself to frustrate this ambition, not on grounds of morality, but because she desired an equivalent from France somewhere else. France was to hand over territory to Germany as a price. If Germany, which had no special interests in Morocco, could claim compensation, then every other nation could with equal right do the same. Why should one nation in the world be entitled to levy toll on the expansion of other nations? This dispute was not far from leading to war. On one occasion there was a quarrel between French and Germans at Casablanca. Refer it to arbitration, said the French. You must first apologize, said the Germans, though France claimed that she was the wronged party. When Germany was shamed out of this demand, the matter went to arbitration, and the arbitrators decided that no one should apologize on either side. These things were merely pieces of tactless irritation. The full merits of the dispute between France and Germany concerning Morocco are matter of controversy. So far as can be judged, there were faults both in substance and in manner on both sides.

An incident like this fairly exemplifies the spirit in which the Military Party in Germany regarded other nations. France was a decayed Power, Great Britain a decaying Power. The Russian Army was a horde of savages. This is not the attitude of well-balanced minds. But it would not necessarily end in war, for there was another and a very different Germany rapidly striding to power. Mr. Bonar Law, a very judicious observer, said before the war—and what is significant, has repeated since the war—that if it could have been averted for ten or fifteen years, it might have been averted altogether. The whole of Europe became alarmed. If they took counsel together how to avoid the menace of Germany, the German Government said that they were all making a ring around her in order to attack her at the right moment. It actually seems to be believed that this was the object of Sir Edward Grey. Whatever his faults, that was not one of them. If there was a conspiracy to make an attack on Germany, Sir Edward Grey was no party to it. He wished to live with her on neighbourly terms.

* * *

Enough has been said about the Storm Centre in Alsace-Lorraine to show what a source of danger it might become. There was a grievous wound, and German policy caused it to remain an open wound. So long, however, as France remained single-handed, the practical common sense which has always abounded in that country appreciated how desperate an affair it would be to encounter without an ally the enormous organized strength and great numerical superiority of the German Empire. Even those Frenchmen who wished to win back by force of arms what had been surrendered in 1871, saw that such an enterprise, single-handed at all events, was too dangerous. It is believed that the great majority of the nation looked forward to some other solution in which they might by cession of colonial territory or by some other method of equivalents recover at least that part of Alsace-Lorraine which was racially and characteristically

French, when saner ideas should get a hearing in the Council Chamber at Berlin. But the whole nation was unquestionably anxious to secure foreign support in view of the menacing cloud that overhung their eastern frontier. Nothing could be more natural. And the opportunity came in 1896, as everything comes to those who know how to wait.

Since the reversal, for it was nothing less, of Bismarck's policy by Kaiser Wilhelm II, Germany had been on far less intimate terms with Russia, though, as we learn from the Kaiser's telegram to the Czar on 31st July 1914, he had received from his dying grandfather a strict injunction to maintain friendship with that country. Probably the espousal by Germany of a strict Austrian alliance, which involved a support of Austrian policy in the Balkans, largely contributed to this estrangement. Probably the dictatorial patronizing methods of the Kaiser were distasteful to the Czar. Whatever the motive, in 1896 Russia contracted a Treaty of Alliance with France. Its terms have not been published, and Sir Edward Grey stated in August 1914 that they were unknown to him. But the publication of our own White Book in that month and references in the Diplomatic correspondence to the obligations of France to give Russia her military support in the event of war place it beyond doubt that the Treaty included a mutual promise of that kind. Sir Edward Grey has stated in Parliament he knew that the "French Government could not contemplate an attitude of neutrality in the event of Russia being attacked by Germany as well as by Austria." France obtained in this way a most valuable promise of support so long as she refrained from provocation. On the other hand, she paid for it

what has proved to be a terrible price, for it was by
virtue of this engagement that she has been drawn into
the Great War. Tolstoy, with the foresight of genius,
said that the Franco-Russian Alliance would be a great
injury to France. He knew the knavery of the Czar's
entourage and of the Kaiser's.

This Franco-Russian Treaty of 1896 is one of the
most important in all history. It gave France a considerable measure of security, and enabled her again
to stand upright in the Councils of Europe without
bowing before the constant menace of a neighbour
whose whole outlook on life was so different from her
own, whose ideas of government were the exact opposite to those of the Republic, material not spiritual,
despotic not Republican, resting upon mediæval
traditions. And it was a great gain that France could
breathe freely again. It is of the very essence in
human progress that the individual man and the individual nation should develop in their own way and
on their own lines. We are not all made to pipeclay
military accoutrements and get out of the road whenever an officer chooses to shove us into the gutter.
That was a great gain. The Franco-Russian Treaty
had another effect more far reaching. Thenceforth
the feud between German and Slav was linked up with
the feud between German and French. If anything
went wrong in the Balkans it would react in the West.
If Berlin and Paris fell out, St. Petersburg would
have to look to its weapons. For the Allies on both
sides would almost inevitably be brought in. Germany
had an alliance with Austria. France now had an
alliance with Russia. Italy had an alliance with Germany. A single quarrel between two of the Great

Powers on the Continent would bring the gravest
danger.   If a third Power intervened then the quarrel
automatically became general.   They were like Alpine
climbers who are roped to one another.   If one stumbles
fatally, all must perish.   That was what Tolstoy saw.
To walk alone on the edge of a precipice is dangerous.
To be fastened to a comrade who may stumble is still
more dangerous.

＊   ＊   ＊

There can be no question that the Franco-Russian
Alliance caused great uneasiness in Berlin, as it naturally might.   For a long time the besetting apprehension
of German Governments has been a combination
against them of France and Russia.   It was Bismarck's
great aim to prevent such a combination, and the
German people have always dreaded it.   We often
have asked ourselves how Germans have been led to
tolerate the remarkable predominance of military men
and the military discipline which has been there applied
in civil affairs till the country almost came to bear the
aspect of a huge armed camp.   We must come to understand it if we are to understand recent events.   It was
the fear of a Franco-Russian combination that chiefly
made them endure it.   A strong army was for them
a prime necessity of existence.   They suffered for want
of it in the reigns of Louis XIV and Louis XV when
those sovereigns constantly meddled with one German
State or another, and almost regarded an inroad into
Germany as a diversion in which they might indulge
with impunity unless some other Power interposed.
Even in the days of Frederick the Great a Russian
invasion, while he was also at war with France,
brought him near to suicide, and his Kingdom near

to ruin. In Napoleon's time again Germany suffered
more than will ever be told, and some of the suffering
was inflicted by Russia. Then came the great
patriotic rising of the German nation, and the
work of Stein and Hardenberg in Prussia. All had
suffered because all had not stood together. Union
became the great aim of patriotic Germans, and
who shall say they were wrong ? It is not union
but the way it has been used of which other nations
have such unanswerable reasons to complain. Once
their union had been accomplished, the memory
of past afflictions taught the whole nation that it
must be maintained. Past history has had a very
full share in making the Germans what they are.
It was the fear of France and Russia which led
Germans to accept that rigid military system which
has led to such frightful results.

Mr. Lloyd George has on two occasions very frankly
and very properly directed attention to this most important consideration. He said, on 28th July 1908 :
" Here is Germany in the middle of Europe, with
France and Russia on either side, and with a combination of their armies greater than hers. Suppose
we had here a possible combination which would lay
us open to invasion—suppose Germany and France,
or Germany and Russia, or Germany and Austria had
fleets which, in combination, would be stronger than
ours, would not we be frightened ? Would not we
arm ? Of course we should." Five or six years later,
the same speaker is reported in the *Daily Chronicle*
as saying : " The German Army is vital, not merely
to the existence of the German Empire, but to the
very life and independence of the nation itself, sur-

rounded as Germany is by other nations, each of which possesses armies about as powerful as her own. We forget that, while we insist upon a 60 per cent superiority (so far as our strength is concerned) over Germany being essential to guarantee the integrity of our own shores, Germany herself has nothing like that superiority over France alone, and she has, of course, in addition to reckon with Russia on her eastern frontier." It is true these things were said before the war, and the relative strength of the German Army as compared with the French Army was understated, as we can now see. But the central fact was indisputable. Germans became united and maintained a vast army because their geographical position between two very powerful military nations made it necessary for them alone among the Great Powers to defend themselves, if attacked, on two frontiers against superior numbers. If they had kept their army to its proper function of defending their own country there would have been no cause for complaint. The evil was that they allowed its chiefs to dictate the national policy, and that policy has been purely selfish, without regard either to the rights or feelings of others.

*   *   *

When it was announced that an alliance had been contracted between France and Russia, the German Government drew the reins still tighter. True to their theory that force is everything, they pushed their military organization yet further, and adopted a still more peremptory attitude in their dealings with other Powers. It is the history of every military Government that has afflicted mankind. From the Franco-

Russian Treaty must be dated the rapid increase of armaments in Europe, which had been bad enough already. The Czar of Russia made a memorable attempt to limit them. Great Britain attempted first by example and then by negotiation to limit them. Of their very nature they remain illimitable so long as the causes which give rise to them remain unaltered. When Germany increased her expenditure on armaments, Russia and France did the same, Italy and Austria did the same. A demand for weapons came from the Balkans. Turkey followed suit in a perfunctory way. Great Britain enormously increased her estimates. And if there were showed at any time a disposition in any quarter to diminish this ruinous outlay, there were always the great armament firms with their privately owned newspapers and their unlimited command of money to insist that not concurrent diminution but still further increase was necessary for the preservation of every country in turn. Armaments depend on policy. Is it not also sometimes true that policy depends upon armaments ?

* * *

For the sake of clearness the story of Alsace-Lorraine, of the bitter feeling its usage aroused in France, of the alarm created in France, and of the support obtained by her in the Russian Treaty of 1896, has been briefly told without any reference to Great Britain. And indeed there is no direct connection between that Treaty and the gradual steps by which the subsequent Entente between the French and ourselves came into existence. But the same motives which led Frenchmen to desire an alliance with Russia must naturally have inclined them to secure, if they could, something of the same kind with us as well.   It must have seemed at first an almost impossible aspiration.   Nevertheless it was accomplished.   We must now see how it was accomplished.

CHAPTER IV

GREAT BRITAIN IS DRAWN INTO A
FRENCH ALLIANCE

FRANCE has been prolific of consummate diplomatists all through history, but her annals record no more brilliant achievement than that of M. Delcassé and M. Cambon when they brought Great Britain into a French alliance. Even those who hold that the happiness of the world would have been better secured without it must admit the skill and the pertinacity with which these two statesmen pursued their purpose. It was a perfectly honourable purpose, always honourably pursued. Their difficulties were stupendous. British Governments had for years stood aloof from the dangerous quarrels of the Continent. When these two men began their task, France had for years been singularly ill disposed towards us. It was the Period of Pinpricks. We were meeting her in many parts of the world. Everywhere, notably in Egypt and Newfoundland, disagreeable incidents followed by unedifying wrangles were apt to occur. The partition of Africa was in progress. Those were the days of Cecil Rhodes, of Empire-building and of a new Imperialism, personified in Mr. Chamberlain. Though this new temper of Imperialism undoubtedly tended

towards a departure from the old traditional foreign
policy of Great Britain, it did not tend in those
days towards good relations either with France
or Russia. Quite the contrary. Short as public
memory is, we cannot have wholly forgotten how
Mr. Chamberlain told the French in 1899 that they
must "mend their manners," and said in 1898 that
we needed "long spoons" to sup with Russia. Nor
can we have forgotten Fashoda. How far off these
memories seem now. Yet it is only twenty years ago.
What is still more remarkable has been quite forgotten
to-day. Mr. Chamberlain in a public speech advocated an alliance between this country and Germany.
The German Government would not entertain it, lest
it might embroil them with Russia or because they
had in view projects of which we were sure to dis-
approve.

A state of ill-suppressed irritation existed between
this country and France for some years before the
Franco-Russian Alliance of 1896 and continued for
some five or six years after that date. There were
moments when it became alarming. In 1898 a serious
crisis arose. Major Marchand and a few score of French
troops marched through great waste regions of Africa,
only to find Lord Kitchener and a vastly superior
British force in Fashoda. A collision was averted by
the good sense of the two distinguished soldiers, but
the settlement had to be made at home. It proved
a little difficult. There is a story that the British
Ambassador at one stage had in his pocket something like an ultimatum, and intimated as much
to M. Delcassé. "Do not show it to me," said the
latter. "You know what must be a French Minister's

answer to a communication of that kind." An admirable attitude, which ended in a peaceful settlement. One other incident may be recalled. France as a whole bitterly opposed our action in regard to the Jameson Raid. And when we were at war with the Boer Republics, France extended an enthusiastic welcome to President Kruger.

General Botha is reported to have said in September 1915: "At the time of the South African War, other nations were prepared to assist the Boers, but they stipulated that Germany should do likewise. The Kaiser refused." It suggests strange thoughts, if it be true, as it seems to be, that the refusal of Germany to join in this project caused it to fall through. In all history there had been antagonism between France and England. It had become very pronounced just prior to 1904, and that is the point here.

* * *

Nevertheless, in that year common sense came to the rescue. We on this side of the Channel had no desire to quarrel, and Frenchmen began to see that it would be insensate on their part to provoke our hostility if they could have our friendship instead. Accordingly, in 1904 a Treaty was signed under the auspices of Lord Lansdowne between the two Powers. Certainly there could have been no intention on Lord Lansdowne's side of making this country a party to aggressive designs, if such existed in Paris, or of engaging us in any war in which France should be embroiled. The Treaty simply provided for our future relations in Egypt, Newfoundland, and other places where we might otherwise cross each other's paths. Morocco is named as a place where France should have practically a free hand, but there as elsewhere nothing beyond diplomatic assistance is promised. Lord Lansdowne intimated that he hoped for friendly agreements of a like order with other Powers also, among whom Germany was undoubtedly included, and no secret was made either here or in France of our desire to make friends with other nations as well.

Amply justifiable though this Treaty of 1904 was, as a means of adjusting troublesome differences, and innocent though it must be considered of any offence towards other States either in its contents or in its intention, yet it proved to be a milestone on the road that led this country into the present war. In the relations existing between France and Germany, though there could be no possible objection to our contracting a friendship with either, there was always a danger lest it might develop into hostility toward the other. That was the one thing that our Foreign Office ought most scrupulously to have avoided, so as to maintain goodwill toward all other Powers, unless indeed a change of policy were sanctioned by Parliament and its consequences duly provided for.

This was doubly true when becoming tied to France might mean being indirectly obliged to support Russia also.

*   *   *

The French Government, once they had resolved in 1904 upon a conciliatory policy toward Great Britain, followed it out with complete thoroughness and loyalty. They fulfilled their obligations as regards Egypt and Newfoundland with scrupulous fidelity. They exerted themselves to the utmost in heralding a new era of friendship. An opportunity of testing its value very soon came. In the autumn of 1904 occurred what is remembered as the Dogger Bank incident. The Russian Fleet, on its way out to Japan, fired on some British fishing vessels in the North Sea. It was an inexcusable act, due to a panic. Reparation was made, but there remained for a little time a dangerous spirit on the Russian side which in the angry feeling that prevailed in this country might easily have led to trouble. France, the Ally of Russia, used her good offices to compose the dispute. A few years earlier she might have been busy to inflame it. Conduct like this on the part of France naturally disposed us to be equally scrupulous in performing our part of the bargain.

Some private telegrams between the Kaiser and the Czar were published in 1917, showing that in connection with the Dogger Bank incident the Kaiser tried to engage both Russia and France in an anti-British combination. At first the Czar agreed, but soon afterwards drew back because France would not concur. Full particulars about this (the Secret Treaty of Bjorke) will be found in Dr. Dillon's *Eclipse of Russia*. He knew it in 1905. Our Foreign Office was sure to be informed, and could estimate the danger of making the British Empire depend upon the caprices of Russia.

Next year, 1905–6, came the turn of Great Britain to fulfil her part of the 1904 Treaty. A serious difference arose between France and Germany in regard to Morocco. It ended for a time, but only for a time, in the Algeciras Conference and an agreement between France and Germany. Both Jaurès and André Mevil, a personal friend of Delcassé, have declared that

Great Britain offered to support France in arms against Germany on this occasion, and that Lord Lansdowne gave some promise of this kind in 1905, and M. Delcassé seems to have said that in the event of war England would be with France.[1] It will be found that so far as Lord Lansdowne is concerned this is wholly without foundation. Sir Edward Grey became, on 12th December 1905, Foreign Secretary in Sir Henry Campbell-Bannerman's Government. He stepped straight into the pending dispute about Morocco, and such was the course taken that, before he had been a month in office, an immense stride was made in the development of intimate relations between this country and France. Very great importance attaches to what then occurred, for it gave a new direction to our foreign policy from that day right up to the outbreak of this war.

Sir Edward has given his own account of it in the House of Commons on 3rd August 1914, describing for the first time in public what passed between himself and the Ambassadors of France and Germany respectively. Date, the end of December 1905 or beginning of January 1906. Scene, the Foreign Office in London. Occasion, a crisis in the relations between France and Germany relating to Morocco, which appeared to be drifting towards danger, unless some expedient could be discovered. The French Ambassador in private asked Sir Edward whether if that crisis developed into war we would give to France our armed support. Here is Sir Edward Grey's answer: [2]

[1] See these statements in Canon Masterman and Mr. Gooch's book, called a *Century of Foreign Policy.*
[2] Speech of Sir E. Grey in House of Commons, 3rd August 1914.

" I said then that I could promise nothing to any foreign Power unless it was subsequently to receive the whole-hearted support of public opinion here if the occasion arose. I said, in my opinion if war was forced upon France then on the question of Morocco—a question which had just been the subject of agreement between this country and France—an agreement exceedingly popular on both sides—that if out of that agreement war was forced on France at that time, in my view public opinion would have rallied to the material support of France. I gave no promise, but I expressed that opinion during the crisis, as far as I remember, almost in the same words to the French Ambassador and the German Ambassador at the time. I made no promise and I used no threats, but I expressed that opinion." Those who remember the House of Commons elected in January 1906, and its strong resentment at the Imperialist War in South Africa, will by no means agree that public opinion would in 1906 have rallied to the material support of France. It would have been vehemently opposed to it. This shows the danger of Ministers shaping the national policy upon their own conjecture of what the public may think instead of ascertaining it in a constitutional way from the representatives of the public.

However carefully the language of promise or threat might be avoided, expectation on one side and apprehension on the other must of necessity be awakened when a Foreign Secretary speaks in that tone. Our obligations concerning Morocco, as expressed in the Anglo-French Treaty, were strictly confined to diplomatic support. This was something quite different. One can imagine the lively satisfaction of M. Cambon at discovering in the new Liberal Minister a man so well disposed toward his overtures. The French Government were naturally enterprising enough to push still farther against the half-open door. The German Government, who, as Sir Edward tells us, were informed of this at the time, were naturally alarmed.

After thus describing what he said in December 1905 or January 1906 to the French and German Ambassadors about Great Britain then going to war with Germany over the Moroccan controversy, Sir Edward Grey's account of how France received what he said proceeds as follows :

" That position was accepted by the French Government, but they said to me at the time, and I think very reasonably, ' If you think it possible that the public opinion of Great Britain might, should a sudden crisis arise, justify you in giving to France the armed support which you cannot promise in advance, you will not be able to give that support, even if you wish it when the time comes, unless some conversations have already taken place between naval and military experts.' There was force in that. I agreed to it, and authorized those conversations to take place, but on the distinct understanding that nothing which passed between military or naval experts should bind either Government or restrict in any way their freedom to make a decision as to whether or not they would give that support when the time arose."

To make plans with one Power for a common war against another Power, should necessity for it arise, is a serious matter, and whatever reservations may be expressed as to preserving freedom of action, the attitude of the one country toward the other will be indelibly affected by such an intimate co-operation. It does not create but it portends a future alliance, and indeed makes such a conclusion almost unavoidable.

These communications with the French and German Ambassadors, and the authorization Sir Edward then gave for military and naval conversations between our officers and those of France, were not told even to the Cabinet. But it is right on such a point to quote Sir Edward Grey's own statement, which will be found in the same speech.

Sir Edward said: " I must go back to the first Moroccan crisis of 1906. That was the time of the Algeciras Conference, and I—spending three days a week in my constituency and three days at the Foreign Office—was asked the question whether if that crisis developed into war between France and Germany, we would give armed support." He then repeated the answer he gave, and the authority he gave for military and naval conversations with France, which has been already transcribed in his own language, and proceeded to state that he had not informed the Cabinet at the time, and gave his reason for not doing so. " As I have told the House, upon that occasion a General Election was in prospect : I had to take the responsibility of doing that without the Cabinet. It could not be summoned. An answer had to be given. I consulted Sir Henry Campbell-Bannerman, the Prime Minister : I consulted, I remember, Lord Haldane, who was then Secretary of State for War, and the present Prime Minister (Mr. Asquith), who was then Chancellor of the Exchequer. That was the most I could

do, and they authorized that, on the distinct understanding that it left the hands of the Government
free whenever the crisis arose. The fact that conversations between military and naval experts took
place was later on—I think much later on, because
that crisis passed and the thing ceased to be of
importance—but later on it was brought to the
knowledge of the Cabinet." He does not say when.

*   *   *

We are considering what was the policy which preceded and guided this country into war, and even the
briefest parenthesis ought to be avoided if possible.
But one of Sir Edward Grey's then colleagues may
be permitted, in view of his statement about with-
holding the information from the Cabinet, to offer
certain criticisms. Sir Edward's phraseology rather
conveys that his selection of confidants was casual.
But Mr. Asquith and Lord Haldane were with himself Vice-Presidents of the Liberal League, a con-
tinuation of the Liberal Imperialist movement which
had supported the South African War and opposed
Sir Henry Campbell-Bannerman on that subject.

There was no difficulty whatever in summoning
the Cabinet during the Election to consider so grave
a matter. A good many members of the Cabinet were
in London or within an hour of it, while those whom
he consulted were at a distance. And there are
railways and post offices in Great Britain.[1]

The Cabinet met in January 1906. They might

---

[1] The weekly meetings of the Cabinet were regular in December
1905, and were held on 3rd and 31st January 1906. From 1st
February they were again regular throughout the year 1906. The
Cabinet might have been told within a very short time.

then have been told of the " conversations " between
military experts, and of the statement made to the two
Ambassadors of which latter Sir Edward does not say
that they were ever informed at all. The military
conversations must have lasted some time, and after
January 1906 the Cabinet was meeting regularly.

Sir Edward does not say when these " conversations " between experts were brought to the knowledge
of the Cabinet, whether it was months or years, and
how many years later.

The reason he apparently gives for not informing
the Cabinet, which he says " could not then be
summoned," as soon as it did meet (31st January),
is that " that crisis passed and the thing ceased to be
of importance." On the contrary, events have unhappily proved that it was of the utmost abiding
importance. It was the first recorded communication pointing to our making war on behalf of France
if she should come to blows with Germany.

The thing of which Sir Edward Grey made light
proved to be the parting of the ways in our relations
with France. Enmity had already given place to
goodwill, but we had not yet espoused the quarrel of
France or held out the prospect of fighting by her side.
In the beginning of 1906 her statesmen learned that
even this was possible. This concealment from the
Cabinet was protracted, and must have been deliberate.
Parliament knew nothing of it till 3rd August 1914,
nor anything of the change in policy which the suppressed communications denoted.

* * *

His Majesty's Government have published in their
Collected Diplomatic Documents some documents

6

which throw a fresh light on what passed between the British and French Ministers at the commencement of 1906. Shortly after the beginning of the war a German newspaper issued in facsimile copies certain papers which had been found by the Germans in Brussels. Their authenticity has not been denied, though it is obvious that they are merely selections from the numerous papers of the Belgian Government which came into German hands. It will be convenient to summarize their contents. They are undoubtedly authentic and may be found both in the Belgian Official Book and in our Blue Book, Cd. 7860 of 1915.

The Chief of the Belgian General Staff reports to his Minister of War in 1906 that he has had conversations with Colonel Barnardiston of the British Army. Colonel Barnardiston saw him first in the middle of January 1906, and told him that the British General Staff was preoccupied about the possibilities of war and that, should Belgium be attacked, it was proposed to send (from England) about 100,000 men. Colonel Barnardiston asked how such a step would be interpreted. The entry of the English into Belgium would only take place after the violation of Belgian neutrality by Germany—so says a marginal note in the facsimile.

Colonel Barnardiston proceeded to say, according to this Report, that the disembarkation of the British troops would take place on the French coast, and that the question of their transport and other incidental questions remained to be decided. He also asked about the condition of Belgian defences, and emphasized the following points : that the con-

versation was absolutely confidential, that it was
in no way binding on the British Government,
that his Minister (Mr. Haldane), the British General
Staff, he, and myself (the Chief of the Belgian
General Staff) were the only persons then aware of
the matter, and that he did not know whether his
Sovereign (King Edward) had been consulted. At a
further interview Colonel Barnardiston asked him to
study the question of transport and of the chief command. Further conversations ensued in regard to
details of the disembarkation, and as the plans of the
British General Staff advanced, "the details of the
problem were worked out with greater precision." At
another interview, says the Chief of the Belgian
General Staff, " Colonel Barnardiston and I examined
the question of combined operations in the event of a
German attack directed against Antwerp and on the
hypothesis of our (Belgian) territory being crossed
in order to reach the French Ardennes," and subsequently Colonel Barnardiston "signified his concurrence in the scheme I had laid before him, and
assured me of the assent of General Grierson, Chief
of the British General Staff." In the course of these
conversations "Colonel Barnardiston confided to
me," continued the Chief of the General Staff, "that
his Government intended to move the British base
of supplies from the French coast to Antwerp as
soon as the North Sea had been cleared of all German
warships." This began in the middle of January
1906 and all happened between the middle of January
1906 and the 10th of April 1906, for the latter is
the date of the Report made by the Belgian Chief
of the Staff containing the narrative. During this

time the Cabinet was meeting regularly. It has
never been stated that these conversations, if they
took place, were brought to the knowledge of our
Cabinet, and they were proceeding long after the
General Election was ended. It does not even appear that any Minister knew of them except Colonel
Barnardiston's Minister, though it is difficult to suppose
none knew.

Another document relating to military conversations between Belgian and British officers was published in the German Press after the war commenced,
but as it relates not to the year 1906 but the year 1912
it will be dealt with a little later on.

*　　*　　*

Now these documents were published by the German
Government through their Press at the end of 1914
in order to establish their contention that Great
Britain and France with the privity of Belgium had as
early as 1906 arranged to encircle Germany and attack
her in concert with France.　A despatch of Baron
Greindl, Belgian Minister at Berlin, was also published,
presumably to show that he shared in that opinion
in 1911.　Baron Greindl does not there say so, and his
opinion, if he had said so, has no weight in interpreting
the intentions of Great Britain.　Nor did Colonel
Barnardiston say so.　The conversations with Belgium
of January–April 1906 show no more than that
Colonel Barnardiston and those who commissioned
him were apprehensive of a German attack on Belgium
and desired to make preparations for resisting that
attack by force of arms.　Whether or not it was wise
or straightforward toward Parliament and the Cabinet
that these communications should pass in secret, as

the Report says they did, is quite a different question, or, rather, two different questions, but Germany could not with any show of reason complain of communications to meet the contingency of her violating the neutrality of an unoffending neighbour.   In fact, it is clear from the documents numbered 1, 3, 5, 6 in the Appendix to the Belgian Grey Book printed in the Collected Diplomatic Documents, that the British Government did not make any agreement with Belgium, and did not at any time contemplate such a thing as violation of her neutrality by Great Britain, unless it had been first violated by Germany and our action should meet with the assent of Belgium, in which case, of course, it would not be a violation.

We are not, however, concerned with this point of view at the present moment, nor with our duty toward Belgium.   What concerns us is the gradual growth of the Entente between Great Britain and France till it came to be virtually the equivalent of an Alliance.   In that connection the conversations between the British and Belgian Staffs in 1906 are important, for they show that France was a party to the design of sending British troops to Belgium in the event of a German invasion.   These troops were to be landed at French ports and conveyed over French railways to the Belgian frontier, and this could not of course be contemplated without French co-operation. It was not indeed an engagement, but was it not just the material out of which a duty from one nation to another takes its origin ?   And it was being done secretly.   That is a feature of our diplomacy which cannot safely be allowed to continue.

A couple of years later, in 1907, the British Govern-

ment publicly entered into a convention with Russia
which was no doubt facilitated by the friendship of
France. Its purpose was to remove causes of difference
such as had arisen in regard to Persia and Afghanistan.
It threatened no one. Indeed, when the annexation of Bosnia and Herzegovina in the following year
led to danger of war between Austria and Russia and
brought out Germany in " shining armour," Sir
Edward Grey told the Russian Minister that he
could not promise him anything more than diplomatic
assistance. But our new friendship with Russia
facilitated still closer relations with France. Step
by step we were drawing nearer and nearer. M.
Delcassé and M. Cambon must have felt that they
were on the road to the goal of their ambitions. An
excellent thing it certainly was, to become friends
with France, provided it did not bind us to enmity
towards others or fetter our control of our own policy.

*   *   *

Presently the same subject, Morocco, which had
given rise to such serious trouble within a month
of Sir Edward Grey's accession to office, presented
itself again in an alarming aspect. Even the war
has not made us forget the Agadir crisis of 1911—
how the smouldering animosities between France and
Germany burst out again, France being obliged, as
she said, to establish what amounted to a Protectorate,
Germany complaining that this was a violation of
Treaty engagements. All of a sudden the Kaiser in
1911 sent a ship to Agadir. Whatever may have been
the merits of the dispute between the two countries—
and there have been many conflicting versions—this
step could only be regarded as a direct challenge and

menace by the German Government. It was the worst possible way of doing the wrong thing.

Diplomatically, as by Treaty bound, in the Agadir affair Great Britain took the side of France. Did our Government go further? In the Round Table of March 1915 a specific statement is made that on 21st July 1911 Great Britain informed the German Government of her intention to stand beside France if Germany demanded the whole of the French Congo (as compensation for giving a free hand in Morocco), and especially if she proposed to take Agadir as a naval base. The same authority adds that after a War Council at Potsdam, at which it was decided that Germany was not ready for war, she gave way and consented to the occupation of Morocco by France and Spain, obtaining for herself some compensations in Africa. This statement means that Sir Edward threatened in 1911 to stand by France in arms. But it would be unjust to Sir Edward Grey were it accepted without proof, for he said nothing of it when giving his explanation to the House of Commons in the speech from which we have already quoted on 3rd August 1914. He devoted only one sentence to the Agadir crisis: " throughout that I took precisely the same line that had been taken in 1906." Undoubtedly in 1911 Great Britain supported France diplomatically, as we were bound to do by the Treaty of 1904. He says nothing about the Cabinet, or the information given to the Cabinet, or when it was given in regard to the Agadir affair. But "precisely the same line " implies that there was some concealment.

*   *   *

One of the documents published by the German

Government in the Press after the war had begun has a direct bearing upon what passed in 1911 between our Government and the French. It is the facsimile of a memorandum found by them in Brussels, dated 24th April 1912. It has a bearing on the Agadir affair of 1911. The British Military Attaché, Colonel Bridges, was asked to meet General Jungbluth, the Belgian Officer, and met him on 23rd April 1912. Colonel Bridges, the British Military Attaché, then said, according to this memorandum, that Great Britain had 160,000 men available for despatch to the Continent, and that " the British Government, at the time of the recent events (clearly the Agadir crisis of 1911), would have immediately landed troops on our (Belgian) territory, even if we had not asked for help, and that General Jungbluth protested that our (Belgian) consent would be necessary for this. The British Military Attaché answered that he knew that, but that as we were not in a position to prevent the Germans passing through our territory, Great Britain would have landed her troops in any event. As to the place of landing, the Military Attaché was not explicit." The statement that Colonel Bridges so expressed himself has not been denied, nor does it anywhere appear from whom he derived authority to make so serious a statement. Whether or not this was in fact said, and whether it was said by direction of the Military Staff or by the authority of a Minister, is not known—Lord Haldane has denied that the British Government ever arranged with Belgium to " trespass " on her country in case of war (see his letter to Dr. Shipley, Cd. 7860 of 1915 at p. 365). Till further information is available the matter must be left there. It is not stated whether Lord Haldane informed anyone of these conversations, or, if he did, whom he informed and when.

* * *

It is, however, certain that the events of 1911 made a strong impression. In France a confident expectation began to be entertained that the Entente would be regarded in England as involving military support in the event of a Franco-German war. In Germany it was believed that we would have stood by France in arms if the Agadir affair had led to war. As is well known, Germany did in the end compromise the dispute in 1911 by giving France a free hand in Morocco in exchange for some territorial cessions in Africa. The military party at Berlin affected to treat the whole affair as a humiliation, and threw upon Great Britain the blame for having inflicted it. Thus we were steadily being drawn deeper and deeper into the Continental system. And the Continental system itself, the august fabric of European States, with its code of usages and old-world ceremonious intercourse and seeming stability and vast strength undermined by hatred, was itself being rapidly whirled away to unknown fearful depths, as if by some inexorable destiny. It subsisted on credit and confidence. Confidence had been woefully impaired. That was the secret fountain of despair. The Continental States stood in fear of being overreached or caught of a sudden by some unexpected attack. Treaties came to be no longer trusted after the action of Austria and Germany in 1908 in regard to Bosnia and Herzegovina. And so everyone looked to his weapons, wondering what would come of it all. Armageddon came within

less than three years of the Agadir settlement.
Certainly it was not an inviting European system
to enter, especially if you were not armed to the
teeth.

* * *

But a great effort was made at the end of 1911,
lasting during those three years 1911–1914, to lay
the foundations of peace. A feeling of alarm became
pronounced among business men. The fear was that
we were drifting into an alliance with France which
might lead us into a war with Germany. That
was probably the impulse which led to the serious
efforts that were then made for a friendly accommodation between Great Britain and Germany. In
Germany there were two opposing parties. One of
them, supported by the military and the Junkers or
agricultural magnates and squires, by some of the
diplomatists, and those classes which in every country
regard force as the only means of attaining greatness,
courted a warlike policy, though they neither wished
nor expected to find England among their enemies
so soon. The other party, consisting of artisans and
peasants, merchants and manufacturers, and the great
world of business, together with the seven million
inhabitants of the provinces conquered by Prussia
and all the Socialists, though differing in other opinions,
yet favoured peace. In the French Yellow Book
(Yellow Book, No. 5) may be found an interesting
Report made in July 1913 to the Minister for Foreign
Affairs on the strength and motives of these contending
parties—pride, jealousy, fear of reform at home,
hatred of hereditary enemies, need of markets, a per-
verted education, and false ideals of patriotism on the

one side; democratic aspirations, fear of economic injury, love of quiet, hatred of Prussian methods on the other side. The conflict was very genuine in Germany, and both sets of antagonists sincere enough ; but the War Party had a great advantage in the station and authority of its leading men and in the disproportionate parliamentary power they possessed owing to electoral contrivances which we should call jerry-mandering. After all, there as elsewhere, the great bulk of the people were too much engrossed in maintaining themselves and their families to exert persistent influence, even if popular opinion had much weight under the German Constitution. It is probable that the Kaiser desired peace, till he was finally overborne. It is certain that the commercial classes as a whole desired it. However that may be, sustained efforts were undoubtedly made by Sir Edward Grey and also by the German Government in the three years 1911–1914 to create friendly relations between Great Britain and Germany. They began in the end of 1911, immediately after the Agadir crisis had been settled, and the Governments concerned saw the danger clearly.

In discussing how the entente between this country and France eventually became equivalent to an alliance, our relations with Germany are an indispensable ingredient.

         *   *   *

The settlement of their Moroccan dispute between France and Germany was signed on 4th November 1911. Its terms had been agreed a few weeks earlier. Now that the whole business of Morocco was settled and done for, the stumbling-block which had led us into conflict with Germany disappeared from the scene, and the road was thus cleared for a new departure. Why should we not adjust our compasses and set up better relations? The Civil Government of Germany at once indicated a readiness to try. Sir Edward Grey displayed an equal readiness. Setting aside differences now ended with the agreement about Morocco, which had been their source, it was the duty of all British Ministers to remove bad feeling with Germany. Our goodwill with France and Russia commenced with a frank discussion of existing . differences and a frank settlement of them. Friendship followed in the wake of those settlements. Why not attempt the same thing with Germany also, now that Morocco no longer stood in the way? Both London and Berlin assented. Negotiations commenced near the end of 1911 for an understanding in regard to our respective possessions and prospects in Africa to prevent future controversy and ensure present harmony. They progressed favourably, and before the war broke out an agreement had been attained. Further negotiations were undertaken in regard to the whole controversy about the Bagdad Railway and its attendant problems, which involved German activities in Asia Minor. Here also we came to terms with Germany shortly before the war broke out.[1] For a great part of the two or three years with which we are here concerned, winter 1911–August 1914, these *pourparlers* proceeded, and their influence in enabling the one Government to understand the other, in softening asperities, grew apace, as always happens when antagonists are brought

[1] See Prince Lichnowsky's memorandum entitled *My London Mission.*

together. It seems strange to think of it now, but the British and German Governments had come to be on excellent terms by the summer of 1914. There was only one danger, the danger that Germany might be brought into antagonism with France and we might be drawn into the quarrel. But we had been assured by Mr. Asquith and Sir Edward Grey that we were free from all engagements as regards France. Sir E. Grey still thought so on 3rd August 1914.

* * *

In other directions also the two Governments of Great Britain and Germany approached one another with a view of removing discord in the same two or three years. We in this country felt legitimate anxiety at the immense growth of the German Navy. An exchange of views upon this subject took place, not for the first time, very soon after the Franco-German Settlement of Morocco. In February 1912, on an intimation from Germany that a visit by some British Minister would be welcome, Lord Haldane went to Berlin. The Government has refused to publish his report of what passed during this visit. It is a pity that they thus decline to set at rest various quite untrue versions. Some facts, however, have been publicly stated by Mr. Asquith. The German Government in February 1912 proposed that both nations should agree to observe neutrality if either of them should be engaged in war. If this offer were made in good faith, it is not easy to see anything necessarily disgraceful in it. Treaties of alliance often bind two nations to go much further than neutrality and actually to take up arms for their ally. There is nothing discreditable in asking for a Treaty of neutrality,-

unless it involves a request for the violation of some
other national engagement. And our Ministers have
always maintained that we had made no such other
engagement. The Foreign Office published a statement at the end of August 1915 in which they explain
that the main German proposal of neutrality would
have left each party free to fulfil its existing Treaties,
and that this would give a great advantage to Germany,
which had a Treaty with Austria, while we had no
Treaties that would affect our neutrality except with
Japan and Portugal. This was one point on which
they indicate that this German proposal was declined.
So far, however, from treating it as an unworthy
proposal, our Government continued to deal with the
German Government and to speak of it publicly in
the most cordial terms through 1912 and 1913. There
is quite a constellation of utterances to this effect.
In order to present an accurate view of the relations
with Germany which the war violently terminated,
here are a few quotations. On 14th February 1912
Mr. Asquith spoke of "unmistakable evidence
of a sincere and resolute desire upon both sides to
establish a better footing." Three days later Sir
Edward Grey said also, referring to Lord Haldane's
visit to Berlin : "Something, I trust, has been achieved
which will remain permanent, which has made the
sky brighter and clearer, and dispelled some of the
mists of suspicion and distrust." On 25th July 1912
Mr. Asquith said : "Our relations with the great
German Empire are, I am glad to say, at this moment—
and I feel sure are likely to remain—relations of amity
and goodwill. Lord Haldane paid a visit to Berlin
early in the year ; he entered upon conversations and

an interchange of views which have been continued since in a spirit of perfect frankness and friendship, both on one side and the other."

In April 1913 Mr. Asquith said : " The Governments of the Great Powers—I say it without qualification or reserve—are animated by a common purpose, which, while it overrides any selfish or particular interests of their own, is in no sense otherwise than friendly, subject to the conditions of equal justice, to the development of free, self-governing communities." The language is a little involved, but the clear sense is that in the speaker's opinion Germany was friendly to free self-government.

At the time they made these speeches, both Sir Edward Grey and Mr. Asquith knew, of course, the German proposal that we should make with them a Treaty of mutual neutrality. They were not shocked by it at the time. It is not that proposal but the subsequent action of Germany that merits condemnation.

These were not isolated individual Parliamentary statements made with a purpose of propitiating a powerful adversary. They represented a settled opinion. After the worst had come, Mr. Lloyd George said in a speech on 10th November 1914 : " When this war broke out, we were on better terms with Germany than we had been for fifteen years. There was not a man in the Cabinet who thought that war with Germany was a possibility under the present conditions." [1]

*　*　*

[1] In 1913, nearly a year after he had left the Cabinet, the present writer publicly drew attention to these assurances of Mr. Asquith

A curious testimony to the prevalence of similar views among the German Civil Ministers may be found in the despatch of 8th August 1914, written by our Ambassador, Sir E. Goschen, after his return from Berlin in August 1914. He had trying interviews with Herr Von Jagow, the Secretary of State, and Dr. Bethmann-Hollweg, the Chancellor. When he saw them for the last time before leaving Germany on the outbreak of war, Von Jagow expressed his poignant regret at the crumbling of his entire policy and that of the Chancellor, which had been, he said, to make friends with Great Britain and then, through Great Britain, to get closer to France. The Chancellor was very agitated, and said that the policy to which he had devoted himself, of friendship with England, had tumbled down like a house of cards. Sir E. Goschen does not express himself as in any way doubting the sincerity of these statements. Both these Ministers belonged to the party of peace in Berlin, and if we must doubt either of them in this matter, then we may refer to the language just cited of Mr. Asquith, Sir Edward Grey, and Mr. Lloyd George, to establish what alone it is sought here to make good—namely, that after the Morocco controversy had been cleared out of the way in November 1911, there remained no subject of quarrel between us and Germany, and a real effort was made to establish goodwill. Our Government did not at the time resent the German proposal for a Treaty of mutual neutrality, though

and Sir E. Grey, and founded on them a strong expression of opinion that there would be no war between us and Germany. This is mentioned only because it has been the subject of public animadversion, and a critic ought not to ignore criticism of himself, whatever its value.

they could not accept it. They could not come to any agreement about limitation of the navies, but that did not preclude friendly relations. And they proceeded with negotiations as to outstanding questions relating to Africa and the Bagdad Railway which resulted in agreements being made a little time before the war.

Not only were good relations growing between us and Germany, but we acted together in 1912-3. When the Balkan War of 1912 and its sequel the Second Balkan War in 1913 brought about the imminent danger of a rupture between Russia and Austria, our co-operation with Germany became intimate and cordial. It prevented a general conflagration. Full acknowledgment of valuable and valued assistance on both sides was made by Ministers both in London and in Berlin. Those who desired peace and could not see any reason why there should be hostility, rejoiced in both countries and thought their wishes now in a fair way to fulfilment. How it all broke down and ended in war we must see presently.

But from the end of 1911 till the actual outbreak of war our Ministers were working in a friendly way with Germany, and speaking of the conduct of that Government in terms of high praise. Did they apprehend that we also might be swept in if France came into war, by reason of our relations with France. It is quite clear from the statements they made in 1913 and 1914 that Sir Edward Grey and Mr. Asquith could have had no misgivings on that score, if they told the truth to the House of Commons in the passages which will presently be cited. They at all events were

7

satisfied—and they knew all we had said and done—
that we had kept our hands quite free from any obligation to take part in such a war.

*   *   *

Nevertheless, our relations with France evidently
caused some anxiety in the Cabinet in November 1912.
The general growth of navies made our Mediterranean
Fleet less equal to possible requirements. Our estimates for the navy were already enormous. Whether
from fear that the House of Commons would make
difficulties in still further increasing them, or from
other reasons, some disposition appears to have been
agreed with France by which the French navy concentrated in the Mediterranean, while we concentrated
our fleet in the North Sea. It seems to have been this
step—a step that would make France expect the British
Fleet to protect her northern coasts—which led the
Cabinet to consider our military and naval relations
towards France in November 1912. At all events the
Cabinet did discuss this subject at that date, and
decided to have a " definite understanding " in writing
with France.[1] Accordingly our Foreign Secretary
sent to the French Ambassador the following letter,
which is transcribed in full :—

" *Nov. 22nd* [1912]

" MY DEAR AMBASSADOR,—From time to time in
recent years the French and British Naval and Military
experts have consulted together. It has always been
understood that such consultation does not restrict
the freedom of either Government to decide at any
future time whether or not to assist the other by

[1] Sir E. Grey's Speech of 3rd August 1914.

armed force. We have agreed that consultation between experts is not and ought not to be regarded as an engagement that commits either Government to action in a contingency that has not yet arisen and may never arise. The disposition, for instance, of the French and British fleets respectively at the present moment is not based upon an engagement to co-operate in war. You have, however, pointed out that if either Government had grave reason to expect an unprovoked attack by a third Power it might become essential to know whether it could in that event depend upon the armed assistance of the other. I agree that if either Government had grave reason to expect an unprovoked attack by a third Power, or something that threatened the general peace, it should immediately discuss with the other whether both Governments should act together to prevent aggression and to preserve peace, and, if so, what measures they would be prepared to take in common. If these measures involved action, the plans of the General Staffs would at once be taken into consideration and the Governments would then decide what effect should be given to them."

The French Ambassador at once wrote accepting in terms Sir Edward's letter. It was obviously a carefully prepared and agreed document.

When Sir Edward Grey came before the House of Commons on the very eve of the war on 3rd August 1914 and claimed to have kept free from engagements to France he disclosed many things for the first time, and among them these letters of 22nd November 1912, and said of them, " that is the starting-point for the Government with regard to the present crisis." He said they made it clear that " as regards our freedom to decide in a crisis what our line should be, whether we should intervene or whether we should abstain, the

Government remained perfectly free and a fortiori the House of Commons remains perfectly free." Other men must be excused if they take a very different view. Obviously consultation between military and naval experts is not of itself an engagement at all. Obviously the disposition of fleets cannot be based upon an engagement to co-operate in war if there was no such engagement. The Cabinet seems to have been satisfied that these letters were equivalent to a renunciation by France of any moral claim to our support in arms based upon the communications that had passed between the two Governments. Why not ask for that express renunciation, if they felt uneasy ? But suppose that, after those letters, M. Cambon or some other gallant gentleman of France came to Sir Edward, when a crisis arose, and said, " There is no express agreement, and neither our military conversations nor the disposition of our fleets constitute an engagement. But look at your own letter of 22nd November 1912. It shows that you have exchanged with us military information, that we have disposed our fleet in concert with you, leaving our northern coasts unprotected, that our General Staffs have made their military plans in common, that you have promised immediately to discuss with us whether to act together or not, and how to act if the general peace is threatened. This promise is not confined to the case of Morocco or to diplomatic support as was our old Treaty of 1904. We are not, as you know, guilty of any aggression. Our very existence is menaced. Did you agree to discuss with us merely about the abstract wickedness of Germany, or did your General Staff make plans of campaign with ours merely for their mutual edification on interesting questions of military strategy? Are you not in honour bound, after all that, to help us when we are perfectly clean-handed and are threatened with invasion by Germany?" Suppose that was put to Sir Edward Grey, what answer would he have made? Would he say, " Pray look at the letter and see that all this is not based on any such engagement "? A gentleman of France, in the agony of his country, would have surely answered, " Away with you! You got this letter for Parliamentary purposes to be able to say you had no engagement." When it came to the point Sir Edward Grey insisted on war. These letters of 22nd November 1912 were in one sense the starting-point. They put the seal of honour on an unrecorded duty. They took the place as regards all policy of the 1904 Treaty, which had promised only diplomatic intervention in regard to policy in Morocco. They implicitly recognized that the duty existed, while agreeing that naval and military conversations and dispositions had not created it—in a formal way.

* * *

Suspicions somehow came to be entertained in Parliament that we were becoming bound to France. These letters were dated November 1912 it will be remembered. Some four months later, on the 10th March 1913, Lord Hugh Cecil said in the House of Commons: " There is a very general belief that this country is under an obligation, not a Treaty obligation, but an obligation arising out of an assurance given by the Ministry in the course of diplomatic negotiations, to send a very large armed force out of this country to operate in Europe. This is the general belief." Thereupon he was interrupted by Mr. Asquith, who said: "I ought to say that is not true."

A few days later, on 24th March 1913, Mr. Asquith, in answer to Sir W. Byles, said: "As has been repeatedly stated, this country is not under any obligation, not public and known to Parliament, which compels it to take part in a war. In other words, if war arises between European Powers, there are no unpublished agreements which will restrict or hamper the freedom of the Government or Parliament to decide whether or not Great Britain should participate in a war." The ordinary man would understand a denial of obligations to include a denial of obligations of honour.

Again, on 11th June 1914, in answer to Mr. King, Sir Edward Grey said that the answer of the Prime Minister, just cited, " remains as true to-day as it was a year ago." This was within two months of war.

If the purpose of Ministerial answers be to give plain information, it is very difficult to maintain that the letters of 22nd November warranted these Parliamentary assurances. In substance the assurances proved quite untrue. It is not intended by this to suggest that Sir Edward Grey meant to convey what was untrue. He is not a man to do that. It is intended to suggest that he failed to appreciate the true situation. He had not wished to bind himself. He thought, or had been led to think, that he had not bound himself, and gave to Parliament in 1913 and 1914 his own conclusion, without giving the facts on which it was based and so enabling others to form for themselves a sounder conclusion of their own. It must have been a bitter thing to realize that he had imposed so tremendous a responsibility upon the country without the knowledge of Parliament, while desiring to keep free, and he clung to the view that he had not done so. If the whole thing were opened out and all materials made available, it might appear that there were other passages in our relations with France, known only to a very few people in either country, and each perhaps a slight thing in itself, which when put together show still further a course of conduct carrying with it an unseen bond. This is pure conjecture, and there may be nothing of the kind. What is known suffices to explain what happened, the demand of France for our support in arms and Sir Edward's compliance.

* * *

The alliance with Great Britain for which M. Delcassé and M. Cambon laboured so long and so patiently was at last attained—in fact though not in form, in substance though not in words. And among other risks which it imposed was the risk of this country being brought into war on behalf of France, not at all in that nation's own interests, not because of any French quarrel with Germany, but because of Treaty obligations from France to Russia.

A remarkable discussion on this subject took place in the House of Commons on 7th August 1918, according to the authorised version circulated next morning. Mr. Lloyd George said that, when the war began, " we had a " compact with France that if she were wantonly at- " tacked the United Kingdom would go to her support." This seems to have shocked Mr. Herbert Samuel, then spokesman of Mr. Asquith's followers. For he said : " It is essential that the country should not think " there was anything in the nature of a secret Treaty

"or any private compact which obliged us at the
"beginning of August 1914 to enter this war. It was
"our sense of duty, our obligation under the Treaty
"that safeguarded the independence of Belgium, and
"our sense of duty to safeguard the reign of public law
"and the freedom of Europe against the wanton aggres-
"sion of the moment, and that alone and no specific
"contract with a French Government which required
"us at that time to enter this war." Being thus
challenged, Mr. Lloyd George referred to the letter
to the French Ambassador of 22nd November 1912
(above transcribed), and said that the word "compact"
was too strong to use in that connection. "In my
"judgment," he continued, "it was an obligation of
"honour." He added: "I think the phrase 'obligation
"of honour' would be a more correct description of what
"actually took place rather than the word 'compact,'
"and certainly it was not a Treaty. I had nothing in
"my mind except that letter when I spoke, and I think
"the matter ought to be put right at once." Where-
upon Mr. Samuel said that in the opinion of Sir E.
Grey there was no obligation of honour. It is to the
credit of Mr. Lloyd George on this occasion that he
told the truth. There was an obligation of honour
which compelled us to intervene, though Sir Edward
might not think so, and it had been entered into
without the public knowing of it.

This was the end, after many years, of the policy
inaugurated by Mr. Asquith, Sir Edward Grey, and
Mr. Haldane, when within a month of Sir Henry
Campbell-Bannerman's Government taking office they
secretly commenced military and naval conversations
with France for contingent common action against

Germany. Sir Edward Grey has affirmed that Sir Henry Campbell-Bannerman was consulted on this at the time. Some of those who knew Sir Henry Campbell-Bannerman and were in close confidential communication with him in December 1905 and January 1906 will not believe that he understood the scope and significance of what was in fact done, unless some evidence of it is given.

* * *

We must more fully realize the risk imposed upon the British Empire by this course of policy. Three contingencies might arise. France might without provocation undertake either single-handed or in concert with Russia an attack on Germany. Such a thing was extremely unlikely, and we have seen how anxious France was to preserve peace. In any case His Majesty's Government would not have taken part in any such aggressive action against Germany. In the Negotiations of 1912, relative to the German proposal for a Treaty of mutual neutrality, His Majesty's Government offered an assurance that they had not entered into and would not enter into any agreement or understanding for any such purpose. There was a second contingency, namely, that Germany might take aggressive action against France on the occasion of some Franco-German quarrel. Now, in 1870, Mr. Gladstone, with the concurrence of all the leading men of that time, decided that Great Britain should remain neutral. He refused to take sides with France. Sir Edward Grey and his confidants, on the other hand, so handled our relations with France that in 1914 they found themselves under an obligation of honour to take up arms for France if some dispute between that country and Germany led to an aggressive attack by the latter. That was a reversal of our old practice of non-intervention in the secular quarrels of the Continent, and a departure from the precedent laid down by the statesmen of 1870 in a matter of high policy, if anything ever was high policy. Still, it exposed us only to the consequences of French action, and France was known to be peaceful. That, however, was not the shape in which the question presented itself in 1914. In No. 116 of the British White Book Sir Edward Grey says : " Feeling is quite different from what it was during the Morocco question. That crisis involved a dispute directly involving France, whereas in this case France is being drawn into a dispute which is not hers." In fact, the quarrel in 1914 was not between France and Germany, but between Germany and Russia. France was bound by her Alliance with Russia. Though Sir Edward Grey did not know the terms of that Treaty, yet he did know, as he has told us, that if Germany and Austria attacked Russia France could not stand aside from her Ally. Everyone also knew that the relations between Russia and Austria were acute, because of their antagonism in the Balkans, and that Germany was bound by Treaty to stand by Austria in the event of a Russo-Austrian war. Therefore a conflict between France and Germany might arise indirectly through Russian action even if both France and Germany had no quarrel of their own to provoke war. This was quite a different risk. It is the risk that, in fact, led to this war. And the point which it is desired to make clear is that, in creating these intimate relations with France, our Government did, in fact, not merely renounce the policy Mr. Gladstone approved in 1870, but went much further. They created a situation which indirectly constrained us to abide the consequences of Russian policy in the Balkans, and to stake the British Empire in defence of France against the consequences of her Russian Alliance. In effect it left the peace of Great Britain at the mercy of the Russian Court. That was the effect of the Entente with France as interpreted and enlarged by our Ministers. It was not the Entente itself as created by the agreement of 1904 that did this, but the expectations which the Ministers raised by their secret proceedings.

Now what was the Russian Court ? It has now ceased to exist, and has been replaced by a series of Revolutionary Governments brought into being after an exposure of cruelty, corruption, incompetence, and treachery such as has never been surpassed in history. The Russian people have been the victims of frightful misgovernment for generations, and this has been the outcome. We are as yet imperfectly informed, but so far as is known the Czar of Russia himself was a well-meaning Sovereign, placed by the accident of birth in a position of unexampled difficulty from which nothing but supreme talent and dauntless courage could have extricated him. He was an autocrat, governing without any check (for the Duma might imperfectly assist, but could not overrule him), a population of 180 millions, and a territory extending from the German frontier to the shores of the Behring Straits, and from the frozen seas on the north right down to Persia and the Black Sea. A man of the highest genius, like Julius Cæsar or the Great Napoleon, might in a lifetime have contrived the means of providing a tolerable administration for this vast Empire. Such men rarely make their appearance. The late Czar was totally destitute of the titanic force that these men wielded. Another Czar had been recently assassinated by anarchists. Czar Nicholas' own life was continually threatened by anarchists. For a Czar to die in his bed was becoming a doubtful chance. There were attempts at Revolution in Russia very recently repressed with extreme brutality. If German Government was founded on exaggerated State control with force in the background, it was, at all events toward Germans, orderly and precise and genuinely desirous of promoting industry and material progress and education. In Russia, on the other hand, the administration in all respects was hopelessly defective. The officials were corrupt beyond belief. The secret police waged war incessantly against liberal opinion and exercised a petty tyranny for their own profit as well as for the supposed advantage of the Government. Governors of provinces and various civil, military, and naval chiefs had little hesitation in disobeying orders and no hesitation at all in feathering their own nests. Whatever policy, or course, the Czar might resolve upon he was always liable to be deceived in the information on which he acted by treacherous advisers, or to be disobeyed and betrayed. The Russian people were devout, industrious, estimable, and brave. Their Czar was an honest man in a perfectly impossible position. Around him in control of great departments or possessed of great influence were to be found, alongside of patriotic Ministers, a number of people utterly unworthy of confidence. At the end of his volume, *The Eclipse of*

Russia, Dr. Dillon speaks of the foul weapons used by the Russian Government, and says: " The main " object of these diabolic methods was to perpetuate " a system which for iniquity had no parallel in " Christendom, and to keep 140 million peasants in a " plight which makes one wonder as much at their pre- " revolutionary patience as one has since wondered at " their anarchic frenzy." The administration was hopeless, the diplomacy unreliable, and a continuous warfare was incessantly waged between uncompromising Nihilists and Anarchists on the one side and a Secret Police quite as unscrupulous on the other side. No one could tell when a Revolution might break out. All these things were perfectly well known to every Government in Europe. The events of the Russo-Japanese war in 1904–5 proved that the Russian Government was unstable and unreliable, and that there were traitors in high places. The horrible excesses of the Russian Revolution do not displace these facts. They are the consequences of these facts.

What has happened since this war of 1914 began has been very imperfectly known in this country and very charily expressed in our newspapers under the system of secrecy and suppression of news which has prevailed. Some part of the terrible history has, however, appeared. It shows what was the true measure of the risk taken by our Ministers when they placed us at the mercy of the men who in reality influenced Russian policy, and how incompetent those men were.

A correspondent of the *Manchester Guardian* on 22nd September 1917, for example, gives an account

of certain facts which seem to have come out on
a criminal trial. In the early days of the war
there was a very great deficiency on the Russian
side in cartridges and artillery ammunition. Then
appeared a deficiency of rifles. On 25th August
1914 it was decided to send Russian troops to the
front with only one-half of the rifles needed, and
gradually in the course of the first two months of
the war it came to such a pass that units were sent
to the front with only one-fifth of the number of rifles
required, and subsequently men were sent down
wholly unarmed. Hundreds of thousands of soldiers
were in consequence obliged to go into the trenches
or even to battle unarmed. It was the same with
the machine guns, so that over and over again whole
units had to leave their positions for lack of arms
and munitions, or were massacred by the enemy
artillery, while in their rear there stood vast hosts of
unarmed men waiting for rifles from the dead and
wounded, and totally inexperienced in the use of fire-
arms. The Chief of the Russian General Staff reported
on 9th April 1915 that on the previous day the Germans
fired three thousand heavy shells " against the sector
of our first regiment," and had swept clear everything,
while the Russians could only fire one hundred shells.
On 22nd June 1915 he reported, " We have no rifles,
and 150,000 men stand without arms." This deficiency was due to corruption and treachery, which
prevented the supplies being kept up as required by
various military authorities and by the Duma Committee of national defence. The sums granted by
the Duma for this purpose were not made full use of,
tenders were rejected, and there was distinct evidence

of corruption. During the war, notwithstanding the great need, offers of rifles were not accepted. It is not necessary to pursue the subject beyond saying that though the Czar himself was personally anxious to stop the Russian mobilisation, which was the direct occasion for the outbreak of the war, his order was disregarded by some of those under his authority. Thus, though there might be reliance on the Czar, there could not be much reliance on his commands being carried out. Treachery and incompetence ruled supreme.

That was the nature of the Government into whose hands the destinies of France were placed by the Alliance between France and Russia, and into whose hands also the fate of the British Empire was entrusted when the Franco-British Entente was interpreted, as it was interpreted or applied. We became liable to be destroyed, and would possibly have been destroyed but for the unexampled conduct of our seamen and soldiers.

This volume deals only with the question how we came into the war, and is not concerned with the management of it. But who can forget the immense debt which the country owes to Lord Kitchener, whose energy and example procured and trained for us the men who at the crisis saved all from ruin? And, whatever mistakes were made, it would be wrong not to acknowledge that every one, including Mr. Asquith and his colleagues, as well as the officers and men in the field, laboured unremittingly in those days to further whatever means of defence commended itself to their judgment. Without the common effort of the whole nation we might have been overwhelmed, and it was a very near thing at one time.

CHAPTER V

ATTITUDE OF GREAT POWERS IN 1914

THE frightful war which has desolated Europe arose on the occasion of the Sarajevo murder, which brought Austria and Russia face to face. Diplomacy failed to effect a reconciliation, and the system of alliances among the great military Powers brought the Continent of Europe into war. This network of alliances, until its fruits became manifest, had often been vaunted as a security for peace. It created two camps in Europe, each standing in genuine fear of the other. One redeeming merit might no doubt be claimed for this system, had not experience proved the claim to be fallacious. It was expected that when so many Powers were exposed to the danger of being brought into war, not by any quarrel of their own, but by some quarrel of an ally in which they might have only a trifling interest, strong pressure would be brought to bear from all sides to compose the dangerous dispute at an early stage. But the event has shown that the temptation of furthering one's own ambitions by the strong arm of an ally is not easily resisted, and that statesmen are rather feeble folk, and military panic in the presence of so many armed millions overwhelms all prudence, if only a few days of hesitation allow it to grow. And above all it has shown the

utter hopelessness of what may be called the old style
of managing foreign affairs, when each nation, including
our own, was encouraged or cajoled into regarding
them as enveloped in mystery and needing to be handled
exclusively by " experts," with as little interference
as could be contrived on the part of anyone outside the
Foreign Office ring. It was the same pretension as
that of Queen Elizabeth in the old days—that foreign
affairs were " too high " for the House of Commons—
only this time the pretension was advanced by Ministers.

Immediately after the Austrian Crown Prince and
his Consort were assassinated on 28th June 1914,
Austria fixed the guilt on the Servian Government,
if not as the deliberate contrivers of the crime, at all
events as the patron of Secret Societies that procured
it. In their manifestos and Notes they say that the
Servian Army Arsenal provided the bombs with which
the crime was committed, that the murderers were
armed by Servian functionaries and enabled to cross
the frontier by the Chiefs of the Servian Frontier
Service, and the crime planned by a Secret Society
at Belgrade of which generals, diplomats, and judges
in that country were members. They say also that
acts of terrorism and a series of murders had been
perpetrated by the same Society, which regarded
assassination as its best weapon against Austria, and
that its foul deeds were publicly glorified in the Servian
Press. Finally, they say that this was the criminal
game of Russian diplomacy, in whose hands Servia
was a mere catspaw. If these things were true they
would cover Servia and Russia with infamy. On
the other hand, there was a long record of harsh
Austrian conduct and the memory of the " shining

8

armour " incident to inflame anger in both countries. This was the atmosphere into which the growth of the Entente had introduced our diplomacy. Very bitter resentment had been felt in Vienna for some years at the persistent agitation carried on by these Societies. Their object was unquestionably the dismemberment of Austria, and their methods were unquestionably unscrupulous. Servian Governments had not succeeded in repressing them; Vienna thought that they had not succeeded simply because they had not tried, and also thought that so small a State would not have dared to countenance so provocative a policy if it had not been encouraged by the Russian Government. We know from debates in the Italian Parliament that in the previous year (1913) Italy had been sounded by Austria about an invasion of Servia, on account of her unfriendly conduct. The project was for a time abandoned owing to the opposition of Italy and Germany.[1] On receiving news of the assassination, however, the Austrian Government recurred to their former idea. Externally they maintained a calm attitude and gave it to be understood that their action would be moderate. The German Kaiser went on a yachting cruise in July. This may have been, of course, an artifice. Both the Russian and the French Ambassadors left Vienna for a holiday. Then all of a sudden, on 23rd July, the Austrian Government sent an ultimatum to Servia, full of the most violent accusations, and requiring its acceptance of ten degrading conditions within forty-eight hours. The precise character of these demands

[1] See Appendix to Servian Blue Book in Collected Diplomatic Documents.

need not be scrutinized. Insistence upon rigorous measures for the suppression of crime and the punishment of offenders could be regarded as legitimate, but the sting lay in a vague dangerous demand for the interposition of Austrian officials in the internal judiciary and administration of Servia. This indicated an intention to establish Austrian ascendancy in the Balkan Peninsula. The Austrian Government indeed maintain in their despatches that their claim to interpose in the affairs of Servia was limited; that they merely desired to share in the inquiry and not in any adjudication.

Everyone at once recognized that this step portended danger to the peace of Europe. In fact, only nine days elapsed between 23rd July, the day when this ultimatum reached Servia, and 1st August, the day when Germany declared war. The history of those nine days must be extricated from the mass of documents under which it has been buried. No one who studies the documents closely can doubt that many others, probably those which most conclusively prove secret springs of action, notably the Austro-German documents, have been withheld. They will not see the light for many years. Enough, however, has been disclosed to make fairly clear the main features of this fatal story, and the factors which drove Europe into war.

* * *

But, before telling that story, at the outset let us try to realize the aims and attitude toward this particular quarrel of the various Great Powers in Europe. Did any of them wish for war in August 1914 ? In 1914, be it observed. What action any of them may have contemplated for a later date is not in question at this moment. Here was a quarrel between Austria and Servia, in itself serious, in its possible development full of infinite danger, for it might reopen the Near Eastern Question in a far more formidable aspect than ever before. Take the Great Powers one by one, and see how they were inclined, and in what frame of mind they entered upon the negotiations which have presently to be examined. Italy had no direct concern in the quarrel, but her interests might be affected if the quarrel extended. She had Italian territories under the Hapsburg sceptre, and, though allied to Austria, really hated Austria, with whom she was in rivalry on the Adriatic. Yet Italy unquestionably desired peace and strove for it. France had no special interest in the Near Eastern Question or in the Servian quarrel, except that she might be drawn into a war by reason of her alliance with Russia. France eagerly desired peace and strove for it.[1] The German Foreign Secretary says he knew France did not desire war, and everyone else knew it. No one has disputed it. She had given her promise to Russia, and meant to be true to her promise, cost what it might; but she knew what that cost would be, and within the limits prescribed by honour longed intensely to spare her children.

* * *

Equally clear was the position of Russia, if by Russia we mean the Czar. The Austrian Ambassador at Berlin said himself that Russia did not want war in 1914. At that time the Czar was in control. It is certain that he wished to avoid war. "The inten-

[1] British White Book, No. 98.

tions of the Emperor of Russia and his Ministers could not be more pacific," reports the French Ambassador at St. Petersburg on 24th July.

Testimonials are not needed. One simple fact places it beyond all doubt. Throughout the nine days of negotiation a series of suggestions for settlement was put forward. To all of them, almost without exception, Russia at once and cordially assented. If in one or two cases she offered a qualification, it was in no case a qualification hostile to the proposal or unreasonable in itself. Russia went so far in her desire for peace that on 29th July 1914 the French Ambassador at St. Petersburg was able to say to his Government: " I am from this moment able to assure you that the Russian Government acquiesces in any step that may be proposed to it by France and England for the safeguard of peace." [1] The Czar had a military party to deal with, and an intense national feeling against the oppression of Slavonic Servia also to deal with. He had an enormous frontier to defend against Germany, if war should come, and against Austria as well. The former could mobilize and could deliver an attack much more rapidly than Russia. The latter actually did attack Servia at an early stage of the negotiations. But the Czar did no more than follow Austrian mobilization and German preparations, as they were truly or falsely reported to him, by like measures. And, even after he had received the German ultimatum, he tried to prevent, by arrangement, any fighting while negotiations should continue. On one point alone he was perfectly resolute throughout. He would not consent to anything which could

[1] French Yellow Book, No. 86.

" encroach on the independence and integrity of Servia," to use M. Sazonoff's language in the Duma.[1] Had he acted otherwise, there must have been a Revolution in Russia. His action in ultimately mobilizing will be considered in its place. It was an act of great folly, but up to that date all that he did was in the direction of peace. His anxiety to preserve peace is indisputable, even to the extent of forbearance while Belgrade was under bombardment. We in this country would have felt as he felt about Servia if we had seen a little nation of our own race threatened with ill-usage by tyrannical neighbours, however we might condemn the misconduct of its Government. But behind the Czar there were undoubtedly dangerous and disloyal influences who might prevail at any moment, and who, in fact, did infinite mischief at the end of July in the premature Russian mobilization.

Such being the dispositions of Italy, France, and Russia when the ultimatum to Servia was delivered on 23rd July, we must come to the three other Great Powers—Austria, Germany, and Great Britain.

* * *

It was Austria that began the quarrel. No one questioned, not even the Czar's Minister, that she had cause of serious complaint against Servia. She might have procured satisfaction without embroiling the whole Continent, as will amply appear. But the Austrians seem to have thought, however much they might deny it, that the punishment of Servia might safely be used as an occasion for readjusting in their own favour the balance of power in the Balkans. They never had liked the Balkan settlement of 1913,

[1] On 8th August 1914.

which followed the Balkan internecine war of that
date. Count Berchtold, their Prime Minister, admitted this dislike. Germany was tied to them in
alliance. The acting French Minister perceived that
the Vienna Cabinet was carried away by the Press and
the military party. They evidently thought that with
this immense force by their side they could repeat the
" shining armour " incident of 1908 with impunity.
Accordingly Austrian troops were at once posted along
the Servian frontier in a serene confidence that they
might do as they pleased without a chance of inter-
ruption. Italy warned them that Russia might intervene. No, said the Austrian Minister, she will not
and cannot, because her strategic railways are not
complete and she is not ready. You are wrong,
replied the Italian, and Great Britain will come in
too. Not in the end, said Count Berchtold; she has
internal (the Irish) trouble. " So just was the cause
of Austria held to be," reports the British Ambassador
in Vienna,[1] " that it seemed to her people inconceivable
that any country should place itself in her path."
The Austrians could see nothing in the background.
The whole thing concerned no one but themselves,
Servia should be brought to her knees, her friends
should mind their own business, and all would be well.
That was the expectation. An ultimatum of unexampled severity to Servia, an answer to be made in
forty-eight hours, when Ministers and Ambassadors
were scattered all over the Continent. These were
the methods. It was not to be a war, merely an
" execution." A temper of this kind would be incredible were it not proved beyond dispute by repeated

[1] Cd. 7860 of 1915, p. 116.

passages in the official despatches. But Austria was not really a Great Power, only a secondary Great Power, dependent for her very existence on her German alliance. Therefore everything turned on the attitude of Germany.

If, however, we desire, as all surely must desire, to see the action of Austria-Hungary in its true light, one important consideration must be kept in mind. The course of European history has placed the Dual Monarchy, as it is called, in a position of extreme difficulty. Four races—German, Latin, Magyar, and Slav—divided up into nine nationalities occupy the dominions of the Hapsburgs. The Germans and Magyars, who number twenty-two millions, have been allowed to exercise a supremacy over the more numerous millions of Latins and Slavs. This has no doubt been the fatal fault and the fatal weakness of the Austro-Hungarian Crown, but it has been still more the fault of the two dominant races, who have been very often intolerant toward the religion and the liberties of the subject majority. For this reason Austria-Hungary has always had difficulties on her frontiers, notably on her Slavonic frontiers, where the depressed Slavs have been of late years increasingly attracted toward their kinsmen in Servia. Austria has often acted with much harshness toward Servia. Now, however deeply and legitimately we may sympathize with the Servian people, it is indisputable that an active Slavonic propaganda has been diligently pursued by Servian nationalist organizations within Austrian territory. It has been from the nature of the case full of danger to the Austro-Hungarian Empire. The obvious remedy was the grant of free institutions, but that in its turn would be strenuously resisted by the " Ascendancy Party " of German and Magyar blood, between whom in turn there was open war as recently as 1848, and a latent antagonism ever since. It can easily be seen how formidable an engine the Pan-Slavonic movement might be to Austria-Hungary. The Austrian Red Book is full of complaints against Servia on this subject, and neither the Germans nor the Austrians have ever concealed the opinion that so small a State could never have entertained such high pretensions without secret support from St. Petersburg.

We are certainly not at liberty to assume that the Russian Government countenanced disloyal action of that kind, but there is conclusive proof that, in the opinion of disinterested judges, the Servian Government had in fact failed to carry out their engagement of 1909 to live as good neighbours toward Austria-Hungary. A few citations will amply establish this statement.

On 20th July 1914, Sir Edward Grey expressed to the German Ambassador the opinion " that any of them (the Great Powers) should be dragged into a war by Servia would be detestable." [1]

On 24th July he told the French Ambassador that " a war on behalf of that country (Servia) would never be sanctioned by British public opinion." [2]

On 25th July he wired to the British Ambassador at St. Petersburg: " I do not consider that public opinion here would or ought to sanction our going to war over a Servian quarrel." [3]

[1] British White Book, No. 1.
[2] *Ibid.*, No. 6.
[3] *Ibid.*, No. 24.

On 26th July Austria had already sent her ultimatum to Servia, charging her in effect with conspiracy to procure murder, and demanding an abject reparation ; upon which the British Ambassador says: " One naturally sympathized with many of the requirements of the ultimatum if only the manner of expressing them had been more temperate." [1]

On 26th July the Russian Minister for Foreign Affairs " agreed that much of the Austro-Hungarian Note to Servia had been perfectly reasonable." [2]

On 28th July the British Ambassador at Vienna told the Austrian Minister for Foreign Affairs that if the British point of view somewhat differed from his " this would arise not from want of sympathy with the many just complaints which Austria-Hungary had against Servia," but from the fact that Sir Edward Grey was anxious in the first instance for the peace of Europe. [3]

On 30th July the Russian Ambassador at Vienna says: " Russia must have an assurance that Servia will not be crushed, but she would understand that Austria-Hungary is compelled to exact from Servia measures which will secure her Slav Provinces from the continuance of hostile propaganda from Servian territory." [4]

All this did not of course justify the violent courses of the Vienna Cabinet or its deafness to Sir Edward Grey's appeals till the opportunity for a settlement had passed, but it does show that the provocation given by Servia was real. In short, the attitude of Austria in July and August of 1914 was that of a

---

[1] British White Book, No. 32.   [2] Ibid., No. 56.
[3] Ibid., No. 62.   [4] Ibid., No. 95.

nation which had just cause for complaint but could not see, beyond its own grievance, the infinite danger to European civilization. And if the Russian Government did not support these Servian provocations many influences at St. Petersburg did.

* * *

Come now to Germany. Beyond doubt the key to the situation was to be found at Berlin, because if Berlin were not ready to support her, Austria would never dream of war with Russia. In the opinion of the Russian Foreign Minister Germany did not want war.[1] On the other hand, M. Jules Cambon, the French Ambassador, pitilessly pointed out to the German Government that their action was leading Europe to ruin.[2] The truth is that the German Military Staff wanted war and forced it on their probably reluctant Civil Government after the Russian mobilization. Have we not already learned from the French Yellow Book, and is it not well known, that there were two Germanies, with two policies and two ideals, whereof in the end the worst prevailed ?

But it would be better to see what the Germans themselves have to say in their Denkschrift or official memorandum published in August 1914, shortly after the commencement of hostilities. Its authors evidently regard it as a complete vindication of their conduct. In reality it reveals, as nothing else can, the disastrous step taken at the beginning which crippled the efforts of those at Berlin who wished for peace, and retarded the steps that otherwise might have been taken, till panic arrived with the news of

[1] British White Book, No. 17.
[2] French Yellow Book, No. 74.

Russian mobilization. And then all sobriety of judgment was overwhelmed by irresistible military clamour.

The fatal step was neither more nor less than this. The German Government, inured to autocratic methods, seems to have regarded it as an intolerable affront that its one powerful Ally should be flouted by any small State like Servia, and in blind resentment placed its own sword unconditionally at the disposal of Austria, as soon as the Crown Prince was assassinated, leaving her an unfettered discretion to act as she pleased. Had the Kaiser and Dr. Bethmann-Hollweg reserved the right to be consulted in the course that Austria might take, there might have been no war. The plague could have been stayed just in time before the military faction could get the upper hand. Or if the Kaiser and his Minister had been strong enough even at the last moment to resist panic and pressure, there would have been no war. What made the catastrophe possible was the folly of these men at the outset in parting with control over their Ally, and their weakness afterwards in yielding to their Military Staff when the hour of crisis came, assuming always that these two men desired peace. No one can be sure, but it is probable that they did desire it. But let us see the Denkschrift itself.

It begins with a statement that Servia, with Russian connivance, had aimed at stripping Austria of her Bosnian and Herzegovinian territories by means of secret conspiracies, which ended in the Sarajevo murder. It then says that, the very existence of the Austro-Hungarian Monarchy being thus threatened, the Government of Vienna had apprised Germany of its resolve no longer to tolerate Servian agitation, and had asked the opinion of Berlin. " With all our heart we were able," says the Denkschrift, " to agree with our Ally's estimate of the situation and assure him that any action considered necessary to end the movement in Servia directed against the conservation of the Monarchy would meet with our approval. We were perfectly aware that a possible warlike attitude of Austria-Hungary against Servia might bring Russia upon the field, and that it might therefore involve us in a war in accordance with our duty as Allies." The Denkschrift proceeds to say that nevertheless Germany could not advise Austria-Hungary to take a yielding attitude in view of her own vital interests and dignity, and adds that German interests also were menaced through the continued Servian agitation. For the collapse of Austria and the subjection of all the Slavs under one Russian sceptre would be the consequence, " thus making untenable the position of the Teutonic race in Central Europe." A single sentence follows which lights up for us dark places in the history of these negotiations. " We therefore permitted Austria a completely free hand in her action towards Servia, but have not participated in her preparations." The remainder of the Denkschrift gives the German account of the negotiations, and copiously affirms her continued efforts to obtain a peaceful settlement. All this will be better appreciated when the course of the negotiations themselves has been examined.

What the Denkschrift itself says about giving Austria a free hand is amplified in a statement published by the *Times* that there was a meeting at Pots-

dam on 5th July 1914, at which the Kaiser with the
German and Austrian Prime Ministers and other civil
and military chiefs were present.   At this meeting,
says the *Times* correspondent, the principal points in
the Austrian ultimatum to Servia were decided upon,
and a resolution taken to accept war if Russia refused
to accept this humiliation.   The *Times* also says that
three weeks later Bethmann-Hollweg tried to withdraw
but it was too late.   A Dutch newspaper gave fuller
particulars of this meeting in its issue of 7th September
1914.   It says that both the Kaiser and Bethmann-
Hollweg were anxious to avert war, but the soldiers
strongly pressed for vigorous action.   It says also
that very strong pressure was needed later on to make
the Kaiser send his ultimatum.   There was, it says,
a belief in Germany that France and Russia would
attack them in March 1916.   All this is in accord with
what will appear in the sequel, so far, that is, as it
relates to the resolutions taken by the Central Powers
and the effort of Bethmann-Hollweg to draw back
later.   A curious memorandum by a Dr. Mühlon was
reproduced in the *Times* of 28th March 1918.   This
gentleman learned from Herr Krupp von Bohlen that
he had seen the Kaiser about the middle of July 1914,
and " the Kaiser had told him that he would declare
" war immediately if Russia mobilized, and that this
" time people would see that he did not turn about.   The
" Kaiser's repeated insistence that this time nobody
" would be able to accuse him of indecision had been
" almost comic in its effect."   No antics, to be sure,
are more ludicrous than those of a weak man who
wants to be thought strong.   And vanity lies at the
root of many tragedies.

What, then, in estimating the forces that were making for peace or against it from the very beginning, was the position of Germany ? Not wishful of war, says the Russian Minister. Yet the Berlin Government knew and say that they knew the possibility of Russian intervention. They knew, and say elsewhere in the same document, that this might mean the intervention of France and of themselves, by reason of existing Treaties. They knew also how difficult Austria was to manage, and how hard put to it they had been to restrain her only two years previously. Indeed everyone knew the furious spirit that prevailed in Vienna. In these circumstances, with the whole peace of Europe at stake, they left Austria a completely free hand. It is difficult to understand how, even if it desired war, any enlightened Government, which cared even for appearances or valued the good opinion of the world, could bring itself to place all in the hands of any other Government, especially of the Austrian Government. The records of the negotiations show what a fatal obstinacy this produced at Vienna, how in this mood Austria spent in mere provocation and defiance the few early days during which a settlement was easy, till bombardments and panics about mobilization blinded statesmen and made peace impossible, and how all the efforts made at the end by many Powers to prevent war, even repentance at Vienna itself, failed to avert the horror which has engulfed the world. This frightful initial mistake must be debited to the Kaiser and his Ministers, not to the soldiers. It happened before the ultimatum to Servia and no doubt explains the ferocity of that document. Perhaps the ideas entertained by the Kaiser of the

peculiar sanctity of Royal blood made him lose his
head, but the Ministers ought surely to have seen the
absurdity of giving carte blanche to such a neighbour
as Austria. They saw too late the danger of what
Austria was doing. All that will appear presently.
Meanwhile let it be noted that the first false step came
from the Civil Government of Berlin which probably,
in part at least, favoured peace. It weakened them
and their policy, and strengthened the powerful fire-
eating faction.

That faction is fully described in a Report to the
French Government in 1913 [1] (which has been already
mentioned on an earlier page), and its aims disclosed
in a remarkable secret Note to the German Government, clandestinely procured in 1913 by the French
Minister for War. These two documents deserve a
notice here, though the first of them is not new to us.
We are told in the French Report how there was a powerful party in Germany that wished for war and possessed
redoubtable means of intimidating the Government.
Some wished war because it was inevitable and had
better come now. Others wanted new markets or
wanted a diversion to check democracy or socialism.
Economic reasons influenced the military aristocracy,
which meant much the same as the landed nobility.
They were afraid of Succession Duties and Free Trade
in food if the democracy gained power. The middle
classes inclined to the same view from a dislike of
democracy. Then there were the armament firms
and the people who thought that war would be good
business. Of the same mind were the professors and
philosophers with their acolytes, who abounded in

[1] French Yellow Book, No. 5, and *ibid.*, No. 2 Annexe (1).

that country. And these people had a powerful Press
and Parliamentary support. We find from this Report
that there was also a great Peace Party, but the others
are what we are now concerned with. They were the
people who put on pressure in favour of war, and the
Peace Party proved powerless to resist it.

Some idea of their policy and methods, now that
we have glanced at the composition of this military
party, may be seen in the confidential German Note
which is published in the French Yellow Book (Annexe
1 to No. 2). It is a secret official German document
procured by the French Minister for War, and dated
19th March 1913. This Note sets forth quite bare-
facedly the German military view, and may be usefully
summarized. There is no doubt, it says, of an Entente
between Russia, France, and Great Britain. The
German Fleet is not strong enough. England had
meant to send 100,000 men to the Continent at the
time of the Algeciras Conference.[1] Germany had to
reply by better formation of reserves. Then the
Agadir incident had showed that the French were well
equipped and an attack by the British Fleet had to be
expected. So Germany increased her army. Then
came the Balkan War, which weakened Austria, and
the French had still further strengthened their army.
Opinion is being prepared, continues the Note, for a
further strengthening of the German active army,
and the object is the strengthening and extending of

[1] If this statement is true, which surely requires proof, it has not
at any time been affirmed by any British Minister. If it be true
it means that some British authority in 1906 had resolved upon
taking part in the Continental quarrel between France and Germany
without consulting Parliament. We were then even less prepared
than in 1914.

9

Germanism throughout the entire world. The Note proceeds to say that the idea must be " instilled into the German people that their armaments are a reply to the armaments and policy of the French." . . . " The people must be accustomed to think that an offensive war by Germany is a necessity to combat the adversary's provocations." . . . " Things must be so managed that under the weighty impression of powerful armaments, of considerable sacrifices, and of political tension, an outbreak shall be considered as a deliverance, because after it would come decades of peace and of prosperity, such as those which followed 1870." Suggestions follow for stirring up trouble in Russia, Egypt, Tunis, Algiers, and Morocco in the event of war. And, when the war has been won, the old county of Burgundy and parts of Lorraine still held by the French, and the Baltic Provinces held by Russia, so thinks the author of the Note, are to be restored to Germany. Such is the pith of this instructive Note. It represents the German military ideals.

Next to it in the French Yellow Book is printed a despatch of the French Ambassador at Berlin, who gives what General Von Moltke, Chief of the General Staff in Germany, says about methods. It is curious reading and in M. Cambon's opinion depicted exactly the state of mind in German military circles. Here it is : " The commonplaces as to the responsibility of the aggressor must be disregarded. When war has become necessary, it must be waged by ranging all the chances on one's own side. Success alone justifies it. Germany cannot and must not give Russia time to mobilize, or she will be obliged to maintain on the eastern frontier a force which would leave her in a position of equality, if not of inferiority, in front of France. Therefore we must forestall our principal adversary immediately there are nine chances in ten that we are going to have war, and we must begin war without waiting, in order brutally to crush all resistance." That was said in 1913 and acted on in 1914. It is the doctrine of preventive war.

A great part of the Press in this country and many political speakers are in the habit of regarding all Germans as if they were cast in the same mould, devoured by ambition, and using the sword like the ploughshare as an instrument of industry in their favourite vocation of destroying other nations in order to steal their wealth and territory. This may be true enough of the military aristocracy, and the generalization is attractive from its very simplicity, but German psychology is much more complex than that. Since their triumph in 1870 Germans have been so skilfully drilled in the arts of peace and so tyrannically drilled in the arts of war, that an enormous anti-military party, already comprising a majority of the people, had been created before the war. When war came these millions fell into the ranks, as our own people have done, to fight for their national existence. Nevertheless there was in 1914 a very widespread anxiety for peace throughout Germany. If only a little time had been gained, would not that feeling soon have directed German policy? The fear that it would be so was one of the motives that led the military party in Germany to strike while they could in 1914.

It is quite possible that the Kaiser wished for peace

when the crisis began in July 1914, as he has since
most solemnly affirmed, and that his Ministers wished
it also. Throughout the despatches there is persistent
evidence of a dual policy and a divided purpose. But
behind the throne a mighty Power, strengthened by
the military traditions of the Kaiser's family and by
his own encouragement, stood ready for war. One
can almost hear what they said—the French military
reforms are incomplete, the Russian railway system
is incomplete. If you give them time, they will fall
on you when their moment arrives; this is your
moment; we can secure our route to Constantinople
and Asia Minor, make an end of French resistance
and settle the Eastern Question in our own favour,
and the Slav race will then never be united under the
Russian sceptre. While Dr. Bethmann-Hollweg and
the other highly placed and shining individuals who
spoke for Germany in the Chancellories of Europe
were trying to coax Austria, after having renounced
their right to interfere, the sands were running out.
Russian mobilization furnished the opportunity and
the Kaiser was overborne by the soldiers. He might
perhaps claim some of the pity which is commonly
bestowed upon guilty men who have failed from weakness of character if he had not subsequently earned
the execration of all honest men by the horrors perpetrated during the war. So much for the attitude
of Germany. On the whole the Civil Government
did not want war. The soldiers did. The soldiers
entertained no doubt that in a few months the
German armies would drive everything before them
and secure a complete victory. Most probably they
were encouraged in these views by the Austrian military

party, and certainly they were provoked by the Russian military caste. But neither encouragement nor provocation can justify their action.

* * *

The attitude of the British Government remains to be considered. Our Government in July 1914 undoubtedly desired to preserve peace. It represented, or professed to represent, the political party in these islands which for generations had inscribed on its banner the words, Peace, Retrenchment, and Reform. It had heartily accepted the necessity of a very powerful Navy, but as heartily repudiated the idea of conscription or of its equivalent, compulsory military training. Accordingly our military armaments, though sufficient for the defence of our own dominions, were transparently inadequate in numbers to take part in a Continental War. Ministers also thought, and say in their despatches, that we had no interest which would justify our intervention in a war between Austria and Russia, even if Germany came in, unless France also came in,[1] and that we had no interest in a Servian quarrel. They also said that our hands were perfectly free. This is repeatedly stated in Sir Edward Grey's despatches. But their entire policy was frustrated, when the pinch came, by two circumstances. First, by the fact that we were not free if France became involved and were attacked without having given provocation. Mr. Lloyd George in terms admitted this, in the passage already quoted. We were bound in honour so far as a Foreign Secretary can bind his country. And secondly, whether bound or not, our Ministers had never made up their minds

[1] British White Book, No. 89.

what they would do either in regard to France or in regard to Belgium from the very beginning of the crisis till after war had been declared between Germany and Russia.

The condition of things from the commencement was that the German military authorities wished for war but would not run the risk of it if Great Britain as well as Russia and France were to fight against them, and there were many people in Germany who wished for peace, though they were ill-organized. It was also clear to those who knew what had happened, always excepting His Majesty's Ministers, that we had become bound in honour to fight for France if she were attacked without giving provocation. We ought to have been kept free to choose our own course, but we had not been kept free. In these circumstances the proper course for Ministers was to announce openly that we were bound to France, and thus enable the friends of peace to prevail in Germany. Indeed the war party themselves would not have gone to war if they knew we should come in. Our course of conduct was prescribed to us by the fact that we were bound to France, however foolish it may have been to bind us. But our Ministers would not see that they were bound. They had denied it in Parliament, and still thought the same. How were they to unsay that now? And so they went on repeating in despatch after despatch that they had kept their hands free, and persuading one another that it was true, whereas it was intrinsically untrue. The faculty of believing what you wish to believe was never more signally illustrated. When at the end it became clear that Sir Edward Grey had tied himself so that he could not

desert France, then and not till then did they, by promising naval support to France, take a decisive step
which led to our taking part in the war.   If their policy
had been announced earlier it would in all probability
have led to peace being preserved all over Europe.
In short, the attitude of the British Ministry was that
of men who had not realized the true position in which
they were placed, and had not the force of character
to take a timely resolution.

Still less did they realize the fearful character of
the war on which they were embarking.   Lord Esher
wrote a letter to the *Glasgow Herald* on 10th August
1915 in which he says: " From the outset of the war
I have been thrown into the company of practically
every one of our leading statesmen, and I have found
them all wrong in their forecasts without exception.
They genuinely believed in a short war.   They
prophesied its conclusion in anything from three to
nine months.   They jeered at a less optimistic view,
and hardly one of them but held that before now
(August 1915) the British Army, accompanied by
political plenipotentiaries, would be marching through
Berlin."   We may now understand a little better the
want of foresight in the matter of food, recruits, and
munitions which have cost us so dear.   Like Emile
Ollivier in 1870, like Lord North at the time of the
American War, they had no conception at all of the
task they were taking in hand.   Lord Kitchener is not
included in Lord Esher's description.   He knew better.

* * *

In describing how the several Great Powers were
predisposed toward the impending Austro-Servian
crisis some light has been borrowed from ahead by

anticipating what they did when the crisis came. What they did when they had to act helps to show what they thought and wished from the beginning. The whole story of how they acted and of the negotiations that preceded the war must be examined minutely and separately. Meanwhile if, for preface, a sketch plan, so to speak, is furnished beforehand on the lines of which the story can be reconstructed, it will make the sequel easier to follow, and will at the same time fitly illustrate what has been said already.

＊　　＊　　＊

There were four stages, fairly distinguishable, in the negotiations which preceded the war from 23rd July down to 1st August 1914. Hardly any communications between the Powers are recorded before the Austrian ultimatum to Servia was delivered on 23rd July. Then began the first stage of negotiations, the First Aid Stage it might be called. Austria sublimely unconscious that anyone could be wounded by her proceedings, Germany rather in the same humour but disposed to get Austria and· Russia to talk it over and come to terms, Russia accessible but resolved not to allow Servian independence to be destroyed, Great Britain and France trying to suggest remedies. Notwithstanding the stiffness of the Central Powers, unduly troubled about forms and dignities, this First Aid Stage ended fairly well on 26th July, with a highly satisfactory direct communication on that day between the Russian Foreign Minister and the Austrian Ambassador, in which they almost agreed on terms, and Russia expected a renewal of the conversation.

The Second Stage lasted two days, 27th and 28th July, and may be called the stage of Austrian infatuation. Great Britain and France making further suggestions for a settlement, Russia ready to make terms if only Servian sovereignty and independence were preserved, and awaiting a renewal of conversations with Austria, Germany refusing to put pressure on Austria, to whom she had promised a free hand. Austria therefore kicks clean over the traces, will not hear of the British suggestions, refuses any further conversations with Russia, and declares war against Servia, notwithstanding a submissive reply by Servia to her ultimatum. So ends the Second Stage, in gloom deepened by the shadow of military and naval preparations, and indeed mobilizations, which all the Powers have now more or less taken in hand. It was the shadow that portended the coming of the storm. War had now broken out on the 28th July between Austria and Servia. Hope yielded for the moment to despair.

The Third Stage also lasted for two days, 29th and 30th July, Great Britain and France still trying to find expedients for composing the original dispute and also to counteract the new and hourly increasing danger of military preparations, Russia still anxious to renew conversations with Austria but deeply moved by the action of that Power. For Austria proceeds to bombard the Servian capital quite indifferent to the consequences. But at this point the German Government seems to have realized whither all this must end. On 29th or 30th July, or on both days, the German Civil Government while not, so far as is known, trying to restrain Austria's military action, does put strong pressure on Austria to change her diplomatic attitude and listen to reason, and above all to resume conversations with Russia. Upon the instant, Austria

gets off her high horse, professes readiness to listen
to several of Sir E. Grey's proposals, and resumes
conversations with Russia. So ends the Third Stage
on 30th July, and it is fairly certain that if a day or
two could have been allowed, in one way or another,
the whole dispute would have ended in peace. But
the day or two needed were not allowed.

The Fourth Stage of these amazing negotiations
lasted only twenty-four hours, beginning and ending
on 31st July. That which had been the nightmare from
the beginning took shape and proved to be no spectre
but a terrible reality. Just when everything was in
train for a settlement, a few hours before, in the opinion
of the British Ambassador at Vienna, everything had
practically been settled by conversations between
Austria and Russia at St. Petersburg,[1] Russia received
very alarming news of military preparations and
intentions on the part of the Central Powers, and at
midnight of 30th July ordered a general mobilization,
which was immediately followed on 31st July by an
ultimatum from Germany and a declaration of war by
Germany twelve hours after its delivery. By the
afternoon of 1st August Russia and Germany were
at war, and the rest followed automatically. Was
there ever a tragedy quite like this ? The original
quarrel had been practically disposed of at St. Petersburg within a few hours of the declaration of war
being despatched from Berlin.

The hurried despatch of this declaration of war is
the main point which makes many people believe
that the German Government meant war from the
beginning.

[1] See Sir M. de Bunsen's despatch, No. 161 of British White Book.

CHAPTER VI

HOW THE CONTINENT CAME TO WAR

WE must now fill in the sketch plan and tell the fuller story of the negotiations which hurried the Continent into war. The part which the British Government played in trying to prevent war altogether, that is to say, in trying to keep peace between the Central Powers on the one side, and Russia and France on the other side, ought to be made clear. But while our Government were trying to do that, they had also to consider at the same time whether, if . war broke out, we should take part in it or not. They were being pressed on the one side to promise support and on the other side to promise neutrality. This chapter deals only with the way in which war came to break out on the Continent, and therefore, for the moment, we merely take note of passages which specially affect our own subsequent intervention. How we came into the war, and why, is indeed for ourselves the most momentous of all questions. It incidentally appears here, but it admits of and requires examination in detail later on. How did the war begin on the Continent ? That is the question now.

There were five chief centres of negotiation, Vienna, Berlin, St. Petersburg, London, and Paris, each with Ambassadors from all the other Governments, Rome also figuring but less prominently. So a little interval elapses before what is said in one capital reaches the others, though as a rule the interval will be very brief in important matters. Nearly all the documents are telegrams. There is much repetition in them, and a good deal of detail. All that seems vital is presented here, omitting unimportant matter, preserving what is essential.

From 28th June, the date of the Sarajevo murder, beyond general statements that Austria intended to act with moderation, very little that we know of is said till 23rd July, the date of the Austrian Note or ultimatum to Servia. Still there is a little. On 20th July Sir Edward Grey is told by the German Ambassador that it would be " very desirable if Russia could act as a mediator with regard to Servia." If this had been done, the quarrel would have soon been composed, but the thought, whether it was the thought of the German Government or merely of the Ambassador, is cast aside and never reappears. Sir Edward Grey says he hates the idea of a war between any of the Great Powers, " and that any of them should be dragged into a war by Servia would be detestable." With this sentiment the German Ambassador whole-heartedly agreed. Quite a different note was sounded the next day (21st July) at Berlin, when the German Foreign Secretary expressed the opinion that the question at issue was one for settlement between Servia and Austria alone without interference from outside, and adds that " he had therefore considered it inadvisable that the Austro-Hungarian Government should be approached by the German Government on the matter." No affair of ours or of yours either, says the voice of wisdom at Berlin.

About this time also the German Ambassador asks the French Government to exercise a moderating influence at St. Petersburg, which France interprets as an attempt to drive a wedge into the Franco-Russian Alliance—perhaps a natural suspicion.

Before the delivery of the Austrian ultimatum to Servia, but on the day of its delivery (23rd July), the Austrian Ambassador privately explains to Sir Edward Grey what it is to be. It is to be an ultimatum, as we know, violent and offensive in tone, demanding the punishment of offenders, the suppression of Secret Societies, and a participation of Austrian officials in the execution of these demands. An answer is required within forty-eight hours. This evidently shocks Sir Edward, who greatly regrets the time limit, and fears the result on Russian opinion. He sees prophetically and warns the Ambassador that " if as many as four Great Powers went to war there might be complete collapse of European credit and industry, and, irrespective of who were victors in the war, many things might be completely swept away." The Ambassador did not demur to this statement, but said that " all would depend upon Russia." Sir Edward hoped very much that if there were difficulties Austria and Russia would discuss them directly with each other. That is the first suggestion of " direct conversations."

On 23rd July the Austrian Note or ultimatum, with its peremptory forty-eight hours' limit, is delivered to Servia. The supine diplomatic world is at once roused into activity. From that date commences a series of

efforts and suggestions, chiefly from London but also
from other quarters, to prevent a collision, and the
views of the various Powers begin to make themselves
clearer, while Servia considers what to say in her
reply, which is due on 25th July. The Great Powers
begin to exchange views. Here opens what may be
called the First Stage of negotiation.

In considering these negotiations we must bear in
mind a few facts. The Austrian Note arraigns the
Servian Government in severe contemptuous terms,
and demands ten acts of submission or atonement.
As to eight out of the ten nearly everyone thought
them appropriate, and they were in substance accepted.
The remaining two required the intervention of
Austrian officials. Did that mean that Austria was
to have authority within Servia? Austria affirms that
she explained from the beginning that she only desired
to collaborate in the preliminary police investiga-
tions, and certainly she made that clear on 27th July.
But Russia and Servia thought she would do much
more. The Italian Foreign Secretary wished that
the entire Note should be accepted at once as it stood.
Servia said on 24th July that she would accept all
that Russia desired her to accept. But Russia was
distrustful and none of the other Powers supported
the Italian view.[1]

*   *   *

July 24.—Germany issued a circular on 24th July
speaking of the Austrian Note to Servia as equitable
and moderate, and urging that no State ought to in-

[1] See British White Book, Nos. 4, 64; French Yellow Book,
No. 72; Russian Orange Book, No. 6; Austrian Red Book, Introduction and Nos. 27–34.

terfere, because " every interference of another Power
would, owing to the different Treaty obligations, be
followed by incalculable consequences." In short,
Germany said "Hands off " to Europe at large. That
was her first position.

Russia begins by asking Great Britain to announce
her " solidarity " with France and Russia in the war
which she thought would be forced upon them. This
Sir Edward Grey declines to do, but asks Austria to
extend the time limit of forty-eight hours so as to give
the Powers time to prevent a collision, which Austria
refuses. Russia asks the same, and is refused.

Sir Edward Grey declared that " the merits of the
dispute between Austria and Servia were not the
concern of His Majesty's Government," and that he
would " look at it solely from the point of view of the
peace of Europe." With this object, he made a variety
of suggestions. As already stated, he joined Russia
in asking that the time limit should be extended. But
he went further. He proposed that France, Italy,
Great Britain, and Germany should act as mediators.
By all means, said Russia, and added that " if Servia
should appeal to the Powers, Russia would be quite
ready to stand aside and leave the question in the
hands of England, France, Germany, and Italy."
France and Italy agreed to the proposal, but Austria
would not hear of it. No one had a right to interfere
while she was punishing Servia. And Germany, while
saying that if the relations between Austria and Russia
became threatening she would agree that the four
disinterested Powers should work together for peace
at Vienna and St. Petersburg, took up the position
" that mediation should not extend to the Austro-

Servian conflict, which is to be considered as a purely
Austro-Hungarian affair, but merely to the relations
between Austria-Hungary and Russia." One does not
understand the point of this distinction, because there
could not at that time be anything to mediate about
between Austria and Russia, except the Austro-Servian
conflict. Truly, the diplomatic mind is fearfully and
wonderfully constructed. A subsequent suggestion of
Sir Edward Grey that there should be a Conference
between the Ambassadors of France, Germany, and
Italy with himself in London, to discuss an issue which
would prevent complications, was met in the same
spirit. Yes, said Russia and the others. No, said
Austria. And Germany added that she would not
bring her ally before a European Tribunal.

Sir Edward urged upon the German Ambassador
(24th July) that Austria should not precipitate military
action. The British Ambassador expressed also at
St. Petersburg " his earnest hope that Russia would
not precipitate matters by mobilizing until he had
time to use his influence in favour of peace," to which
the Russian Minister replied that Russia had no
aggressive intentions and would take no action till it
was forced on her. Sir Edward expressed the hope
that, even if there was mobilization, the four Powers
would ask Austria and Russia not to cross the frontier
while the Powers were trying to settle matters, and
impressed on the German Ambassador the necessity of
Germany participating in that case, " for alone we
could do nothing." Sir Edward Grey also asked the
German and other Governments to influence the
Austrian Government to take a favourable view of
Servia's reply to her ultimatum, if it should corre-

spond (as in fact it did) with the forecast he had privately received of it.   Instead of doing that, Austria treated the Servian reply as a mockery, almost as an insult, conciliatory though it was.   At each rebuff, naturally an impression was left that Austria simply aimed at war.   For these proposals seem in them-selves extremely reasonable.

July 25.—The reply of the Servian Government to the Austrian ultimatum was delivered.   It conceded eight points out of the ten, and offered to submit to the Hague Tribunal.   Austria without a word broke off diplomatic relations with Servia the same day.

In the *Times* of 18th March 1919 a document is printed from the *Debats*.   It is a telegram of date 25th July 1914, from the Austrian Ambassador at Berlin to the Foreign Minister in Vienna, saying what follows : " It is generally supposed here that the " negative Serbian reply (to the Austrian ultimatum) " will be followed on our part by an immediate declara-" tion of war and military operations.   Any adjourn-" ment of military operations would be considered very " dangerous here because of the intervention of other " Powers.   We are urged strongly to come to acts at " once and thus confront the world with an accom-" plished fact."

If the telegram is authentic, it proves that there was somewhere at Berlin a German instigator actively at work to bring about war, and that he had access to the Austrian Ambassador.   Was it a Civil Minister or a Military Chief ?   We do not know.

All this looked very alarming, and in fact was so. But alongside of these fruitless suggestions another of greater hope was maturing—namely, that Austria and

10

Russia should endeavour by direct conversation to bring about some settlement. This idea had originally been mentioned by Sir Edward Grey, and received the support of the German Government, as may be seen from various passages in the diplomatic correspondence. The German Ambassador suggested to the Russian Foreign Minister that this method should be tried.[1] It was not, of course, a settlement, but it was a road by which that result might possibly be attained. M. Sazonoff, the Russian Foreign Minister, who throughout listened favourably to anything which might lead to a solution, assented.

July 26.—Accordingly, an interview took place on 26th July between him and the Austrian Ambassador at St. Petersburg. There are several accounts of it in the official papers, from which an adequate summary may be compiled. M. Sazonoff pointed out to the Ambassador that, though he perfectly understood Austria's motives, her ultimatum to Servia had been so drafted that its demands could not possibly be accepted as a whole by the Servian Government. Some of them were, he said, reasonable enough (a notable admission); others could not be put into immediate execution because they entailed a revision of existing laws and were incompatible with Servian independence. A conversation ensued, and we learn from Sir Maurice de Bunsen's telegram of the next day that M. Sazonoff and the Austrian Ambassador on 26th July had " practically reached an understanding as to the guarantees which Servia might reasonably be asked to give to Austria-Hungary for her future good behaviour."[2] The Russian Minister expressed

[1] British White Book, No. 78.   [2] *Ibid.*, No. 56.

the hope that these conversations might be continued
and that the Ambassador should be authorized to
deal with him, and said he would advise Servia to
yield all that could be fairly asked of an independent
Power. Nothing better than this could be expected
as a beginning. Indeed, with goodwill it would have
ended the whole thing. To settle the terms that
Servia ought to accept was to close the whole quarrel
at once; and if Austria would ratify her own Ambassador's views, the thing was done already. For
whatever Russia ordained, Servia could not help
accepting. Even a pessimist might feel cheerful
when he heard of this interview.

But a few hours before this highly satisfactory
interview of 26th July, on the night of 25th July, a
serious set-back to the prospect of peace had intervened. The Servian reply to Austria's ultimatum was
delivered. It was conciliatory. It yielded nearly all
of Austria's demands, and half yielded the remainder,
which related exclusively to infringements of Servian
sovereignty. Yet the Austrian Government at once
unceremoniously rejected it, and instantly broke off
diplomatic relations with Servia.

• • •

On 26th July ends what may be called the First
Stage of these negotiations, and the Second Stage
begins with the world distinctly nearer war. True,
there remained a hope in the prospect of renewed
interviews at St. Petersburg, but the rupture of
relations between Austria and Servia had slit the fine-
spun thread of diplomacy, and all had to begin again.
Despondency began to show itself. Austria had
proved herself strangely unapproachable. Would she

invade Servia and so force Russia into war, wonder the
diplomatists. Could anything be done to stop actual
invasion ? Could Russia be appeased if Servia were
invaded ? Would it be possible to induce Germany
to put pressure on her ally instead of leaving her a
free hand ? The despatches are full of these specula-
tions. And now, as the hours were flying, even if these
things could be dealt with, it obviously must be done
at once or never would be done at all. For the very
advance of civilization, with its telegraphs and railways and facilities of all kinds for organization and
its deadly weapons, has created immense new difficulties in the way of maintaining peace, because it
gives such an incalculable advantage to the nation
which gets ready in time and is able to strike first.
What everyone dreaded above all else was that his
adversary would amuse him with negotiation and
prepare for war behind that screen. Therefore everyone watched with intense anxiety the military preparations of his neighbours. In this atmosphere of
alarm began the Second Stage of these fatal negotiations. It covers 27th and 28th July.

Notwithstanding this alarm, hopes were still entertained for two or three days after the rejection by
Austria of the Servian reply, due no doubt to knowledge
of the satisfactory interview at St. Petersburg on
26th July between M. Sazonoff and the Austrian
Ambassador, due also to the knowledge that Great
Britain was working hard for peace, and to a belief
that the German Government desired the same thing.
The *Times* served as an index of well-informed opinion
when its Berlin correspondent on 27th July declared
that Germany was " certainly and no doubt sincerely

working for peace." This accords with other Press opinions, and is, so far as can be judged, quite true—not indeed of the military party at Berlin, but of the German Civil Government, as it is beyond all doubt true of the Czar, France, Great Britain, and Italy. But there is not anything to show energetic action by Germany at this stage. We must treat the conversations and negotiations between the Powers during these two days (27th–28th July) briefly and elliptically, if a sharp impression of them is to be left. Otherwise the impression will be blunted by mere tediousness.

July 27, 28.—Austria means to punish Servia, and Russia will keep quiet, says the German Ambassador at Vienna. So will France, he thinks, for she cannot face a war. One sympathizes with Austria, observes the British Ambassador at Vienna, if the tone of her ultimatum to Servia had been more temperate. Will the Ambassadors of France, Italy, and Germany meet me here to try and find a way out? asks Sir Edward Grey. Yes, say the others. No, says Germany; it would be a Court to try Austria. Will you defer mobilization as long as possible, and, even when mobilized, stop your troops crossing the frontier, says the British Ambassador to the Russian Foreign Minister. If we wait too long, replies the Minister, our enemies will profit by the delay to complete their preparations. Germany accepts mediation as between Austria and Russia on 27th July, and says to Sir Edward Grey, Do use your influence at St. Petersburg in favour of peace (meaning against mobilization). To which Sir Edward replies, Russia must have influenced Servia in making her submissive reply; pray urge Austria to treat that reply as " a basis for discussion and pause." Russian Ambassador says to Sir Edward Grey, Both Germany and Austria believe that Great Britain will stand aside if war comes, and this has a deplorable effect. We have given orders that our fleet (which had been assembled as usual for autumn manœuvres) is not to disperse, answers Sir Edward, but, he adds, " this must not be taken to mean that anything more than diplomatic action is promised." We must appeal to force against Servia, observes the Austrian Ambassador to Sir Edward Grey, and we feel we can count on British sympathy. Sir Edward in answer says nothing about sympathy, one way or the other, but warns the Ambassador that Russia will come in, and asks, Why do you treat the Servian reply as a blank negative ? We shall take no territory, says the Ambassador, and Sir Edward Grey tells him about the British Fleet not being dispersed, but adds that it is no menace. A significant passage may be found in No. 63 of the French Yellow Book. The French chargé d'affaires reports from London as follows on 27th July: " The German Ambassador and the " Austrian Ambassador allow it to be understood that " they are sure that England would preserve neutrality " if a conflict were to break out. Sir A. Nicholson " has told me, however, that Prince Lichnowsky can- " not after the conversation which he has had with " him to-day entertain any doubt as to the freedom " which the British Government intended to preserve " of intervening in case they should judge it expedient."

Apparently in the opinion of our Government the last word in statesmanship throughout this business was to preserve entire freedom of action. But this was just what they had not done.

That brings us up to 28th July.

July 28.—It was on 28th July that Austria, which had provoked all the trouble, took her next step toward the ruin of Europe. She declared war on Servia, and proceeded to bombard Belgrade, causing a very massacre of its inhabitants. Had not Germany given her a " complete free hand " ? Until this happened, the prospects of peace had not been vitally impaired, but this action of Austria immensely increased the difficulties of the Czar in view of the racial and religious sympathies of the Russian people. Still, there had been that satisfactory interview at St. Petersburg between the Russian Secretary of State and the Austrian Ambassador on the 26th July, and hopes might rest on a continuance of like interviews. Russia was anxious to continue them. But Austria proceeded to dash these hopes also to the ground, as if to make peace impossible. On 28th July, the same day on which she declared war on Servia, Austria also refused definitely to continue these conversations,[1] even though they had been commenced on the recommendation of her German ally. How is this astonishing recklessness to be explained ? Probably Vienna was benighted enough to believe that Russia neither could nor would go to war,[2] even when shot and shell were being poured into the Servian capital, though every level-headed man could have told her the contrary. But even if Russia did fight, what then ? Was not Germany strictly tied to support Austria, not merely by their formal alliance, but by an express promise, given beforehand in reference to this particular occasion, that Austria might

---

[1] See British White Book, No. 78.   [2] *Ibid.*, No. 71.

take what measures she pleased and her ally would
be by her side ?   Austria had received some mortifica-
tions of late.   It was not in the Austrian nature that
she should forgo this chance of settling the Balkan
Question in her own favour, when she could dispose
of the most powerful army in the world.   Rattling
other people's sabres is an enticing pursuit.   But
Austria's action on the 28th may have been influenced
from Berlin, for on the preceding day the Austrian
Ambassador at Berlin wired to Vienna as follows, if
the *Times* of 13th March 1919 is well informed :
" Berlin, 27th July 1914.—The Secretary of State has
" just positively assured me, under a vow of the greatest
" secrecy, that very shortly it is probable that British
" proposals for British mediation will be communicated
" to your Excellency.   The German Government states
" in most convincing terms that it is in no way identified
" with these proposals, that it is absolutely opposed to
" considering them, and they only transmit them to
" us in order that we may take note of the British
" request."

If this wire is authentic, then it proves that the
German Foreign Secretary was working for war while
professing anxiety for peace.

*   *   *

So ended the Second Stage of the nine crucial
days, in a renewal of Austrian provocation.

Another source of infinite danger now began to
emerge—the progress of military preparations.   In
the condition of universal distrust which had come
over Europe what men most feared was being caught
unprepared and destroyed before they could defend
themselves.   This is the consideration which made

the loss of golden hours between 23rd and 28th July
so deplorable. For till tension is removed nothing
can be more certain than that the States which are
in danger of attack will begin to get ready. This is
precisely what happened. How, when, where, to
what extent, is obscure. No more is possible than an
outline based largely on conjecture. As early as
25th July, Russia decided upon a partial mobilization
for the military districts bordering upon the Austrian
frontier. Perhaps preliminary steps were also taken
in Kovno and elsewhere near the German frontier
at about the same time. Some measures, of precaution, not of mobilization, seem on the whole to have
been taken in France, such as bringing the various
corps up to full peace strength, and recalling officers
on leave, up to 28th July. The same kind of thing
was certainly done in Germany, if not more. Much
more than this occurred in Austria in those early days
before anyone else moved, and there is ground for
thinking that full mobilisation itself secretly began
then. Each nation, of course, either denied or represented as mere trifles the steps it had taken. Each
received reports, probably exaggerated, from its agents
of the steps taken by others. But when the process
has once been commenced, it goes forward progressively
faster each day. Those are wise men who hasten their
action and make light of forms, so as to agree terms
before the panic comes and the fate of nations passes
into the hands of military men. Just when this kind
of terror about military preparations began to become
pronounced, Austria, instead of hurrying on her
conversations with Russia, on the 28th July, as we
have seen, broke them off, and on the same day declared

war against Servia.   That seemed to make the outlook hopeless.

* * *

July 29, 30.—Now comes the Third Stage, 29th and 30th July. One Power alone could prevent war at this point, and that Power was Germany, for Germany was omnipotent at Vienna. And Germany did wake up, after Austria's escapades on 28th July. Berlin became very uneasy, probably now recognizing what was really involved in an unconditional promise of support with all your heart and of a completely free hand to so violent an ally as Austria, with a Kaiser nearly ninety years old to shape her policy and a military party in the background.   The military party in Germany pointed to the mobilizations, and would have struck at once, if rumour is true.   It is believed that three days' grace were given to the Civil Government at Berlin to save the situation if they could by diplomatic methods.   Sir Edward Grey urged on Germany that mediation was ready to be put into operation by any method that Germany could suggest, if his own method was not acceptable, and on 29th July asked, would not Germany " press the button " in the interest of peace.   The German Chancellor expressed in reply his warm anxiety to work with us.[1]   On 29th July he declared that he was " pressing the button " as hard as he could, so hard indeed that he feared his insistence had caused Austria to precipitate matters.   This idea, that it might do harm to press Austria, is often put forward by the German Ministers in their dialogues.   It is doubtful whether we ought to regard these statements of Dr. Bethmann-Hollweg as mere falsehood and

[1] British White Book, Nos. 84 and 107.

hypocrisy. We know from independent sources how perverse Austria was. On the two days following 28th July (the date of Austria's outburst) the civil Ministers at Berlin and the Kaiser did really insist upon more rational conduct at Vienna.[1] They told Austria that if she did not mean to annex Servian territory she should say so openly. They assured Russia that the Austrians had no territorial designs, and went so far as to tell Russia that Germany would guarantee the integrity of Servia. These steps, whether sufficient or not, were in the interests of peace. Also Kaiser William accepted the Czar's request that he should act as mediator. How critical the situation had become appears from the pathetic statement in the Czar's telegram of 29th July: " I " fear that very soon I shall be unable to resist the " pressure exercised upon me, and that I shall be forced " to take measures that will lead to war." All these things were done on 29th July.

There is further proof that at this stage the German Civil Government was bestirring itself. The most promising way to prevent war was for direct conversations to be continued between Austria and Russia.[2] They had been originally suggested by Sir Edward Grey, with the immediate assent if not on the independent initiative of Germany, and Sir Edward thought them " the most preferable method of all."[3] Clearly he was right, for by this method a settlement would admittedly have been reached a few days later, had not the military men interposed, as we shall see. The German Ambassador had been the person who

[1] British White Book, Nos. 75 and 97. Denkschrift, Exhibit 22.
[2] British White Book, No. 3. [3] *Ibid.*, No. 67.

advised Russia to commence these conversations which began so well on 26th July.[1] And after Austria had refused to continue them on 28th July, the German Government most strongly urged that they should be recommenced. They said so to Russia on 29th July, and next day, 30th July, the French Ambassador at Vienna hears[2] that the German Ambassador is instructed to speak seriously to the Austro-Hungarian Government against acting in a manner calculated to provoke a European war. And the Italian Minister hears[3] that Austria had broken off conversations with Russia, but believes that Germany was now disposed to give more conciliatory advice at Vienna. There is really no doubt that it was so—on the part of the German Civil Government, that is to say.

All these things support and are supported by two authoritative statements of the German Government as to their action on these two days, the 29th and 30th July. The first of the statements in question was made by the German Chancellor when addressing the Reichstag in November 1916. He then said: "Lord Grey well knows that I transmitted to Vienna, with the most peremptory recommendation, the mediation proposal which he made to our Ambassador on 29th July, and which appeared to me a suitable basis for the maintenance of peace."

This mediation proposal, which Sir Edward Grey made to the German Ambassador on 29th July, is to be found in the British White Book, No. 88. Sir Edward said to the German Ambassador: "In a short

---

[1] British White Book, Nos. 78 and 93 (2). See also Russian Orange Book, No. 38.
[2] British White Book, No. 95.   [3] *Ibid.*, No. 106.

time I supposed the Austrian forces would be in Belgrade and in occupation of some Servian territory. But even then it might be possible to bring some mediation into existence, if Austria, while saying that she must hold the occupied territory until she had complete satisfaction from Servia, stated that she would not advance further pending an effort of the Powers to mediate between her and Russia." That was Sir Edward's mediation proposal. In answer to it on the 30th July, the German Ambassador informed him, " that the German Government would endeavour to influence Austria,[1] after taking Belgrade and Servian territory in region of frontier, to promise not to advance further, while the Powers endeavoured to arrange that Servia should give satisfaction sufficient to pacify Austria. Territory occupied would of course be evacuated when Austria was satisfied." This was an acceptance by Germany of Sir Edward's own suggestion—an event of enormous importance, for London and Berlin were at one. We must appreciate that London and Berlin were at one on 30th July in a plan which would have preserved peace, if we are to realize the full horror of what followed.

Continuing his speech in November 1916, the German Chancellor then read to the Reichstag the terms of his message to Vienna recommending acceptance of Sir Edward Grey's mediation proposal. It contained the following sentences : " We urgently and emphatically ask the Vienna Cabinet to consider the acceptance of mediation on the proposed conditions. Responsibility for the consequences which may otherwise arise must be extraordinarily severe for Austria-Hungary and

[1] British White Book, No. 103.

ourselves." He added that Austria agreed to this. Lord Grey has not denied that he was aware of this step being taken, nor need he do so, for it is an additional proof of his exertions to keep the peace. But all this does show that on 29th July the German Chancellor also was working for peace.

The second authoritative statement from Berlin that supports the same conclusion is also confirmed in the same speech of the German Chancellor, but it was originally made public on 2nd August 1914 by the *Westminster Gazette*. That journal then published a telegram which had been officially communicated to it by the German Government, in the hope no doubt of satisfying public opinion here that Germany was trying to avert war, and in order to prove that Germany was trying to make Austria resume conversations with Russia. No reason has been given for doubting its genuineness. This telegram is dated 30th July 1914, and is addressed by the German Chancellor to the German Ambassador at Vienna. "The Report," it says, "of Count Pourtales (German Ambassador at St. Petersburg) does not harmonize with the account which your Excellency has given of the attitude of the Austro-Hungarian Government. Apparently there is a misunderstanding which I beg you to clear up. We cannot expect Austria to negotiate with Servia, with which she is in a state of war. The refusal, however, to exchange views with St. Petersburg would be a grave mistake. We are indeed ready to fulfil our duty. As an Ally we must, however, refuse to be drawn into a world-conflagration through Austria-Hungary not respecting our advice. Your Excellency will express this to Count Berchtold with

all emphasis and great seriousness." This is plain
speaking. On the same day, 30th July, the Austrian
Government at once changed its tone and caused direct
conversations to be recommenced with Russia.[1] It was
a great step in the right direction. All this certainly
indicates that Bethmann-Hollweg was at that date
endeavouring to bring Austria and Russia together.
On the other hand, there were the two telegrams
recently mentioned from the Austrian Ambassador
at Berlin to his Chief at Vienna, if they are authentic.
It is possible that different members of the Civil
Government in Berlin were privately working in
different directions, some for war, others for peace.
The military men at Berlin were certainly for war.

*　　*　　*

That day, 30th July, was fruitful also of other proposals for a sane treatment of the dangerous crisis.
In the small hours of the morning (2 a.m.) the German
Ambassador at St. Petersburg saw the Russian Secretary of State and completely broke down in his presence
on seeing or thinking that war was inevitable. He
implored the Russian Secretary to give him some
suggestion that he might send to Berlin.[2] This seems
to have touched the Russian Secretary, and he accordingly drew up the following formula: " If Austria,
recognizing that her conflict with Servia has assumed
character of question of European interest, declares
herself ready to eliminate from her ultimatum points
which violate principle of sovereignty of Servia,
Russia engages to stop all military preparations." [3]
This was at once wired to Berlin, Vienna, and London.

[1] British White Book, No. 96.　　　[2] Ibid., No. 97.
[3] Russian Orange Book, No. 60, and British White Book, No. 97.

Sir Edward suggested a slight modification, and next day the proposal in its final form was delivered to the French and German Ambassadors. It was in these terms: " If Austria will agree to check the advance of her troops in Servia, and if, recognizing that the dispute between her and Servia has assumed a character of European interest, she will allow the Powers to look into the matter and determine whether Servia can satisfy the Austrian Government without impairing her rights as a Sovereign State or her independence, Russia will undertake to maintain a waiting attitude." This too looked hopeful. But it was cut short by the German ultimatum following upon the Russian mobilization resolved upon at midnight on 30th July, and promulgated early on 31st July.

* * *

Indeed, the 30th July 1914 proved to be the day of Fate. That evening the hope of peace was at its zenith. Next morning it had almost vanished. We have just seen how Great Britain and Germany were agreed on a plan, and how Russia had her plan and Germany was pressing Austria.

Other projects also were on foot that fateful day. What had hitherto hindered a settlement more than anything else was Austria's refusal to give an assurance that she would respect Servian sovereignty and independence, and her refusal to accept mediation as between Austria and Servia, or to continue conversations. On 30th July her attitude completely changed. Every one of the proposals which she had scorned now found favour in her eyes. And then, in the twinkling of an eye, negotiations broke down.

* * *

July 31.—The Fourth Stage of these negotiations began at midnight of 30th July with the Czar's decision to mobilize the entire Russian Army, and ended at midnight of 31st July when the German ultimatum was delivered at St. Petersburg. Within these few hours the last hopes of peace flickered to their extinction. After that there were some despairing efforts by the Czar and by Sir Edward Grey, and then all was over. If we are to see this closing scene in a true light, we must look at it in the light of what went before and what came after.

On 30th July Austria was ready to accept almost anything. Germany had spoken, and her ally's illusions disappeared. Arrogance and obstinacy disappeared with them. She became of a sudden gracious, conciliatory, even genial.[1] Austria assured France that she had no wish to impair the sovereign rights of Servia. Austria begged the Russian Ambassador at Vienna " to do his best to remove the erroneous impression in St. Petersburg that the door had been banged by Austria-Hungary on all further conversations," and the Austrian Prime Minister repeated " that neither the infraction of Servian sovereign rights nor the acquisition of Servian territory was being contemplated." Sir Edward Grey heard on 1st August " from a most reliable source that Austrian Government have informed German Government that though the situation has been changed by the mobilization of Russia they would, in full appreciation of the efforts of England for the preservation of peace, be ready to consider favourably my [Sir Edward Grey's] proposal

[1] British White Book, Nos. 96, 110; French Yellow Book, No. 104; Austro-Hungarian Red Book, Nos. 49–51.

11

for mediation between Austria and Servia." [1] What
Sir Edward thus heard had occurred on a previous
day.   Dr. Bethmann-Hollweg said in November 1916
that it was the result of his pressure.   Austria had
indeed changed.

The proposals just mentioned, however, only aimed
at getting machinery to settle the Austro-Servian
quarrel.   Much more than this was on the point of
being attained.   The machinery would have lain idle,
had it been set up, for the Austro-Servian quarrel
was itself put in training for a direct and final settlement on 30th July, and was practically settled on
31st July or 1st August (which of these two days is
not quite clearly stated in our Ambassador's despatch), by direct conversations between the Austrian
Ambassador and the Russian Secretary of State at
St. Petersburg.

July 31 began with no less than three irons in the
fire in favour of peace, Sir Edward Grey's proposal
that Austria should hold a definite part of Servia as
guarantee while the Powers were mediating, the
Russian offer to stop arming if Austria would accept
mediation, and the direct renewal of conversations
between Russia and Austria.   What happened to
them all ?   Let us take them in turn.

Sir E. Grey's proposal had the support of France and
Italy.   He thought Russia would accept it, and he
ought to know.   Germany thought the same (see
statement in German Denkschrift at p. 411).   Would
Austria agree?   The Kaiser handed to the American
Ambassador a written statement in which he said,
" His Majesty [the British Sovereign] asked me if I

[1] British White Book, No. 135.

would transmit to Vienna the British proposal that
Austria was to take Belgrade and a few other Servian
towns and a strip of territory as a main mise to make
sure that the other Servian promises on paper should
be fulfilled in reality. This proposal was in the same
moment telegraphed to me from Vienna for London,
quite in conjunction with the British proposal. Besides
I had telegraphed to H.M. the Czar the same as an idea
of mine before I received the two communications
from Vienna and London, as both were of the same
opinion. I immediately transmitted the telegrams
vice versa. I felt that I was able to tide the question
over and was happy at the peaceful outlook." The
Kaiser placed this transmission of telegrams to London
and Vienna *vice versa* as of date 30th July, for he says
that next morning he got news of the Russian mobilization, and he got that news on 31st July. Now there is
no trace in any of the official papers of any such transmission. The Austrian Red Book, No. 51, shows that
on 31st July Vienna notified Berlin that Austria
accepted Sir E. Grey's offer of mediation, but on
condition that Austrian military action in Servia
should continue and Russian military preparations
should be suspended. This shows that Austria would
agree, though the news may not have been transmitted.
Was there foul play somewhere? Or was the Kaiser
romancing? Or were the telegrams held up when
news of the Russian mobilization arrived? At all
events Sir E. Grey's proposal came to nothing
on 31st July, owing to the German ultimatum to
Russia.

The Russian offer to stop arming if Austria would
accept mediation shared the same fate. Nothing

came of it from 31st July. The first and second iron in the fire were extinguished on 31st July, obviously for the same reason, namely the Russian mobilization and the German ultimatum which followed it.

In regard to the third iron in the fire, namely, direct conversations between Austria and Russia, these conversations had been broken off by Austria on 28th July, and resumed on the 30th July. Sir M. de Bunsen tells us what followed from the reopening of the conversations, in his despatch of 8th August, which appears in the British White Book (No. 161), and tells at the same time how everything was wrecked by the German Declaration of War.

" From now (30th July) onwards the tension between Russia and Germany was much greater than between Russia and Austria. As between the latter an arrangement seemed almost in sight, and on the 1st August I was informed by M. Schebeko (Russian Ambassador in Vienna) that Count Szapary (Austrian Ambassador at St. Petersburg) had at last conceded the main point at issue by announcing to M. Sazonoff that Austria would consent to submit to mediation the points in the Note to Servia which seemed incompatible with the maintenance of Servian independence. M. Sazonoff, M. Schebeko added, had accepted this proposal on condition that Austria would refrain from the actual invasion of Servia. Austria, in fact, had finally yielded." Sir Maurice de Bunsen proceeds to say that Austria was showing the most conciliatory spirit, and the condition as to invading Servia " could probably have been settled by negotiation." He ends this part of his despatch with a statement which is perhaps one of the saddest on record. " Unfortunately, these conversations at St. Petersburg and Vienna were cut short by the transfer of the dispute to the more dangerous ground of a direct conflict between Germany and Russia. Germany intervened on the 31st July by means of her double ultimatums to St. Petersburg and Paris. The ultimatums were of a kind to which only one answer is possible, and Germany declared war on Russia on the 1st August, and on France on the 3rd August. A few days' delay might in all probability have saved Europe from one of the greatest calamities in history." And so it all ended in war. Peace had practically been agreed in one capital when war broke out in another.

* * *

That was the crucial fault which Germany committed. It is a mistake to find the fatal fault in her pedantic punctilio or even her slothfulness during the early negotiations. It is to be found in the fact that when the original quarrel was all but settled, and with a few days or even hours of patience would in all probability have been completely settled, she drew the sword. When all this was in sight, Russia mobilized on 30th July, and Germany at once sent off her ultimatum next day.

This catastrophe supervened by reason of alarm about mobilizations, which gave the German General Staff their chance. Up to 28th July there had already been some military preparations and even some partial mobilization of the various armies, which caused anxiety from the first. Great stress is laid upon it in the German official Denkschrift. The Germans say that they first heard of Russian partial mobilization on 26th July, and at once warned Russia. They say that in the succeeding days news of Russian mobilization came at a rapid rate, that some of it related to the Russo-German frontier, and that news of French preparations first came on 27th July. It was clear that Russia partially mobilized only after Austria had mobilized. She wholly denied any mobilization against Germany. Her assurances were, however, disbelieved at Berlin. Berlin began to be very seriously alarmed on this subject as early as 28th July, and the *Times* correspondent noted the development of military opinion there, " which is now making itself felt, and may be difficult to control." Germany was in fact making military preparations herself at the same time—secretly, it would seem. That kind of thing was perfectly certain to happen. Berlin and indeed all the capitals were greatly perturbed about mobilization, each watching and warning the other of the consequences which it might bring.

On 30th July Prince Henry of Prussia telegraphed to our King George his assurance that the Kaiser was with the greatest sincerity working for peace, but that the military preparations of his neighbours may compel him at last to follow their example, or his country would remain defenceless. To which the King replied that his Government were doing all that is possible to induce Russia and France to stop their military preparations, " if Austria would content herself with occupying Belgrade and the adjacent portions of Servian territory as a pledge for the conclusion of an agreement satisfying her claims, while at the same time other countries stop their preparations for war." This was one of the proposals already mentioned. The Kaiser sent a telegram next day, 31st July, saying

that he agreed with the proposal, but had just learned
that Russia had ordered the mobilization of all her
army and navy.

*   *   *

Turn to Russia.   Was Russia to blame for mobilizing as she did?   According to the despatches the
orders for a general mobilization in Russia were
determined upon late at night on 30th July and promulgated on 31st July.   Fuller information was given
at the trial in 1917 of General Sukhomlikof, the Russian
Minister for War, published in some detail by the
Manchester Guardian of 22nd September of that year.
Though this evidence does not affect the main story it
does throw light on the question whether or not the
militarists of Russia must share some part of the
blame.   It appears that the Czar was induced to sign
an order for general mobilization on 29th July.   But
after signing it he received a telegram from the Kaiser,
probably No. 22 of the Russian Orange Book, and he
then ordered his Minister for War to stop the general
mobilization and to mobilize only against Austria.
But the Minister for War and the Chief of the Staff
disobeyed and let the general mobilization go on.
The Czar was left in ignorance of this disobedience,
and a deliberate falsehood was told to the German
officer who complained that mobilization was going
forward.   But on 30th July the Russian Ministers for
War, Navy, and Foreign Affairs met and definitely resolved that general mobilization must be proceeded with
and the Czar's consent obtained.   They did obtain it
on the night of 30th July, though both Great Britain
and France were led to think that only mobilization
against Austria was proceeding (see British White

Book, No. 78, and French Yellow Book, No. 102).
Heavy blame is cast on Russia for this step taken at
a time when her conversations with the Austrian
Government had just been renewed. It is true
enough that the day before they took this resolution to mobilize, the Russian Government received
most serious communications. One was from the
Russian Ambassador at Paris (possibly inaccurate)
to say that while keeping up conversations at St.
Petersburg Austria was planning active measures,
and, if they were permitted, her demands would increase proportionately.[1] Another, accurate no doubt,
was on the same day (29th July) from the German
Ambassador at St. Petersburg, who communicated
to the Russian Minister for Foreign Affairs " the decision of his Government to mobilize if Russia does
not break off her military preparations." [2]

It must be added that on 30th July a Berlin newspaper announced that mobilization had been, in fact,
ordered in Germany. All the accessible copies of this
news-sheet were immediately seized and urgent telegrams sent from Berlin to all the European Courts
contradicting the statement. The statement may
have been wholly false, as the German Government
have always maintained, but it might well be believed,
all the same, in St. Petersburg, coming as it did
on the top of other pieces of intelligence pointing
to military measures in Germany. But this was
not all. Official news reached Russia of complete
Austrian mobilization as well.[3] This is the main
cause which Russia has always alleged for her own

[1] Russian Orange Book, No. 53.   [2] Ibid., No. 58.
[3] Ibid., No. 77.

mobilization, and it must be remembered that Austria had not only declared war against Servia, but was also still attacking Servian territory and bombarding Belgrade. The news that reached Russia on 29th and 30th July may have been untrue. No one will ever know the whole truth. But this was the information on which Russia appears to have acted, and these were the broad circumstances under which Russia decided on a general mobilization late at night on 30–31st July. None the less this general mobilization by Russia was inexcusable. It was accompanied by falsehood to Germany, and was contrary to the wishes both of France and England. It was just the kind of act which would infuriate the Germans when peace was in sight. But it did not make peace hopeless, for, as we shall see, the Czar still offered to continue negotiations and to stop all military action while they were continued. And the Kaiser ended it all by his ultimatum and his declaration of war. Germany had the advantage in her power of rapid mobilization. Russia had very superior numbers of fighting men. It is probable that the Germans were afraid of losing their advantage if Russia could get time to mobilize But that was no reason for refusing to negotiate, because if negotiations were needlessly protracted they could have been broken off at any time.

* * *

The efforts that had been already commenced were continued a little longer, but negotiation, in any true sense of the word, ceased when Russia mobilized. It need not have been so. Even after the step taken by Russia, the situation might have been saved had Berlin been reasonable. For mobilization is not the same thing as war, though it too often leads to war. The proper answer to mobilization is mobilization. That still leaves a chance of peace. It ought not to be matter of complaint in itself that on receiving news of what had been done in Russia the Kaiser proclaimed Kriegzustand on 31st July—that is to say, a military " stand at attention." It might have been legitimate even for Germany to mobilize fully on that day. But that alone was not the course taken. At midnight on 31st July Germany delivered to Russia an ultimatum requiring her to stop her military preparations in twelve hours—that is, by midday on 1st August—not only against Germany but also against Austria, or Germany would be compelled to mobilize.[1] A compliance would leave Russia defenceless on both frontiers. A refusal would obviously, indeed avowedly, mean war. Why did not Germany take what steps she might think right to defend her own frontier instead of making a demand which could only meet a refusal, and so bring to a point at once the issue of peace or war which, had it been postponed even for a few hours, would have come out differently ? For it is one thing to place your own country in a position of self-defence against a neighbour and quite another thing to threaten him with war unless he places himself in a posture of defencelessness. Russia furnished the opportunity for war, but it was Germany that seized the opportunity. How did this come about ?

No answer except one is possible to this question. The German military chiefs had resolved to close negotiations and to declare war unless Russia would at once submit. It was to be the same as she had

[1] Russian Orange Book, No. 70.

done, and won, in 1908. Germany was not content merely to mobilize herself, but if she mobilized she would at once also declare war. This is clear from the telegram of the same date (31st July) sent by the German Chancellor to his Ambassador in Paris, which is printed in the Denkschrift.[1] He states that unless Russia stops within twelve hours Germany will mobilize, and adds : " Mobilization inevitably implies war." In the same telegram he says: " Please ask French Government whether it intends to remain neutral in a Russo-German war. Reply must be made in eighteen hours." Proof could not be more complete that Germany meant not merely to take steps for defending herself but to make Russia disarm or to make war at once. If Russia disarmed she would be in no position to make terms for Servia. Russia did not comply within the twelve hours, and on 1st August, at 12.52 p.m. according to the Denkschrift, the German Ambassador at St. Petersburg was ordered to declare war against Russia.[2]

In their statement of how the war arose the German Government say that on 1st August in the afternoon Russian troops marched into German territory; but neither place nor proof are given, and it is admitted that the German declaration of war was on its way at the time. If Russian troops had disobeyed their orders, which is nowhere confirmed, that had nothing to do with the outbreak of war. For the Germans had sent their declaration of war before the time at which they allege the Russian violation of their

[1] German Denkschrift, No. 25.
[2] *Ibid.*, Exhibit 26.

frontier took place. It was sent at 12.52 p.m. on 1st August.

*   *   *

Those who defend the action of Germany in sending her ultimatum, and the German Government itself, justify this action upon the ground that Russia had not only ordered a general mobilization but also meant to strike. It is therefore important to note again that, after he had ordered mobilization, and again even after the receipt of the German ultimatum, the Czar made a last effort to avoid war. The proof of this comes from the German Official Memorandum.

There are reproduced in the German Denkschrift two telegrams from the Czar to the Kaiser. One of them is dated 31st July, and sent at two o'clock that afternoon, before the Czar had received the German ultimatum. It is as follows :

" I thank you cordially for your mediation, which permits the hope that everything may yet end peaceably. It is technically impossible to discontinue our military preparations, which have been made necessary by the Austrian mobilization. It is far from us to want war. As long as the negotiations between Austria and Servia continue my troops will undertake no provocative action. I give you my solemn word thereon. I confide with all my faith in the grace of God, and I hope for the success of your mediation in Vienna for the welfare of our countries and the peace of Europe.—Your cordially devoted
" NICHOLAS "

This crossed a telegram from the Kaiser to the Czar also of 31st July, in which the Kaiser protested that while he was mediating by the Czar's request the latter was mobilizing against Austria and also on the German frontier. The Kaiser refers to the legacy of friendship towards Russia bequeathed to him by his grandfather the Emperor William on his death-bed and which has always been sacred to him. He adds that the peace of Europe can still be preserved if Russia discontinues those military preparations which menace Germany and Austria-Hungary.

The German ultimatum to Russia was delivered at midnight on 31st July. The next day (1st August) after receipt of it the Czar sent another telegram to the Kaiser, worded as follows :

" I have received your telegram. I comprehend that you are forced to mobilize, but I should like to have from you the same guarantee which I have given you, viz., that these measures do not mean war, and that we shall continue to negotiate for the welfare of our two countries and the universal peace which is so dear to our hearts. With the aid of God it must be possible to our long tried friendship to prevent the shedding of blood. I expect with full confidence your august reply."

If in answer to this the Kaiser had agreed that while mobilizing he would take no provocative action and would continue negotiations, peace would have been preserved. But the Kaiser answered that he had received no reply to his ultimatum, that an immediate, clear, and unmistakable reply is the sole way to avoid endless misery, and that until it is received the Kaiser is unable to enter on the subject of the Czar's telegram. How was it possible for the Czar to submit ? On the same day, 1st August, the Kaiser declared war on Russia. The system of Continental alliances came into play. France joined Russia. Germany had

Austria on her side, and we all know what has happened since.

*   *   *

There is no doubt that the action of Germany which
brought on the war, and her subsequent refusal to
suspend actual fighting while negotiation should still
be in progress, were due to the pressure by the military
party at Berlin. Herr von Jagow, the German
Foreign Secretary, told the French Ambassador at
Berlin on 30th July that the German military leaders
were insisting on mobilization because every day was
a loss of strength to the German Army. Herr Zimmer-
mann, the Under Secretary, said the same thing to
another of the Ambassadors on 29th or 30th July.[1]
If anyone has doubts on this subject he has only to
read Ambassador Gerard's book, *My Four Years in
Germany*. The military chiefs gained the upper hand
about 29th or 30th July. Alarm at Russian mobilization gave them their chance. They believed that they
were completely prepared and could gain an early and
decisive victory. Speed was on their side, because they
could mobilize more rapidly ; numbers were on the side
of Russia. So they insisted upon striking at once. It
would be misreading of history to place on the shoulders
of the German Civil Government a responsibility which
belongs to the soldiers. They have a sufficient
burden of their own to bear. They allowed the
military party to overrule them, when they knew
that a very brief delay would result in an honourable
peace.

The Civil Governments or Managers of Foreign
Policy in Europe, under whatever title they be

[1] See French Yellow Book, Nos. 105 and 109.

designated, were very heavily to blame, for drifting helplessly in a situation of unexampled danger. They all knew—in Berlin, Paris, London, Vienna, and St. Petersburg—that the danger lay in one General Staff desiring to forestall the other or fearing to be itself forestalled. This apprehension is clearly expressed throughout the despatches. Therefore time became all-important. If the diplomatists could not settle soon, the chance of settling at all would probably vanish in a few days. A strong, prompt decision by each State as to the course it proposed to steer, and an immediate announcement of that course, where an antagonist was about in ignorance to thwart it, or a friend was about to commit some error which would run counter to it—these surely are necessary in the management of any kind of controversial business. It is fatal, too, to make a blunder as to your opponents' resolution or resources. Blunders on such a point may be excused when the conditions are doubtful or obscure, but no one of intelligence could doubt that Russia would never allow Servia to be trampled in the dust without having her voice heard. Yet Austria proceeded as if she could do as she pleased, and Germany allowed her a free hand. The Civil Government at Berlin did put down its foot at last on 29th and 30th July. Till then, it babbled of its fear that if unduly pressed Austria might present a *fait accompli*. When the foot was once put down, Austria utterly subsided. But then the military spectre had assumed irrepressible strength.

* * *

The action of our own Government must be further considered with reference to our own entry into the war, which is a different chapter. But it is clear from Sir Edward Grey's speech in the House of Commons that he thought we should be disgraced if we did not fight to support France, even should she be attacked by Germany by reason of her supporting Russia according to Treaty. Very well. If he thought so, why did not Ministers make up their minds and tell it, as politely as you please, to Germany before things went too far ? As already stated, President Wilson is reported on 5th March 1919 to have said in America, " We know for a certainty that if Germany had thought for a moment that Great Britain would go in with France or Russia she would never have undertaken the enterprise." Mr. Bonar Law expressed the same opinion, though less emphatically, on 18th June 1918, in the House of Commons. He said, " It has been commonly " said—I think it is very likely true—that if the Ger- " mans had known for certain that Great Britain would " have taken part in this war, the war would never have " occurred." Or they had another course. On 31st July Sir Edward said to Germany that if she would get a reasonable proposal put forward he would tell France and Russia that if they would not accept it Great Britain would have no more to do with the consequences. Suppose he had said at the very outset, instead of saying it on the day when Germany sent her ultimatum to Russia, which as we learn from the Denkschrift was despatched on the afternoon of 31st July. In view of the negotiations that have been discussed, is it not at least probable that this would have proved successful ? Or another course might have been adopted. There never was any thought of our coming in unless France were attacked, for Belgium was merely a road into France, and France had no interest in the quarrel between Russia and Germany except that she was bound by a Russian Alliance. This gave France a clear right to require that Russia should not precipitate war by mobilizing, and if Russia had not mobilized the settlement which just missed fire would have been completed. Jaurès, the most able of living Frenchmen, was urging his Government to notify Russia that if she mobilized without the consent of France, France would not support her in arms. It was a perfectly legitimate demand, like the demand ultimately made by Germany that Austria must not precipitate war by unreasonable conduct. Now our own Cabinet might most fairly have said to the French Government at the outset: "You expect us to help you, but this is no quarrel of yours ; you are being brought into it because of your Treaty with Russia. If you like to give Russia a free hand, well and good, but in that event we will not give Russia a free hand to control our policy as well; and unless you can restrain Russia from mobilizing till we agree that the necessity for doing so is come, we will not join you in arms. We do not intend to be embroiled by your Ally, to whom we are under no sort of obligation." We did repeatedly say to Russia, Be moderate, pray do not mobilize ; but we had no Treaty with her. Surely we had a right to say this. If we had taken up that attitude, Russia would not have thought the delay of a day or two in mobilizing of such vital importance as to forfeit the Alliance with Great Britain in order to mobilize on 31st July, and that day or two would have saved the situation, for it would have given

12

the short time that was needed to settle the whole controversy between Austria and Russia. But our Government could not say it, because they did not make up their minds till after war had been declared whether or not they would in any event support France in arms. They waited on without any policy, and they had no policy because they had proceeded for a long time on their own views without taking Parliament into their confidence.

There is something cynical and repulsive in the attempt to exculpate Germany on the ground that she would not have begun the war had she known that Great Britain would be among her enemies. An ordinary malefactor might as well say that he would not have broken the law if he had known that a policeman was within call. It may be true, all the same, in both cases. But that is no excuse for Germany. The truth seems to be that the Kaiser was tempted by the assurances of his military advisers that they were fully prepared and their adversaries unprepared, and that Great Britain would not interfere in arms. And he could not resist the temptation.

CHAPTER VII

HOW GREAT BRITAIN CAME INTO THE WAR

THE ground is now clear for inquiry how and why Great Britain came into this war shortly after it had broken out between Germany and Russia. Those who hold that His Majesty's Government were unwise before the crisis came, and injudicious when it did come, are all the more bound to insist upon what is in truth incontestable, that Sir Edward Grey throughout desired the maintenance of peace in Europe. A man who tries hard to keep the whole Continent out of war can scarcely be accused of wishing to bring Great Britain into it. And therefore, in face of the opinion so obstinately circulated in Germany that our Government designed and precipitated the conflict from sinister motives of their own, it may be well here to recapitulate the successive proposals made by Sir Edward Grey to prevent an outbreak between the Continental Powers. This will be a fitting prelude to the depressing narrative of his failure to extricate this country from the unforeseen consequences of earlier mistakes. So here is a summary of the more important suggestions made by our Government between 23rd July and 1st August to the Con-

tinental Powers with a view to removing the cause of
quarrel for good and all.[1]

On 23rd July Sir Edward pressed Austria to withdraw the time limit from her ultimatum to Servia,
and urged that Austria and Russia should in the
first instance discuss any difficulties directly with
each other. On 24th July he suggested that Germany,
France, Italy, and Great Britain should act together
for the sake of peace simultaneously in Vienna and
St. Petersburg. He recommended Servia on the
same day to promise the fullest satisfaction if any of
her officials should prove to have been accomplices
in the Sarajevo murder, and urged on Germany that
Austria should not precipitate military action. Next
day, 25th July, the British Ambassador on his behalf
expressed to the Russian Foreign Minister the earnest
hope that Russia would not precipitate war by mobilizing till Sir Edward had had time to use his influence
in favour of peace.

On the same day he expressed the hope that Germany
would induce Austria to take a favourable view of
the Servian answer to their ultimatum, and next
day proposed a Conference in London of the French,
Italian, and German Ambassadors for the purpose of
discovering an issue which would prevent complications. On 27th July he urged the Russian Government through our Ambassador to defer mobilization
for as long as possible, and that troops should not be
allowed to cross the frontier even when the Ukase
was issued. He begged Germany on the same day to
urge at Vienna that the Servian answer should at

[1] The record of Sir Edward's efforts will be found in the British
White Book, Nos. 3, 10, 11, 12, 17, 27, 36, 44, 46, 84, 88, 103, 111, 135.

least be treated as a basis for discussion and pause. By 29th July things had become still more serious, and Sir Edward Grey appealed to the German Ambassador that the German Government should suggest any method by which the influence of the four Powers —France, Italy, Germany, and Great Britain—could be used together to prevent war between Austria and Russia, and suggested that mediation might be possible if Austria, while saying that she must hold the occupied Servian territory till she had complete satisfaction, stated that she would not advance further pending an effort of the Powers to mediate between her and Russia. On Germany signifying her readiness to recommend this at Vienna, Sir Edward endeavoured, not without success, to procure Russia's assent to this idea.

31st July was the day on which Germany sent her ultimatum to Russia. Things had become rather desperate. Nevertheless, on that day Sir Edward suggested that the four disinterested Great Powers might offer to Austria their undertaking to see she should obtain full satisfaction of her demands on Servia, provided the sovereignty and integrity of that country were not impaired. He offered to sound St. Petersburg on this if Germany would sound Vienna. He went even further and told the German Ambassador that if Germany could get any reasonable proposal put forward which made it clear that Germany and Austria were striving to preserve European peace, and that Russia and France would be unreasonable if they rejected it, he would support it at St. Petersburg and Paris and go the length of saying that if Russia and France would not accept it His Majesty's Government would have nothing more to do with the consequences,

" but otherwise I told the German Ambassador that if France became involved we should be drawn in." On 1st August he informed Russia that Austria had agreed to mediation, and suggested that Russia should stop mobilizing. These and other suggestions were repeatedly urged by Sir Edward Grey.

As we have seen, the prospect of a settlement by negotiation was wrecked by fears arising from mobilization; but Sir Edward's efforts were indefatigable, and were fully acknowledged both by Germany and Austria. That in face of these facts anyone should believe Great Britain brought on this war, is one of the strangest delusions recorded in history. It is probable that these facts were entirely unknown to the great bulk of the German people. They have been systematically deceived.

*   *   *

Any inquiry into the action of our Ministers must be regarded in this setting. Still the question remains —When it came, how and why did they bring us into it ? Various answers have been given by the numerous orators and writers who almost alone have obtained a hearing under the Censorship. Some say that we went to war for the sake of Belgium and small nationalities, others that we went to war in the interests of civilization against lawless brutality, and that, as the conflict must have come sooner or later, it was better that it should come now when we could have France and Russia and Italy and Japan on our side. This country was no doubt entitled, according to the canons which have hitherto governed mankind, to draw the sword, either on behalf of Belgium or because of the overbearing conduct of the Central Powers. Neither

Austria nor Germany have the smallest ground of complaint that their methods of violence were met by the rifle and by artillery. Still the question remains —Did our Government of 1914 in fact go to war for these reasons ? What were in fact their reasons ? This must be answered, not by rhetoric but by scrutinizing our official declarations. And until we know how we were brought suddenly to the brink of this precipice we shall not be free from the danger of finding ourselves again unexpectedly conducted to the edge of another like abyss.

The answer to this question, in a single sentence, is that we were brought into the war because Mr. Asquith and Sir Edward Grey and their confidants, by steps some of which are known while others may be unknown, had placed us in such a position toward France, and therefore also toward Russia, that they found they could not refuse to take up arms on her behalf when it came to the issue, though till the end they denied it to Parliament, and probably even to themselves. They were driven from point to point because they would not realize that they had so committed themselves, and accordingly would not take any decisive attitude. Nothing breeds irresolution more certainly than a sense that you are in a false position which you will not bring yourself to recognize. What were the twists and turns along which this nation was guided blindfold till it came to the exit and, on the bandages being removed, was confronted with the awful visage of war ?

*   *   *

From the beginning of the crisis in July 1914 there was visible danger of a war breaking out which would

become general. Stop it altogether at the outset, or
if you cannot do that, then localize it, would be the
first instinct, and our Ministers tried hard to persuade
and to appease the contending Governments. A
simultaneous anxiety obviously presented itself to
their minds—to save our own country from being
embroiled, if it could be done honourably. They
evidently recognized this danger. And upon some
points they had no doubts at all, as may be seen
from their despatches and statements. The original
quarrel, Quarrel number one, was between Austria
and Servia. Would they take a hand in that, a
fighting hand ? Most certainly not. It does not
concern us, they say; our interests in Servia are nil.
Very good. What, then, if out of it should arise Quarrel
number two, between Austria and Russia, the patron
of Servia ? Would Great Britain take a hand in that ?
By no means, say our Ministers. We do not mean to
take part in a Balkan quarrel. But go a little further.
Suppose Germany comes in to help Austria pursuant to
her Alliance ? That would be Quarrel number three.
Would you come in then and help Russia ? No.
Our Government say they do not mean to take part in
a fight between Slav and Teuton, which that would be.
So far it is clear and they are clear. But then comes
the debatable ground, the difficult ground. What if
France is brought in as the ally of Russia, and so
finds herself at war with Germany ? That would be
Quarrel number four. What will you do then ? Our
Government knows throughout that France will come
in as Russia's ally, if there is war, because France
tells them so at the outset. · Will Great Britain join
France in arms if she is thus brought in and attacked

by Germany? This was the crucial question, not only for ourselves but also for all the nations on both sides, because it meant the mastery of the sea. They all knew perfectly well what that is, and they all knew the great power of this country.   It is incredible that a decided answer would not have enormously affected the action of the Continental Powers on both sides.   Yet no decided answer was forthcoming till after the Continental War had actually begun and neither side could well draw back.   Both sides eagerly sought an answer, but none came till too late.

According to the despatches, Sir Edward is often asked, What will you do? What will be your attitude? Will you be neutral, and on what conditions will you be neutral? Will you at once declare that you will support us in arms? Sir Edward refuses to give an answer either way.   He hints at what we may do, but will not say what we will do.   Very late in the negotiations on 31st July, indeed, the day on which Germany sent her ultimatum to Russia, he tells the German Ambassador that if Germany could get a reasonable proposal made, and it was rejected by France and Russia, he would tell them that he would have nothing more to do with the consequences, "but otherwise I told the German Ambassador that if France became involved we should be drawn in." [1]   Later on the same day he told the French Ambassador that he could not give any definite engagement to support France in arms. [2]   A prophecy or expression of a general opinion as to what will happen is a very different thing from taking an en-

[1] British White Book, No. 111; *ibid.*, No. 119.
[2] *Ibid.*, No. 119.

gagement to France, as Sir Edward himself points out
in the same passage, but even a definite statement had
little chance of influencing German action at that
stage.   It was too late.   Russia had ordered mobilization and Germany had sent her ultimatum.

The one point on which Sir Edward persistently
dwells in these discussions is, that he is not committed to France, that his hands are quite free, that
he has no engagements.   He says it so often that
the very repetition seems to betray some misgiving
lest after all he may have bound himself in honour
unawares.   But the question which became vital for
foreign nations was not what hopes Ministers had
held out to France, but what in fact they would do
for France, bound or not bound.   They refused to
answer that question simply because they did not know
themselves.   There was no collective plan or policy.

*　　*　　*

And now we may place in the form of an abbreviated
journal the communications of importance from day
to day which show how the British Government
marched, or, if you will, drifted into hostilities.   A
brief comment is added where necessary.

July 24.—On 24th July (the day after the Austrian
ultimatum had been delivered to Servia) the Russian
Foreign Minister and the French Ambassador urged
upon the British Ambassador at St. Petersburg that the
British Government ought to " proclaim their solidarity
with France and Russia."   The French Ambassador said
the only chance of averting war was for us to adopt
a firm and united attitude.   To this our Ambassador
replied (and all he said was expressly approved by
Sir Edward Grey) that he could see no reason to expect

any Declaration of solidarity from His Majesty's Government, that " direct British interests in Servia were nil, and a war on behalf of that country would never be sanctioned by British public opinion." On being further pressed, our Ambassador added that perhaps Sir Edward Grey might see his way to saying that it would be difficult for Great Britain to keep out if the war became general. The Russian Minister answered that we would sooner or later be dragged into war if it did break out, and we should have rendered war more likely if we did not from the outset make common cause with his country and with France.[1]

July 25.—Next day (25th July) the Russian Foreign Minister again entreated the British Ambassador in the same sense.[2] " He did not believe that Germany really wanted war, but her attitude was decided by ours (the British). If we (the British) took our stand firmly with France and Russia, there would be no war. If we failed them now, rivers of blood would flow, and we would in the end be dragged into war." M. Sazonoff also said that unfortunately Germany was convinced that she could count upon British neutrality. The British Ambassador observed that " England could play the rôle of mediator at Berlin and Vienna to better purpose as a friend, who, if her counsels of moderation were disregarded, might one day be converted into an ally, than if she were to declare herself Russia's Ally at once."

July 26. — The Kaiser told Mr. Gerard, the American Ambassador, in the interview recorded in his book, that his brother Prince Henry saw the British Sovereign in London on a date which the con-

[1] British White Book, No. 6.   [2] *Ibid.*, No. 17.

text shows to have been 26th July. The Kaiser says that King George on that occasion sent him a message, namely, that England would remain neutral if war broke out on the Continent involving Germany and France, Austria and Russia. This statement was instantly contradicted on " the highest authority " as being " absolutely without any foundation." It is in itself wholly incredible, apart from this conclusive contradiction. Not a trace of it appears in any of the official publications.

July 27.—M. Sazonoff questioned the British Ambassador again,[1] who told him that the cause of peace would not be promoted by our telling the German Government that they would have to deal with us as well as with Russia and France, that their attitude would merely be stiffened by such a menace.

On this same 27th July Sir Edward Grey was told by the Russian Ambassador [2] that in German and Austrian circles the impression prevails that in any event Great Britain would stand aside. Sir Edward said that this impression ought to be dispelled by the orders he had given that the British Fleet was not to disperse for manœuvre leave, " but I explained to the Russian Ambassador that my reference to it must not be taken to mean that anything more than diplomatic action was promised."

Another interview between the Austrian Ambassador and Sir Edward Grey took place on the same day, the Austrian Ambassador saying that " the Austrian Government, confiding in their amicable relations with us, feel that they could count on our (British) sympathy in a fight that was forced on them,

[1] British White Book, No. 44.   [2] *Ibid.*, No. 47.

and on our assistance in localizing the fight if necessary." Sir Edward, in reply, said nothing at all about
sympathy, but gave very good advice about the
Servian answer to the ultimatum, and the danger of
incalculable consequences if Russia were brought in,
and pointed out that the British Fleet had not been
allowed to disperse. " We should not think of calling
up our reserves at this moment, and there was no
menace in what we had done about our Fleet, but
owing to the possibility of a European conflagration
it was impossible for us to disperse our forces at this
moment. I gave this as an illustration of the anxiety
that was felt." [1] Merely as an illustration. One
cannot help feeling that this communication as a
whole would lead Austria to think that we should in
the end be neutral. Possibly that reflected the mood
of our Government at the moment. But if we meant
to be neutral, why not say so to Russia ? It would
make her less in a hurry to mobilize. Or, if we meant
not to be neutral, why not say so to Austria in a diplomatic way ? Austria was a very old friend of this
country, and also was well aware of our strength.
Would she have gone on in so reckless a style had she
known our purpose, if we had any, of intervening ?

At this time, 27th July, the British Government
had very strong cards in its hand, had they been skilfully played. Indeed no great skill was needed—merely
the courage to see the truth and say it. Suppose that
we were really so situated that we could not refuse to
help France ? A war between Austria and Russia
necessarily would bring France in. Could we not
have said to Austria, before she burnt her boats:

[1] British White Book, No. 48.

You have strong grievances against Servia, you are entitled to redress and guarantees for the future, and Russia admitted that yesterday (26th July), and we will help to get that for you in a peaceful way. You have been often our Allies in the past, and almost always our friends throughout history. You know the danger of war with Russia, or, if you do not, then we can assure you of it, and that will bring France in and will bring us in, for we are tied to France in honour, or at all events we are tied to France by our own interests, if they did not like to admit their obligation to France. What earthly ground is there for quarrel between you and us ? It would be merely the automatic action of these Treaties which were never intended to bring about an antagonism between old friends like us. There is at all events a good chance of averting all this. Do not make it impossible, because we really cannot leave France to her fate. Suppose that had been said, not necessarily in this language, which, to be sure, is quite possibly undiplomatic, but in some more recondite phraseology that would be palatable to the Olympian personages who make or prevent our wars. Is it not likely that Austria would have reflected on this piece of information ? If Austria had known that going on in her quarrelsome mood would bring her to war with Great Britain, who had been her friend throughout history, it seems very difficult to believe that she would have paid no need to a really well-meant warning. Three or four days later, when the thing was past praying for, Austria did say she would consider mediation with Servia, out of appreciation of England's efforts for peace. Possibly also, if we had spoken plainly, she would have reflected that the

British Fleet was not a wholly useless piece of furniture to be wantonly provoked when England really desired her friendship. Had Austria been told frankly of our true obligations to France, of our regrets, of our intentions, would she have rushed hot foot into a declaration of war on Servia and a rupture of her conversations with Russia? But she was not told that on the 27th July. She was told what we have just seen on 27th July. And on 28th July she declared war on Servia, and broke off conversations with Russia. She counted on our neutrality, believing our hands were free, and even counted on our sympathy. How could it be otherwise? Sir Edward had not repelled her claim to our sympathy, and was constantly repeating that we had kept our hands free. The despatches are full of it, and on the 28th July the British Ambassador at Vienna was saying to the Austrian Minister for Foreign Affairs what follows : [1] " I begged him to believe that, if in the course of the present grave crisis our point of view should sometimes differ from his, this would arise, not from want of sympathy with the many just complaints which Austria-Hungary had against Servia, but from the fact that, whereas Austria-Hungary put first her quarrel with Servia, you (Sir Edward Grey) were anxious in the first instance for the peace of Europe." Sir Edward was informed of this the same day. There is no trace of his expressing dissent. What he ought to have said was: For God's sake, don't drive your oldest friends into war with you. For we are bound to support France in arms and shall do so.

July 29.—Austria in this frame of mind, with the

---

[1] British White Book, No. 62.

support of Germany secured and the sympathy of England assumed, now proceeds on 29th July to open hostilities against Servia. Another most formidable obstacle to the maintenance of peace was thus added. Still the fatal hour had not struck. All the Great Powers were still at peace with one another. If Germany and Austria even now learned for certain that in the event of a general war England would fight against them, they could still accept some submission from Servia without any stain on that code of military honour which both of them so highly prized. Or if Russia even now learned definitely that England would not join her and France in arms over a Servian quarrel, if she mobilized prematurely, she might have stayed for a few days the military steps which Sir Edward Grey was constantly urging her to pretermit, and which ultimately brought on the rupture. But such are the penalties of indecision and of the ambiguities which it begets, that at this very time not only was Austria reckoning on our sympathy, but Russia was counting on our support. Reuter's St. Petersburg correspondent wires on the following day (29th July) that, "confident of England's support, about which doubts have mostly disappeared, the Russian public is prepared to accept war." There is nothing in the published correspondence to show the grounds of this confidence, unless it be Sir Edward Grey's allusion to the British Fleet not being dispersed, and the certainty that our Fleet, if used, would be used against Russia's enemies. But both sides construed an ambiguous attitude as an attitude favourable to their own hope, of British neutrality on the one side, of British support on the other.

Most certainly we must acquit our Government of any Machiavellian duplicity, however we may deplore their want of frankness. Their attitude is to be explained very simply. They had no idea what they would do. Sir Edward Grey tells the French Ambassador to-day (29th July) that " if Germany became involved and France became involved we had not made up our minds what we should do ; it was a case that we should have to consider." [1] They continued considering it till 2nd August, and then took a step which committed us to war, though apparently they did not think so. It consisted of promising France the support of our Fleet, quite irrespective of Belgium.

On 29th July the German Chancellor makes proposals to Great Britain through our Ambassador at Berlin.[2] He said that so far as he could judge Great Britain would never stand by and allow France to be crushed in any conflict there might be, but that was not the object at which Germany aimed. Provided that British neutrality were certain, Germany would give every assurance that they aimed at no territorial acquisitions at the expense of France. On being asked, he said he was unable to give a similar undertaking about the French Colonies. He would respect the " integrity and neutrality of the Netherlands," and " it " depended upon the action of France what operations " Germany might be forced to enter upon in Belgium, " but when the war was over Belgian integrity would " be respected if she had not sided against Germany." He then said his policy had always been to bring about an understanding with England, and trusted that these assurances " might form the basis of that

[1] British White Book, No. 87.   [2] *Ibid.*, No. 85.

13

understanding which he so much desired." In reply
to this the British Ambassador said he did not think
it probable that at this stage of events Sir Edward
Grey would care to bind himself to any course of
action, but would, he thought, desire to retain full
liberty. The German Chancellor's language was of
course immediately communicated to Sir Edward Grey.

A few hours before the above conversation at Berlin,
and on the same day, Sir Edward Grey saw the German
Ambassador in London and told him " in a quite
" private and friendly way something that was on my
" [Sir Edward's] mind. The situation was very grave.
" While it was restricted to the issues at present actually
" involved we had no thought of interfering in it. But
" if Germany became involved in it, and then France,
" the issue might be so great that it would involve all
" European interests, and I [Sir Edward] did not wish
" him (the German Ambassador) to be misled by the
" friendly tone of our conversation—which I hoped
" would continue—into thinking that we should stand
" aside. He said he quite understood this, but he
" asked whether I meant that we should, under certain
" circumstances, intervene ? I replied that I did not
" wish to say that or to use anything that was like a
" threat or an attempt to apply pressure by saying that
" if things became worse we should intervene. There
" would be no question of our intervening if Germany
" was not involved or even if France was not involved.
" But we knew very well that, if the issue did become
" such that we thought British interests required us to
" intervene, we must intervene at once, and the decision
" would have to be very rapid, just as the decisions of
" other Powers had to be. I hoped that the friendly tone

" of our conversations would continue as at present,
" and that I should be able to keep as closely in touch
" with the German Government in working for peace.
" But if we failed in our efforts to keep the peace, and
" if the issue spread so that it involved practically every
" European interest, I did not wish to be open to any
" reproach from him that the friendly tone of all our
" conversations had misled him or his Government into
" supposing that we should not take action, and to the
" reproach that, if they had not been so misled, the
" course of things might have been different. The
" German Ambassador took no exception to what I
" had said ; indeed, he told me that it accorded with
" what he had already given in Berlin as his view of
" the situation." [1]

This statement of Sir Edward's is explicit on one
point—namely, that if France were not involved in the
war there would be no intervention on our part ; but it
still leaves uncertain whether or not we would intervene
in the event of France being involved in war, and
indeed we have seen that on this very day he says
that our Government had not made up its mind.

July 30.—Sir Edward Grey replies (through our Ambassador at Berlin) to the German Chancellor's proposals of the previous day and rejects them.[2] He says
they are unacceptable, that it would be a disgrace to us
were we to make such a bargain with Germany at the
expense of France, and that we could not bargain away
" whatever obligation or interest we have as regards
the neutrality of Belgium," and that " we must preserve our full freedom to act as circumstances may
seem to us to require." He added that " the one way

---

[1] British White Book, No. 89.   [2] *Ibid.*, No. 101.

of maintaining the good relations between England and Germany is that they should continue to work together to preserve the peace of Europe.'' Sir Edward ended by forecasting some arrangement for assuring Germany against any aggressive or hostile policy on the part of France, Russia, or England if the present trouble should blow over.

July 31.—Before the German ultimatum to Russia of 31st July was known, but on the same day, Sir Edward Grey told the German Ambassador[1] that "if Germany could get any reasonable proposal put forward which made it clear that Germany and Austria were striving to preserve European peace, and that Russia and France would be unreasonable if they rejected it, I would support it at St. Petersburg and Paris, and go the length of saying that if Russia and France would not accept it His Majesty's Government would have nothing more to do with the consequences ; but otherwise, I told the German Ambassador that if France became involved we should be drawn in." This most fair suggestion, that Germany should make a proposal, unfortunately came too late, for Germany received on 31st July the news of Russia's general mobilization, and at once sent her ultimatum. Such were the communications between our Government and Germany up to 31st July as regards the possibility of our intervention.

*   *   *

Turn back now to the communications between our Government and France on the same days—29th, 30th, and 31st July—and on the same subject.

July 29.—Sir E. Grey sees the French Ambassador and tells him what he would say and did say to the

[1] British White Book, No 111.

German Ambassador as to not being misled by the
friendly terms of our conversations.[1] Sir Edward then
went on as follows : " But I went on to say to the
" French Ambassador that I thought it necessary to tell
" him also that public opinion here approached the
" present difficulty from a quite different point of view
" from that taken during the difficulty as to Morocco a
" few years ago. In the case of Morocco, the dispute
" was one in which France was primarily interested and
" in which it appears that Germany, in an attempt to
" crush France, was fastening a quarrel on France on a
" question that was the subject of a special agreement
" between France and us. In the present case, the dis-
" pute between Austria and Servia was not one in which
" we felt called to take a hand. Even if the question
" became one between Austria and Russia, we should not
" feel called upon to take a hand in it. It would then be
" a question of the supremacy of Teuton and Slav—a
" struggle for supremacy in the Balkans; and our idea
" had always been to avoid being drawn into a war over
" a Balkan question. If Germany became involved and
" France became involved, we had not made up our minds
" what we should do ; it was a case that we should have
" to consider. France would then have been drawn into
" a quarrel which was not hers, but in which, owing to
" her alliance, her honour and interest obliged her to
" engage. We were free from engagements, and we
" should have to decide what British interests required
" us to do. I thought it necessary to say that, because,
" as he knew, we were taking all precautions with regard
" to our fleet, and I was about to warn Prince Lichnow-
" sky not to count on our standing aside, but it would

[1] British White Book, No. 87.

" not be fair that I should let M. Cambon be misled into
" supposing that this meant that we had decided what
" to do in a contingency that I still hoped might not
" arise." In short, neither France nor Germany was
to be misled into thinking that we had yet made up
our minds what to do. Such was the anxious warning
repeated to both by Sir E. Grey, even though hostilities
had already begun in Servia. M. Cambon recapitu-
lated what Sir Edward had said. " He seemed quite
prepared for this announcement," observes Sir Edward, " and made no criticism upon it." M. Cambon
said nothing. Probably he thought a good deal, and
at once communicated what had been said to the
French Government. For on the following day (30th
July) the French President moves. He is alarmed
by the trouble arising from military preparations,
and fears that negotiations for peaceful settlement
may fail. He tells the British Ambassador that " he
is convinced that peace between the Powers is in
the hands of Great Britain. If His Majesty's Government announced that England would come to the aid
of France in the event of a conflict between France and
Germany as a result of the present differences between
Austria and Servia, there would be no war, for Germany
would at once modify her attitude." The British
Ambassador explained to him how difficult it would be
to make such an announcement; but the President
adhered to his opinion, and said that such a declaration
" would almost certainly prevent Germany from going
to war." [1]

July 30.—France was eager and anxious, as well she
might be. The same day (30th July) a fresh approach

[1] British White Book, No. 99.

was made by France to England.[1] The French Ambassador called and reminded Sir Edward Grey of his letter in November 1912 agreeing that if the peace of Europe were seriously threatened we would discuss with them what we were prepared to do. He did not ask Sir Edward to say directly that we would intervene, " but " he would like me [Sir Edward] to say what we would " do if certain circumstances arose. The particular " hypothesis he had in mind was an aggression by Ger- " many on France." The aggression he anticipated was either a demand that France should cease her preparations or a demand that she should undertake to be neutral, neither of which would France admit. This was a polite way of saying, " We mean to go on arming, and we mean to support Russia in arms—what will you do ? " Sir Edward answered that the Cabinet would meet to-morrow morning, and he would see him to-morrow afternoon—that is, on the 31st July. Here we must leave the French Ambassador, M. Paul Cambon, waiting for an answer to his question, in order to clear up a little what passed in the interval between the time he put his question and the time he got his answer.

When " to-morrow afternoon " came the Russian general mobilization was known, and the German ultimatum followed that same afternoon. All prospect of averting a great war in Europe had vanished, though vain efforts still continued.

Certainly there are few parallels in history to this situation. War between Austria and Servia already commenced on 28th July. Peace or war trembling in the balance between the four greatest military

[1] British White Book, No. 105.

Powers in the world on 29th and 30th July. Each side urgently anxious to know what course England would pursue—a vital question for all of them. No new question this. The possibility of such a crisis had been for some weeks clearly seen, and for a whole week had been actually upon us. His Majesty's Government continued in complete uncertainty, unable to give an answer. Why? It looks as if this proceeded not merely from inability to arrive at a decision, but also from the results of the past, which had placed Ministers in a dilemma between the expectations the Foreign Office had raised in France and the assurances they had given to Parliament. The Ministers who had given those assurances, Mr. Asquith and Sir Edward Grey, together with such of their colleagues as knew all that had been done, must have begun now to see the truth—that this country, though free so far as express written promises went, was in honour bound by a course of confidences and of secret negotiations, including the disclosure of deep military secrets.

However that may be, in the interval between 30th July, when the French Ambassador put his question, and 31st July, when he was to receive the answer, other things came to the front in a menacing way. The military Powers were becoming more and more anxious about the preparations of their neighbours. At any moment a panic might arise on this subject, and some sudden step be taken which would arrest all negotiations and throw everything into the hands of the General Staffs. Germany, Austria, France, Russia were all being accused by their rivals of secret mobilization or something near to it. It had been apparent from the first that unless the peacemakers could come to terms at once, their chance would soon be gone for good. The knowledge that this country would or that it would not join one side in the event of war, or the plain statement of the conditions on which we would remain neutral, if we could honourably remain neutral, must have had enormous influence on the action of all the States affected.

If we were free to take part or not take part in the war, we might have exercised enormous pressure on either side or both; but our whole authority was weakened by the belief that we had already practically taken sides even though we might not fight, and so were not impartial arbiters. Whatever chance there might be lay in our at all events making up our minds now and definitely saying what we would do, one way or other. Either way might have, probably would have, sufficed to keep the peace, if only it had been in time. Neither way was taken.

* * *

Meanwhile, the French Ambassador was waiting for an answer to the question he had, as we have seen, put on 30th July—namely, What will you do if Germany attacks France? A Cabinet meeting was to take place on the morning of 31st July, and an answer had been promised to that question in the afternoon. The Cabinet met in the morning, and M. Cambon saw Sir Edward in the afternoon.

July 31.—On this 31st July, as Sir Edward Grey's answer to M. Cambon will show, he and his colleagues were still not ready to say either that they would or that they would not do anything to support France if Germany attacked her. They were still undecided. But it appears to have occurred to them that the contin-

gency of an invasion of Belgium might appropriately be
introduced, though not hitherto mentioned by Belgium
herself, and something about Belgium might be said
to the French Ambassador instead of a plain reply to
the very different question actually put. That specific
question might run off on Belgium. There had been
at this date no request for assistance by Belgium.
Indeed, three days later the Belgian Government said
in terms that they did not think it necessary to call
upon the guaranteeing Powers for their intervention.[1]
But this country certainly had interests in Belgium,
and there was a general feeling that our duty required
us to protect that small nation so near our shores,
whereas in the case of France, not only had Ministers
assured Parliament that we were free from any engagements to fight for her, but also this was a case, as Sir
Edward had pointed out,[2] in which France would, if
war came, be drawn into a quarrel which was not her
own, but in which her honour and interest obliged her
to engage. "Nobody here," says he on this very
31st July,[3] " feels that in this dispute, so far as it has
yet gone, British Treaties or obligations are involved.
Feeling is quite different from what it was during the
Morocco question. That crisis involved a dispute
directly involving France, whereas in this case France
is being drawn into a dispute which is not hers."
So when a difficult question was asked about France,
might it not be possible to do or say something about
Belgium instead of France? A polite evasion might
be excusable if the purpose was to gain time in order
to continue a policy of " masterly inactivity."

[1] British White Book, No. 151.   [2] *Ibid.*, No. 87.
[3] *Ibid.*, No. 116.

It comes to this. On 31st July public opinion was not favourable [1] to making war for France, the general belief being that we were free. from engagements. But Belgium was a different thing.

But after the Cabinet meeting on 31st July Sir Edward took up the point and asked both France and Germany if they were prepared to respect Belgian neutrality. Yes, said France. Germany gave no answer, intimating that she could not answer either way without disclosing at least partially her plan of campaign.[2] On the same day (31st July) Sir Edward informed Belgium that he assumed she would maintain her neutrality to the utmost of her power. Certainly, said Belgium. We believe we can defend ourselves, and we do not suspect the intentions of our neighbours. She did her duty when the time came, and was nearly destroyed in doing it.

*   *   *

We must now come back to M. Cambon, who put a most important question to Sir Edward Grey on 30th July, and was promised an answer " to-morrow afternoon," after the Cabinet meeting.

July 31.—A good deal had happened since the question had been put when on 31st July, as arranged, the French Ambassador presented himself to see Sir Edward, Grey.[3] It was " to-morrow afternoon." Sir Edward fresh from the promised Cabinet meeting that morning, on being again told that if England declared definitely for Russia and France it would decide the German attitude in favour of peace, said we had not

[1] See Mr. Lloyd George's statement cited in Chap. IX.
[2] British White Book, Nos. 114, 115, 122, 125, 128.
[3] *Ibid.*, No. 119.

left Germany under the impression that we would not intervene. " I had not only refused overtures to "promise; that we should remain neutral, I had even "gone so far this morning as to say to the German "Ambassador that if France and Germany became "involved in war we should be drawn into it." Sir Edward continues : " That, of course, was not the "same thing as taking an engagement to France, and I "told M. Cambon of it only to show that we had not "left Germany under the impression that we would "stand aside. M. Cambon then asked me for my "reply to what he had said yesterday." Namely, what would we do if Germany attacked France ? What now follows is of the utmost importance. " I [Sir Edward] "said that we had come to the conclusion in the Cabinet "to-day that we could not give any pledge at the pre- "sent time. Though we should have to put our policy "before Parliament we could not pledge Parliament in "advance. Up to the present moment we did not feel "and public opinion did not feel that any treaties or "obligations of this country were involved. Further "developments might alter this situation and cause the "Government and Parliament to take the |view that "intervention was justified. The preservation of the "neutrality of Belgium might be, I would not say a "decisive but an important factor in determining our "attitude. Whether we proposed to Parliament to "intervene or not to intervene in a war, Parliament "would wish to know how we stood with regard to the "neutrality of Belgium, and it might be that I should "ask both France and Germany whether each was pre- "pared to undertake an engagement that she would not "be the first to violate the neutrality of Belgium." (In fact this was done that same day). That was Sir Edward Grey's statement. M. Cambon's treatment of it, in its laconic simplicity, is more eloquent than any criticism. Belgium had nothing to do with the question he had put. " M. Cambon repeated his "question whether we would help France if Germany "made an attack on her. I [Sir Edward Grey] said "that I could only adhere to the answer that as far as "things had gone at present we could not take any "engagement." M. Cambon then again pressed upon Sir Edward that Germany had from the beginning rejected proposals that might have made for peace, and asked that his question might be submitted to the Cabinet again, to which Sir Edward replied that we could not give any definite engagement. This conversation, be it remembered, took place on the very afternoon on which Germany sent her ultimatum to Russia.

Another pressing inquiry was made by France on the same day as to what England's attitude will be, addressed to our Ambassador in Paris; but no further answer was given.[1]

At last, on the same 31st July, the French President directly appealed to the British Sovereign. This despatch and the answer to it were first published in the British Press on 20th February 1915, and then found their way into the Collected Diplomatic Documents at pages 542–4. The President solemnly declares that "if Germany were convinced that the "*entente cordiale* would be affirmed in case of need "even to the extent of taking the field side by side "there would be the greatest chance that peace would

[1] British White Book, No. 124.

"remain unbroken." He then says: "It is true that
"our military and naval arrangements leave complete
"liberty to Your Majesty's Government, and that in
"the letters exchanged in 1912 between Sir Edward
"Grey and M. Cambon Great Britain and France
"entered into nothing more than a mutual agreement
"to consult one another in the event of European
"tension and to examine in concert whether common
"action were advisable." And then he dwells upon
the close friendship and confidence between the two
countries which "justify me in informing you quite
"frankly of my impressions, which are those of the
"Government of the Republic and of all France."
Here we see reappearing the formula of November
1912, and can estimate its precise value at the moment
of trial. His Majesty replied with many gracious
expressions, and said that his Government would
"continue to discuss freely and frankly any point
"which might arise of interest to our two nations
"with M. Cambon." This answer was of course, by
our Constitution, an answer given simply on the advice
of Ministers.

It must be noted here that Sir Edward Grey gave
as a reason for his refusing a promise of support that
he could not pledge Parliament in advance. This was
to throw on Parliament the responsibility of deciding
on peace or war, and to relieve the Government of
that responsibility. Now this would be, in the opinion
of very many people, a most excellent principle; but,
if it is to be acted upon, surely it must involve that
Parliament shall be kept really free from all obligations either of honour or of Treaty which could fetter
its free judgment. Nothing could be more dangerous

or unfair than that a Government should be able to
create such relations between us and some foreign
Power that we could not honourably refuse our armed
support, and then should be able to throw the responsibility for war off its own shoulders on to the
shoulders of Parliament at the last moment.   Nothing
more intolerable can well be imagined in a self-governing
country, or in a self-respecting Parliament.

*   *   *

August 1.—1st August 1914 was a day of the deepest
anxiety not only in London but in every corner of the
earth.   On that day war was declared between Germany
and Russia, to be followed, as was universally known, by
war between France and Austria as well.   His Majesty's
Government were still considering what they should
do.   Here is a despatch of Sir Edward Grey, dated
1st August 1914, given textually.   It photographs the
state of mind of the British Government on that day,
and gives an account of a fresh effort by Germany to
secure our neutrality.   It is No. 123 of the British
White Book.

" SIR EDWARD GREY TO SIR E. GOSCHEN,
British Ambassador at Berlin

" FOREIGN OFFICE, 1st *August* 1914

" SIR,—I told the German Ambassador to-day that
the reply of the German Government with regard to
the neutrality of Belgium was a matter of very great
regret, because the neutrality of Belgium affected
feeling in this country.   If Germany could see her
way to give the same assurance as that which had been
given by France, it would materially contribute to .
relieve anxiety and tension here.   On the other hand,

if there were a violation of the neutrality of Belgium by one combatant while the other respected it, it would be extremely difficult to restrain public feeling in this country. I said that we had been discussing this question at a Cabinet meeting, and as I was authorized to tell him this I gave him a memorandum of it. He asked me whether, if Germany gave a promise not to violate Belgian neutrality, we would engage to remain neutral. I replied that I could not say that; our hands were still free, and we were considering what our attitude should be. All I could say was that our attitude would be determined largely by public opinion here, and that the neutrality of Belgium would appeal very strongly to public opinion here. I did not think that we could give a promise of neutrality on that condition alone. The Ambassador pressed me as to whether I could not formulate conditions on which we would remain neutral. He even suggested that the integrity of France and her colonies might be guaranteed. I said that I felt obliged to refuse definitely my promise to remain neutral on similar terms, and I could only say that we must keep our hands free.—I am, etc.,

" E. GREY "

Such is the letter. Sir Edward has since said that the German Ambassador's suggestions came from himself alone and were not authorized by his Government. It is a very strange thing, if that be true. The German Chancellor said in November 1916 that they were authorized, and the question might easily have been asked at the time. But take it that they were not authorized. What is significant in this interview is the answers that Sir Edward gave, no matter who authorized the questions. We know from the answers what his mind was on 1st August. If he could have saved Belgium that day by promising our neutrality he would not do it. Why not? It must have been because of some duty to France. He must have now felt that he at least was in honour tied to France. He was asked by the German Ambassador to formulate himself the terms on which Great Britain would remain neutral, and refused to do so. Why did he refuse? Was it not because he began to feel that he had so bound himself that he could not in honour be neutral on any terms at all, if France were engaged in this war and gave no provocation, even if France came in, not in any quarrel of her own, but purely because of her treaty with Russia? In other words, was he not really tied to Russia? It seems that at this date neither our duties to Belgium nor our duty to make war on Germany in the interests of European independence had been perceived by the Cabinet in the sense that Ministers have since presented to the country, but it does seem as if his duty to France had at all events begun to become visible to Sir Edward Grey, though he had refused to promise that he would fulfil it.

August 2.—How long the Cabinet would have waited before making up its mind, if left to itself, no one can say. They were awaiting " developments," also awaiting " public opinion here." Somehow the thing got wind. How they finally did come to make up their minds has been told by Mr. L. J. Maxse in the *National Review* of August 1918. Many people differ from this gentleman's opinions, but he is a man of honour whose statements of fact within his personal knowledge are entitled to credit. Mr. Maxse says that on Saturday, 1st August, he and his friends were in despair, thinking that our Cabinet was mentally and

14

physically incapable " of giving France any assurance "of support." He procured a meeting of Unionist leaders on the night of 1st August, with the result that shortly after midday on Sunday, 2nd August, the following letter was taken by car to 10 Downing Street :

[2nd August 1914.]

" DEAR MR. ASQUITH,—Lord Lansdowne and I feel it our duty to inform you that in our opinion, as well as in that of all the colleagues whom we have been able to consult, it would be fatal to the honour and security of the United Kingdom to hesitate in supporting France and Russia at the present juncture, and we offer our unhesitating support to the Government in any measures they may consider necessary for that object.—Yours very truly,

"A. BONAR LAW "

Not a word in it, observe, about Belgium. To support France and Russia : that was the thing to be done. According to Mr. Maxse's statement, Mr. Asquith " dexterously used the Unionist missive as " indicating a possible Coalition of Liberals and "Unionists." At once the Government took action, though still some dim idea appears to have survived that at such a moment in the world's history there might be a state of contingent war on a part of the sea without war being actually declared. The very day of Mr. Bonar Law's letter, Sir Edward Grey handed a document to the French Ambassador which will always be remembered. It was handed to M. Cambon " after the Cabinet this morning "—namely, 2nd August.

" I am authorized to give an assurance that, if the German Fleet comes into the Channel or through the

North Sea to undertake hostile operations against French coasts or shipping, the British Fleet will give all the protection in its power. This assurance is of course subject to the policy of His Majesty's Government receiving the support of Parliament, and must not be taken as binding His Majesty's Government to take any action until the above contingency of action by the German Fleet takes place." [1]

Sir Edward in handing this note to the French Ambassador on 2nd August, told him that it did not bind us to go to war with Germany unless the German Fleet took the action indicated, but it did give a security to France that would enable her to settle the disposition of her own Mediterranean Fleet. At the same interview Sir Edward told M. Cambon, about Belgium, " We were considering what statement we should make in Parliament to-morrow—in effect whether we should declare violation of Belgian neutrality to be a *casus belli*."

* * *

Returning to this memorandum of 2nd August, it fixes the date at which Great Britain became definitely and irrevocably committed to war with Germany. War was perfectly certain between France and Germany on 2nd August. It was declared next day. The German ultimatum to France had been sent on 31st July. It was in reference to that imminent war that Sir Edward gave the above written assurance. The assurance is expressed without limit of time, so that it would last throughout the war, and not merely till France could make her arrangements about her fleet, then in the Mediterranean. It amounted to a prohibition against

[1] British White Book, No. 148.

the use of her fleet by Germany against any coast of France or any French shipping during the war. There is no corresponding prohibition against the use of a French fleet against German coasts or German shipping. If we were, as seems hardly disputable, tied to France by engagements of honour, this was right, but whether right or wrong there can be no doubt that it is a promise of direct armed support for one belligerent against the other in the ordinary operations of war. Can anyone imagine that this step was compatible with British neutrality? Can anyone conceive how it could be carried out without war ?

In the text it will be observed that the assurance is given " subject to the policy of His Majesty's Government receiving the support of Parliament." And sure enough next day the House of Commons was asked to take the responsibility of coming to a decision, though it had been told nothing about it till then.

*   *   *

Nothing can be more clear than that our intervention in this war by the promise of naval support to France was dictated by our duty or supposed duty to France ; but if there could be any doubt that this document of 2nd August involved war on behalf of France against Germany, the doubt would be removed by the interpretation put upon it in France and Sir Edward Grey's acceptance of that interpretation.

The French Prime Minister wires to the French Ambassador in London on 2nd August and tells him that he means to indicate to the Chamber England's promise of naval support. " I propose, moreover, to indicate that the assistance which Great

Britain has the intention of giving to France with the view of protecting the French coasts or the French Mercantile Marine, would be so exerted as to afford equal support to our Navy by the English Fleet, in the case of a Franco-German conflict in the Atlantic, as well as in the North Sea and in the English Channel. I will, moreover, mention that English ports cannot be used as points for the revictualling of the German Fleet." [1]

Possessed of that information, the French Ambassador sees Sir Edward Grey on next day (3rd August). Here is the Ambassador's report : [2] " Sir Edward Grey has authorized me to tell you that you may inform Parliament that to-day he was making declarations in the Commons as to the present attitude of the British Government, and that the chief of these declarations was as follows : ' If the German Fleet cross the Straits or go north in the North Sea in order to double the British Isles, with a view to attacking the French coasts or the French Navy or to disturbing the French Mercantile Marine, the British Fleet will intervene in order to give the French Marine complete protection, so that from that moment on England and Germany would be in a state of war.' Sir Edward Grey," continues the Ambassador, " pointed out that the mention of operations through the North Sea implied protection against a demonstration in the Atlantic Ocean." In short, the letter required the German Fleet to be kept in port. If this does not amount to a promise of support against Germany, it is difficult to see what does. It was beyond

[1] French Yellow Book, No. 138.
[2] *Ibid.*, No. 143.

all argument a distinct intervention hostile to Germany.

Early the same morning (2nd August) German troops entered Luxemburg. At the interview of 31st July the French Ambassador had asked Sir Edward Grey as to the violation of Luxemburg's neutrality. Sir Edward answered that our guarantee in common with other Powers of Luxemburg carried with it more " a moral sanction than a contingent liability to go to war. No party was called upon to undertake the duty of enforcing it." That was the substance of the answer. The form of it was to refer M. Cambon to the doctrine laid down on that point by Lord Derby and Lord Clarendon in 1867.[1] Sir Edward had no idea of intervening on behalf of Luxemburg.

* * *

This written assurance of naval support was handed by Sir Edward Grey to the French Ambassador on the morning of 2nd August. On that very night the German Government at 7 p.m. presented an ultimatum to Belgium stating that French forces intended to march across Belgium to attack Germany (which there is nothing at all to prove), and requiring leave to march their own troops across Belgian territory. They offered to maintain the independence and integrity of all Belgian possessions, together with full compensation, but intimated that if a free passage were refused they would treat Belgium as an enemy.

The dates require attention. On 1st August the German Ambassador asked Sir Edward Grey whether

[1] British White Book, No. 148.

Great Britain would remain neutral if Belgium were not invaded. He declined to say. The German Ambassador then asked him on what terms Great Britain would remain neutral. He declined to say. On the morning of 2nd August Sir Edward gave to the French Government the assurance of naval support which has been discussed. That night at 7 o'clock the Germans made their demand on Belgium.

The invasion that followed, the constancy in martyrdom of unoffending men, women, and children, the courage of the soldiers who fought for their country against overwhelming odds, can never be forgotten. Generations will pass away, but the memory of those crimes and those virtues will not pass away.

In order to complete the story, two further citations are necessary here. In the Appendix to the German White Book is printed a speech made by the German Chancellor on 4th August 1914, in which he said: " We have informed the British Government " that as long as the British Government remains " neutral our fleet will not attack the Northern coast " of France and that we will not violate the territorial " integrity and independence of Belgium." And on 3rd August the German Embassy published in the London Press a statement that Germany would be disposed to give an undertaking that she will not attack France by sea in the North or make any warlike use of the sea coast of Belgium or Holland if it appeared that Great Britain would take this undertaking on condition of her neutrality for the time being. On 4th August Sir E. Grey demanded that Germany should refrain from violating the neutrality of Belgium, and on this being refused declared war against Germany the same night.

✦　✦　✦

Now that the narrative has been told and the documents analysed, it is right to present what seem to be the legitimate inferences and conclusions.

1. The military masters of Germany wanted war from the beginning in order to attack France and Russia, and to carry out their ambitions, but always on the condition that they could count on British neutrality, as in 1870.

2. On the formation of the Liberal Government on 12th December 1905, three Ministers, Mr. Asquith, Mr. Haldane, and Sir Edward Grey, laid the foundation for a different policy, namely, a policy of British intervention if Germany should make an unprovoked attack on France. They did this within a month, probably within a few days of taking office, by means of communications with the French Ambassador and of military and naval conversations between the General Staffs of the two countries, who worked out plans for joint action in war if Great Britain should intervene. They did it behind the back of nearly all their Cabinet colleagues, and, what really matters, without Parliament being in any way made aware that a policy of active intervention between France and Germany was being contemplated.

3. As time went on our Entente with France was still further developed by stages which have been already described, and France was encouraged more and more to expect that Great Britain would stand by her in arms if she were attacked by Germany without

giving provocation. By 1913 our Entente with France had become such that, to use Mr. Lloyd George's phrase, we were under an obligation of honour to join her in arms, if so attacked.

4. Under our Constitution such obligations, or even formal Treaties, can be undertaken on behalf of the Crown by the advice of Ministers without Parliament being informed. At all events that is so in theory. Parliament can, of course, refuse supplies to support any engagement of which it disapproves when it comes to know of it, but cannot require to be consulted before it is made.

5. Now it may have been perfectly right, in view of the threatening attitude of Germany, that this country should have a defensive understanding or even an alliance with France in 1906, or in any subsequent year. Obviously that would be a new departure of tremendous importance, and one which could be reliably and effectively taken only if it were known to and approved by Parliament as a national policy, with its limitations fixed by Parliament and proper provision made by Parliament so that we should not be caught unprepared. For it would expose us to the risk of war on land against the greatest military Power in the world.

6. Sir E. Grey made it clear in his speech of 3rd August 1914 that in his opinion our honour as well as our interest required that we should support France in arms, though up to the present moment he and his coadjutors have always maintained that they had kept our hands free and that Parliament was quite free to decide for either peace or war.

7. But Parliament was never warned by Ministers

of the great danger in which we stood of being drawn suddenly into a war which would threaten our national existence. If it had been warned we might have been better prepared with men and ships and guns and ammunition, or might have adopted a wiser and more open policy.

8. The last chance of maintaining peace was when the crisis came in July 1914. A plain timely statement to Germany that if she attacked France we should be on the side of France and Russia would " for a certainty," as President Wilson says, have prevented war. The military masters of Germany would not have faced the fearful risk. That statement was not made. Ministers would not agree to make it, and no wonder. It involved responsibility. They had no firm foothold of Parliamentary support such as would fortify them in giving a warning which, if disregarded, meant a war of unprecedented magnitude. And they had no foothold of Parliamentary support because Parliament had not been either consulted or informed as to the policy.

9. Secret diplomacy has undergone its " acid test " in this country. It had every chance. The voice of party was silent. The Foreign Minister was an English gentleman whom the country trusted and admired, who was wholly free from personal enmities of every kind, and who wanted peace. And secret diplomacy utterly failed. It prevented us from finding some alternative for war, and it prevented us from being prepared for war, because secret diplomacy means diplomacy aloof from Parliament.

Let us have done with it for good.

CHAPTER VIII

SIR EDWARD GREY'S SPEECH OF
3RD AUGUST 1914

WHEN the negotiations had ended and a state of war had arisen on the Continent, and the one remaining question was whether or not this country should take part in it, Sir Edward Grey made a speech on 3rd August 1914 in the House of Commons, strongly urging war. He told the House a number of things they had never heard before. His purpose was, as he said, " to place before the House the issue and the choice." What should be done had to be decided at once from the very nature of the case. Was it to be Peace or War ?

* * *

After assuring Parliament that his efforts to preserve the peace of Europe in this crisis had been strenuous and genuine and whole-hearted, he proceeded at once to deal with the question of British obligations. " I have assured the House," said Sir Edward, " and the Prime Minister has assured the House more than once, that if any crisis such as this arose we should come before the House of Commons and be able to say to the House that it was free to decide what the British attitude should be ; that we would have no secret engagement which we should spring upon the

House, and tell the House that because we had entered
into that engagement there was an obligation of
honour upon the country." He then said that the
Triple Entente was not an alliance but a diplomatic
group, and that in the Balkan crisis of 1908 he had
told the Russian Minister that this country could not
give him more than diplomatic support. He added
that in this present crisis he had until yesterday
(2nd August) given no promise of more than diplomatic
support. Having said that, Sir Edward repeated
that he " must make this question of obligation clear
to the House," and proceeded to disclose what passed
between him and the French and German Ambassadors
at the very beginning of 1906. This has already been
stated on an earlier page. It was, in short, that he had
in 1906 given his opinion to both these Ambassadors,
in regard to the Morocco crisis of 1906, that if it led
to war between France and Germany, " public opinion
in this country would have rallied to the material
support of France," and that he had authorized
military and naval conversations between French
and British experts to prepare for the contingency
of a joint war against Germany. He also admitted
that this authority was given without the knowledge
of the Cabinet.

Sir Edward Grey next referred to the Agadir crisis
of 1911, another Morocco crisis, which he dismissed
in a sentence. " Throughout that I took precisely
the same line that had been taken in 1906." That
statement is made without any qualification. He
then went on to say that in November 1912 it was
decided in the Cabinet that we ought to have a definite
understanding in writing that " these conversations

which took place were not binding upon the freedom
of either Government." And he read to the House
the letters of 22nd November 1912 between himself
and the French Ambassador. They have been already
quoted, and say that " consultation between experts is
not and ought not to be regarded as an engagement that
commits either Government to action in a contingency
which has not yet arisen and may never arise." The
letters also allude to the disposition of the French and
British fleets respectively " at the present moment,"
and say it is not based upon an engagement to co-
operate in war. They need not be transcribed again.
They do not declare that Great Britain is not committed, but only that the consultation of experts does
not commit us and that the naval dispositions are not
based upon an engagement to co-operate in war, which
is quite a different thing.

Upon these grounds Sir Edward Grey then repeated
his claim that he had been justified in telling the House
that the Government remained perfectly free, and
a fortiori the House remained perfectly free, to decide
whether we should intervene in the war or not. He
said the letters of 22nd November 1912 were " the
starting-point for the Government with regard to
the present crisis," and once more affirmed that the
House was perfectly free to decide.

Having given this information, " to prove our good
faith to the House of Commons," Sir Edward entered
upon a passionate but reasoned appeal for support to
France. He dwelt upon the unwisdom and dishonour
of remaining neutral in the war between France and
Germany, which was in fact declared that very day.
He admitted that this crisis did not originate with any-

thing that primarily concerned France; that France
desired peace, and was involved because of her obligation of honour under a definite alliance with Russia,
and that he did not know the terms of that alliance.
He then spoke of our long-standing friendship with
France; " but how far that entails an obligation, let
every man look into his own heart and his own feelings."
The French Fleet was in the Mediterranean, and the
coast of France undefended. " The French Fleet is in
the Mediterranean, and has for some years been concentrated there because of the feeling of confidence
and friendship which has existed between the two
countries. My own feeling is that if a foreign fleet,
engaged in a war which France had not sought, and
in which she had not been the aggressor, came down
the English Channel and bombarded and battered
the undefended coast of France, we could not stand
aside."

Sir Edward then spoke of British interests, and said
it was on that he was going to base and justify what he
was presently going to say to the House. If we said
nothing, it might be that the French Fleet would
be withdrawn from the Mediterranean. Suppose we
took up an attitude of neutrality, and that consequences
not foreseen made Italy join in the war at a time when
we were ourselves forced to fight in defence of vital
British interests, what would be our position, because
our trade routes in the Mediterranean might be vital
to us. And we had not kept in the Mediterranean
a fleet equal to dealing alone with a combination of
other fleets in the Mediterranean. He then said that
France was entitled to know at once whether or not,
in the event of attack upon her unprotected northern

and western coasts, she could depend upon British
support, and read to the House the assurance he had
given the day before (2nd August) that our fleet would
support France against such attack. He added: " I
understand that the German Government would be
prepared, if we would pledge ourselves to neutrality,
to agree that its fleet would not attack the northern
coast of France." I have only heard that shortly before
I came to the House, but it is far too narrow an engagement for us." Sir Edward did not say what would be
a sufficient engagement, or that any engagement would
suffice.

* * *

Up to this point in his speech Sir Edward said
nothing about Belgium. In fact, very little had been
said about Belgium in the entire negotiations by anyone. But after he had urged on the House our duty
to France, he turned to the neutrality of Belgium.
He referred to the Treaty of 1839, under which all the
Powers agreed to respect its neutrality, and without
arguing the effect of that instrument, spoke of it as a
" guarantee " on our part in which our honour and
our interests were concerned. He narrated how he
had asked both France and Germany whether they
would undertake an engagement to respect the
neutrality of Belgium—how France had said Yes, and
Germany had not said either Yes or No, but had said
that any reply on their part would in the event of war
disclose to a certain extent a part of their plan of
campaign. He informed the House that he had quite
recently heard, but was not sure how far it had reached
him in an accurate form, that Germany had sent an
ultimatum to Belgium requiring a passage for her

troops to the French frontier. Sir Edward then told
the House that " we were sounded in the course of last
week as to whether, if a guarantee were given that
after the war Belgian integrity would be preserved, that
would content us," and that he had rejected the proposal. We had great and vital interests in the independence (" and integrity is the least part ") of
Belgium, and it would be gone if Belgian neutrality
were violated and no action taken to resent it. And
if Belgian independence goes, " the independence of
Holland will follow." He did not refer to the questions
put to him by the German Ambassador on 1st August—
namely, on what terms we would remain neutral—or
to his answer.

*   *   *

Sir Edward Grey then returned to France. " If
France is beaten in a struggle of life and death, beaten
to her knees, loses her position as a Great Power,
becomes subordinate to the will and power of one
greater than herself—consequences which I do not
anticipate, because I am sure that France has the power
to defend herself with all the energy and ability and
patriotism which she has shown so often—still, if that
were to happen, and if Belgium fell under the same
dominating influence, and then Holland, and then
Denmark, then would not Mr. Gladstone's words come
true that just opposite to us there would be a common
interest against the unmeasured aggrandizement of
any Power ? " A little further on he said : " I do not
believe for a moment that at the end of this war, even
if we stood aside and remained aside, we should be in a
position, a material position, to use our force decisively
to undo what had happened in the course of the war,

to prevent the whole of the west of Europe opposite to us—if that had been the result of the war—falling under the domination of a single Power, and I am quite sure that our moral position would be such as to have lost us all respect."

Sir Edward then added—that we had taken no engagement yet with regard to sending an expeditionary armed force out of the country, and that " the one bright spot in the whole of this terrible situation is Ireland." The rest of the speech was concerned with emphasizing what he had already said.

* * *

This remarkable speech began with an elaborate effort to prove that the House of Commons was perfectly free to determine either for peace or war. It ended with a passionate declaration that this country would be disgraced if we did not declare war, and the reasoning of the speech proved that Sir Edward Grey had committed himself irretrievably. It left the House of Commons convinced that it had in honour no choice but to join France in arms. It is an epitome of the reasoning by which Sir Edward Grey had been brought to believe that he could say and do what he said and did without limiting his freedom of action. But if this is legitimate we ought not to keep up the pretence that we are a self-governing nation in foreign affairs.

It would have been simpler if Sir Edward's speech had consisted of two sentences something like the following. France is about to be attacked by Germany, not for any act of her own, but merely because she is bound by treaty to Russia and Russia has fallen out with Germany's ally Austria. You are not in honour

15

free to stand out of this war because we have bound
you in honour by a course of policy without your
knowledge : even though this is not a French quarrel
at all, and though I told you we were free, I now find
that I was entirely mistaken and you are not free in
honour.   Every word of that imaginary speech would
have been true, but he could not see it even at that
stage.

It is a very curious thing that Sir Edward Grey
should have dwelt on his letter of 22nd November 1912
and the French Ambassador's answer to it as the
" starting point for the Government with regard to
" the present crisis " when he was endeavouring to
make out on 3rd August 1914 that the House was
perfectly free to decide what the British attitude
should be.   For it was precisely the selfsame letter
which Mr. Lloyd George read to the House on 7th
August 1918 in support of his contention that there
was an " obligation of honour " on our part towards
France.

CHAPTER IX

BELGIUM

A GOOD deal has been said about Belgium in previous chapters. It is, however, desirable to present in a compact form a view of our duties to that deeply wronged country and of the manner in which we endeavoured to fulfil them, because both public writers and public speakers have persistently maintained that we were drawn into this war on account of Belgium.

Very few people will be found to deny that we have great interests in preventing a great military Power, be it Germany or be it France, from securing a mastery of the Belgian coast. Nor can it be denied that the spectacle of some military bully devastating that small kingdom, while we passively looked on across the narrow seas, would be regarded as a dishonour and an affront to the United Kingdom. In these circumstances it does not much signify whether or not we were in 1914 bound by Treaty to defend Belgium against invasion. For the sake of historical accuracy, however, it is right to say that we were not so bound either by the Treaty of 1839 or by any other instrument. All that we did in 1839 was to sign, together with Austria, France, Prussia, Russia, and Holland, an agreement that Belgium should be a perpetually neutral State. We bound ourselves, as did the others, not to violate that neutrality, but did not bind ourselves to defend it against the encroachment of any other Power. That is the plain effect of the document, but it would be a waste of time to enter upon any controversy on this controverted subject, for we had obligations of honour and interest which could not be ignored.

When the Treaty of 1839 was signed the primary purpose was to perpetuate the separation of Belgium from Holland. They had been united against their will in the Napoleonic times though racially and linguistically distinct. But the neutrality of Belgium came before long to have a much wider importance. The neutrality and even the existence of that nation was undoubtedly threatened by Napoleon III, and ever since the consolidation of Germany both the one and the other have been in peril. For, if a war broke out between France and Germany, both those Powers might be tempted to cross the Belgian frontier in order to attack each other. The geographical position of Belgium, as a glance at the map will show, tempted an unscrupulous belligerent to get at his enemy through this neutral territory, and thus turn the powerful frontier defences which both France and Germany possessed. So great is the advantage, in a strategical sense, of adopting this unprincipled method that for some years before the war broke out it had become an axiom among military experts in Germany that in case of war with France their attack must be delivered either through Switzerland, which would be difficult, or through Belgium and Luxemburg, which has been done.

But, though this danger had become more acute
of late, the risk has always been recognized, and it
has been perfectly well known in England for forty
or fifty years that the risk could arise only out of a
war between France and Germany. How should it
be met if such a war came ? Belgium single-handed
could not long resist the overwhelming forces of a
great military Power. And in her interest as well as
our own the thing to be desired was that she should
be kept out of war altogether. She was not strong
enough to deter either belligerent from invasion by the
threat that she would join his adversary. In this
cruel dilemma the Belgians always looked for British
support. " When are the English coming? " was the
question on all men's lips in Belgium when invasion
actually came upon them in 1914. Belgians have
always looked to England as their mainstay.

* * *

And what has been the traditional policy of British
Governments for meeting this possible danger ? That
question may perhaps be more easily answered by an
historical illustration.

The present war is not the first occasion upon
which we have had to resolve what we ought to do if
Belgium is threatened, and how we ought to do it.
In 1870 war broke out between France and Germany.
Great anxiety arose in regard to Belgium, lest one or
other of the belligerents might invade that country
in order to attack its adversary. At that time the
greater fear was that France would invade, because the
disgraceful proposal of Napoleon III, that France
should be allowed to annex Belgium as compensation
for the aggrandizement of Prussia, had just been

brought to light by Prince Bismarck. Mr. Gladstone was Prime Minister in 1870. He and his colleagues in the Cabinet were entirely unfettered by any engagements or obligations of honour as between France and Prussia. They were free to consider what was required for the safety of this country and for the protection of Belgium against lawless violence from either of her great military neighbours. In these circumstances Mr. Gladstone took an eminently wise and strong step, openly in the face of Europe. He proposed both to France and to Prussia a Treaty by which Great Britain undertook that, if either of the belligerents should in the course of that war violate the neutrality of Belgium, Great Britain would co-operate with the other belligerent in defence of the same, " employing for that purpose her naval and military forces to ensure its observance." In this way both France and Germany knew and the whole world knew that invasion of Belgium meant war with Great Britain. Whichever belligerent violated the neutrality must reckon with the consequences. Both France and Prussia signed that Treaty. Belgium was saved. But Mr. Gladstone was also careful to insert in that Treaty both with France and with Prussia a limitation—namely, that Great Britain did not engage to take part in any of the general operations of the war beyond the limits of Belgium. In this way we were safeguarded from being swept into the maelstrom of a general Continental war. We were enabled to save that country without committing ourselves to incalculable risks.

*　　*　　*

This policy, which proved a complete success in

1870, indicated the way in which British power could effectively protect Belgium against an unscrupulous neighbour. But then it is a policy which cannot be adopted unless this country is itself prepared to observe neutrality so long as Belgium is left unmolested, and unless this country is prepared to make war against either of the belligerents which shall molest Belgium. For the inducement to each of such belligerents is the knowledge that he will have Great Britain as an enemy if he invades Belgium, and as an ally if his enemy attacks him through Belgian territory. And that cannot be a security unless Great Britain keeps herself free to give armed assistance to either should the other violate the Treaty. The whole leverage would obviously disappear if we took sides in the war on other grounds.

Accordingly, Mr. Gladstone's Treaties with France and Prussia in 1870 were accompanied by a Proclamation of our neutrality in the Franco-Prussian War, and this was a vital part of his policy. But Sir Edward Grey in 1914 did not and could not offer similar Treaties to France and Germany, because our relations with France and the conduct of Germany were such that for us to join Germany in any event was unthinkable. And he did not proclaim our neutrality because our relations with France, as described in his own speech, were such that he could not in honour refuse to join France in the war. Therefore the example of 1870 could not be followed in 1914, and Belgium was not saved but destroyed. Further, our participation in this war, when we did come in, was not limited to the defence of Belgium, as in Mr. Gladstone's day, but committed us to the full in vast issues extending to almost every corner of Europe. This intervention embarked us upon present or prospective operations all over the world and committed us to support schemes of conquest in Alsace-Lorraine, Poland, Bosnia and Herzegovina, Transylvania, Albania, Dalmatia, the Trentino, Constantinople, the Dardanelles, Asiatic Turkey, North, South, East, and West Africa, and in the vast area of German Colonies all over the world.

There is a great difference between this and the curtailed but effective plan of Mr. Gladstone to save Belgium.

* * *

It will be convenient now to set out chronologically in a condensed form the doings and dealings of His Majesty's Government in regard to that country during the negotiations that preceded the war, as they appear in the British White Book, our authentic source of information.

The despatches in point are numbered 85, 101, 114, 115, 119, 123, 128, 148, 151, 153, 154, 155, 157, 158, 159. Many of them have been already the subject of comment, because it is impossible in such a survey of events as this to keep one thread of the story wholly disconnected from the rest, but a slight repetition may be excused when the purpose is to present a synoptical view.

Negotiation between some of the Powers commenced informally soon after 28th June 1914, and formally commenced among all of them on 23rd July. Till the 29th July, three days before Germany declared war, Belgium is not even mentioned in the British White Book. On the night of the 29th July the German Chancellor adverted to that country in an interview

with the British Ambassador at Berlin, saying that
" it depended upon the action of France what operations Germany might be forced to enter upon in
Belgium, but when the war was over Belgian integrity
would be respected if she had not sided against
Germany." He did not say that Belgian independence would be respected, but pressed us to remain
neutral. This proposal was rejected by Sir Edward
Grey on 30th July. He said that the Chancellor
" in effect asks us to bargain away whatever obligation or interest we have as regards the neutrality of
Belgium," and declared that we could not entertain
that bargain, indicating, as the context shows, that
he considered it would be a disgrace for us to do so.

On that same day (30th July) the French Ambassador
asked Sir Edward what we should do in the event of
an aggression by Germany on France (Belgium is not
mentioned), and Sir Edward told him that there
would be a Cabinet to-morrow morning and he
would see him again " to-morrow afternoon "—the
31st July, that is. On the 31st July Sir Edward wired
to the British Ambassadors both in Paris and in
Berlin directing them to ask whether the French and
German Governments respectively " are prepared to
engage to respect the neutrality of Belgium so long
as no other Power violates it," and asking for an early
answer. This is the first time that any mention at
all is made of Belgium by the British Government
either in official despatches or anywhere else so far as
we know, except that our Ambassador reported what
the German Chancellor said, and Sir Edward Grey
answered him on 30th July. It will be observed
that what Sir Edward Grey then did is not the same

thing as Mr. Gladstone had done in 1870, for Sir Edward Grey merely asked for a promise to respect Belgian neutrality and said nothing about joint Treaties with each of the belligerents for the common defence of Belgium, and did not offer either armed assistance for that purpose or announce that Great Britain would remain neutral in case Belgium were unmolested. But he notified Belgium on the same day of the question he had put to the French and the German Governments, and added: " I assume that the Belgian Government will maintain to the utmost of their power their neutrality, which I desire and expect other Powers to uphold and observe." Belgium did indeed resist to the utmost of her power, with a gallantry which will never be forgotten. Unhappily, Great Britain was unable to give her that military assistance without which her resistance was inevitably unavailing. In answer to these inquiries, France said that she would respect Belgian neutrality; Germany postponed giving an answer, and never gave a formal answer at all. Belgium answered the message of Sir Edward Grey by saying she would maintain her neutrality to the utmost of her power; that her relations with her neighbours were excellent, and there was no reason to suspect their intentions.

At this stage, the 31st July and 1st August, the question of peace or war between the great military Powers on the Continent had come to a head. It was on these two days that Germany despatched first her ultimatum and then her declaration of war to Russia, and it was on 31st July that Sir Edward said to the German Ambassador that if France became involved we should be drawn in. But on the same day he also told the German Ambassador that we were still free and could not promise to remain neutral on terms similar to what the Ambassador suggested, which included respect of Belgian neutrality, but must keep our hands free. The prospect of our remaining neutral, however, was not definitely excluded by Sir Edward's statement to the German Ambassador.

* * *

It was from the beginning possible for the British Government to adopt any one of three courses, which may be enumerated without discussing the wisdom or justice or morals of any among them. We could announce definitely, not as an expectation but as a resolve, that if war came between France and Germany, we would fight on the side of France. Possibly on 31st July that would have come too late to prevent the German ultimatum. But it was a policy. The second course was to announce definitely that we washed our hands of the whole business, being, as Sir Edward maintained, quite free from any engagements and regarding it as detestable to be brought into a war for a Servian quarrel. Whether or not that would have disposed Russia to retard her mobilization and so gain the time to settle the whole controversy is a matter of opinion. Clearly it would not have been honourable conduct toward France on the part of Ministers in view of their previous dealings with France. The view that we were under an obligation of honour has been already presented. Certainly it would have been an abandonment of Belgium, but at all events it was a policy. The third course was to announce definitely that we would remain neutral unless Belgian neutrality were violated, but that if

Germany violated the neutrality of Belgium she would become our enemy and meet with our armed opposition. If that had been said in time, before the German ultimatum to Russia, or even after the ultimatum, it would have had a good chance of saving Belgium, for the power of this country was very well known to all concerned. That course was, however, barred by reason of our Ministers' real obligations with France. But that also was a policy.

It seems clear, from what has been already said, that the British Government had not either on the 31st July or on 1st August decided in regard to either the first or the second of the three alternative courses which have just been enumerated. For the moment, however, we are dealing with the third alternative, namely, would we declare that we would defend Belgium if she were attacked by Germany, and remain neutral if Belgium were left unmolested. Confining ourselves to that alone, it might be concluded from Sir Edward Grey's silence that Ministers had not come to any resolution. This fact, however, is placed beyond all possible question by express statements of Sir Edward Grey himself, one of them made to M. Cambon, the French Ambassador, on 31st July 1914, another made to the German Ambassador on 1st August, and yet another made to the French Ambassador on the 2nd August 1914.

The first statement was made to the French Ambassador on the occasion of his asking Sir Edward on 31st July for a reply to the question what Great Britain would do in the event of an aggression by Germany on France. Sir Edward, while declining to pledge himself on that point, said that further developments might cause Parliament and the Government to take the view that intervention was justified. " The preservation of the neutrality of Belgium might be, I would not say a decisive but an important factor, in determining our attitude. Whether we proposed to Parliament to intervene or not to intervene in a war, Parliament would wish to know how we stood with regard to the neutrality of Belgium, and it might be that I should ask both France and Germany whether each was prepared to undertake an engagement that she would not be the first to violate the neutrality of Belgium." He did ask both France and Germany the same day. It is clear that no definite resolution had been taken as to Belgium at the time this interview took place—namely, 31st July.

The next statement of Sir Edward was made to the German Ambassador on 1st August, when the German Government had omitted or declined to give an undertaking that they would respect Belgian neutrality. Sir Edward said:[1] " The German Government's attitude was a matter of very great regret. If Germany could see her way to give the same assurance as that which had been given by France, it would materially contribute to relieve anxiety and tension here. On the other hand, if there were a violation of the neutrality of Belgium by one combatant while the other respected it, it would be extremely difficult to restrain public feeling in this country." Upon this, the despatch informs us, the German Ambassador came to the point. He " asked me [Sir Edward Grey] whether, if Germany gave a promise not to violate Belgian neutrality, we would engage to remain neutral." Sir

[1] British White Book, No. 123.

Edward has since expressed the view that the German
Ambassador had no authority to offer that his country
would respect Belgian neutrality. He might have
made certain by asking the German Ambassador.
But it does not signify for the matter in hand. What
signifies is not the authority of the Ambassador to give
a promise, but the frame of mind indicated by the
answer which Sir Edward Grey gave to the question
just quoted, whether, if such a promise were given,
Great Britain would engage to remain neutral. " I
replied," writes Sir Edward, " that I could not say
that ; our hands were still free, and we were considering what our attitude should be. All I could say
was that our attitude would be determined largely
by public opinion here, and that the neutrality of
Belgium would appeal very strongly to public opinion
here. I did not think that we could give a promise
of neutrality on that condition alone. The Ambassador pressed me as to whether I could not formulate conditions on which we would remain neutral.
He even suggested that the integrity of France and her
Colonies might be guaranteed. I said that I felt
obliged to refuse definitely any promise to remain
neutral on similar terms, and I could only say that
we must keep our hands free."

If language means anything, this means that whereas
Mr. Gladstone bound this country to war in order
to safeguard Belgian neutrality, Sir Edward would
not even bind this country to neutrality in order to
save Belgium. He may have been right, but it was
not for the sake of Belgian interests that he refused.

One further statement of Sir Edward's on the 2nd
August must be quoted. It was made to the French

Ambassador, and is to be found in No. 148 of the British White Book. Lord Lansdowne and Mr. Bonar Law had sent on that day a letter to Mr. Asquith offering him their help in supporting France and Russia, but they said nothing about Belgium. When Sir Edward saw the French Ambassador after the " Cabinet this morning "—2nd August—he handed to him the memorandum containing a promise of British naval support to France against the German Fleet, which need not be again canvassed. The French Ambassador asked him about Belgium, and then he said : " We were considering what statement we should make in Parliament to-morrow (3rd August)—in effect whether we should declare violation of Belgian neutrality to be a *casus belli* "—and told him what had been said to the German Ambassador on this point. At last they made up their minds. We learn from No. 26 of the Belgian Grey Book that on 3rd August our Foreign Minister informed the Belgian Minister that if their neutrality were violated it meant war with Germany.

For events moved rapidly as regards Belgium as soon as it became clear that Great Britain would not declare to Germany on what conditions she would remain neutral, which we refused to do on 1st August, and that we had decided to give France our naval support, as we promised to do on 2nd August. The same night, at 7 o'clock, the German ultimatum was delivered to Belgium, requiring a passage for German troops through Belgian territory on pain of war. The German Chancellor admitted that it was a wrong and an injustice. It has been aggravated a thousandfold by the outrages since perpetrated in that country.

* * *

It has so often been stated in public and in private by those concerned, as to be no longer private information, that there were differences of opinion among Ministers. Some held that we ought to keep out of the war altogether, crediting Sir Edward Grey's and Mr. Asquith's assurances that we were not bound to France. Others thought that we ought to join France irrespective of Belgium. Others thought that we ought to keep out of the war if Belgian neutrality were respected. There is also clearly visible in these despatches much more than a trace of the comfortable reflection that after all it was for Parliament to decide. A reflection of that kind by executive Ministers in moments of difficulty ever has when quartered, three parts desire to avoid responsibility and one part respect for constitutional doctrine. Respect for the Constitution requires that Ministers should decide when decision is needed, and that if the policy is critical, so that the approval of Parliament ought to be obtained, that policy should be submitted to Parliament in time for a real determination, and not withheld till there is no choice but to accept what the Minister proposes or incur what in the face of the world he declares would be national dishonour.

*   *   *

The remaining facts are very few. Keeping to dates, on Saturday 1st August we recall that Sir Edward refused to state conditions on which we would remain neutral. On 2nd August he gave the naval undertaking to France, and said the Government were still considering whether or not to treat violation of Belgian neutrality as a *casus belli*. At 7 p.m. on 2nd August Germany presented her ultimatum to Belgium,

and on the morning of 4th August invaded Belgium.
It is certain that this attack was the thing which
enabled Mr. Asquith to retain for a few months all the
members of the Cabinet except two. It is also certain
that as soon as the Germans did attack Belgium the
whole of the Ministerial Press and the Ministerial
Speakers with few exceptions dwelt upon that as the
reason for the war. It was perhaps natural on their
part to select this argument. The best way of obtaining popular support for the war, which in the days of
voluntary recruiting was of the highest importance,
would be to dwell on an outrage which could admit of
no excuse. But this does not alter facts.

* * *

A highly interesting and important statement has
been made by Mr. Lloyd George in an interview published by *Pearson's Magazine* in its number of March
1915. " Why are you so whole-soully for this war,"
asked the interviewer. " Belgium," was the reply.
" The Saturday after war had actually been declared
on the Continent (Saturday, 1st August) a poll of the
electors of Great Britain would have shown 95 per cent
against embroiling this country in hostilities," continued Mr. Lloyd George. " Powerful City financiers
whom it was my duty to interview this Saturday on
the financial situation ended the conference with an
earnest hope that Britain would keep out of it. A
poll on the following Tuesday would have resulted in a
vote of 99 per cent in favour of war." Mr. Lloyd
George then asked : " What had happened in the
meantime ? " and answered his own question as
follows : " The revolution in public sentiment," he
said, " was attributable entirely to an attack made by

16

Germany on a small and unprotected country which had done her no wrong, and what Britain was not prepared to do for interests political and commercial, she readily risked to help the weak and helpless. Our honour as a nation is involved in this war, because we are bound in an honourable obligation to defend the independence, the liberty, the integrity of a small neighbour that has lived peaceably ; but she could not have compelled us being weak. The man who declined to discharge his debt because his creditor is too poor to enforce it, is a blackguard." Such is Mr. Lloyd George's account of it.

It is a strong claim, and of a kind that appeals to everyone. A little later, in the same interview, Mr. Lloyd George, after allusion to German misrepresentations, said : " But this I know is true—after the guarantee given that the German Fleet would not attack the coast of France or annex any French territory,[1] *I* would not have been party to a declaration of war, had Belgium not been invaded, and I think I can say the same thing for most, if not all, of my colleagues. If Germany had been wise, she would not have set foot on Belgian soil. The Liberal Government then would not have intervened. Germany made a grave mistake."

What are we to make of this explosive utterance ? It seems to open a window into the Council chamber of those disastrous days, if there is anything there worth seeing. Evidently Mr. Lloyd George must have been opposed to the giving to France of the naval assurance of 2nd August, for that assurance was

---

[1] The allusion seems to be to a statement publicly made by Herr Kuhlmann in the London Press on 3rd August to this effect.

given prior to any German invasion of Belgium. No doubt at that time he believed the declarations of the Foreign Office that they had kept our hands perfectly free, and that Parliament was free to decide whether to intervene or not, though later on he perceived, as we have seen, that our hands had by no means been kept free. Believing that Parliament had been kept free to decide, he thought apparently that we ought not to be plunged into a ruinous war over what was really a Russian quarrel, and says that most if not all the Cabinet agreed with him. His tone as well as his conclusion is very different from that of Sir Edward Grey's speech, and there was the prospect of a very serious difference inside of the Cabinet and outside of it. Then the Germans invaded Belgium, and Mr. Lloyd George, like every one else, resolved to resist them. What he said at this interview expresses what a very great number of people would have thought and said if they had really been free to decide what the interest of this country required. But the truth was, as Mr. Lloyd George afterwards discovered, that we were not free to decide. The nation found itself bound by obligations of honour contracted toward France in secret, and that was what constrained us to enter upon this war, whether Belgium were invaded or not. We should have gone to war on behalf of Belgium if we had not already done so on behalf of France.

CHAPTER X

WAS IT INEVITABLE?

THERE are some people in this country who are apt to be impatient when the origins of this war are discussed, and would dismiss the whole subject with the summary comment that it must have come sooner or later, and even that it was a good thing it did come in 1914 when we had France and Russia as allies, cost what it might.

Many things incline men's minds, when they look at our awful sacrifices, to acquiesce in that conclusion. Millions of our people, who have lost what was dearer to them than their own lives, shrink instinctively from the thought that their bereavement was avoidable. The Ministers who guided us into the war and their supporters have the deepest interest in believing that the struggle was unavoidable. Few could reconcile themselves to the thought that so terrible a tragedy was in any sense due to their own shortcomings. It has always been so. Whenever any policy which has led to war comes to be arraigned, the last line of defence has always been that the thing must have come sooner or later. It was so notably in the South African War. And then, as now, the influence of Party and of the Press under its control has been used

to support the same plea—that our misfortunes are to
be laid at the door of destiny.

It is not intended to affirm in this place that foresight or firmness or frankness would certainly have
averted a great European war for good. No one can
tell with certainty what would have happened had
these qualities been available. But it is not right to
pass a sponge over all that has happened and so lose
the lessons it teaches by summarily accepting a
predestinarian plea.

Sometimes people say, and the argument is put most
formidably when so put, that the military party in
Germany intended, with the assistance of Austria-
Hungary, to destroy the power of Russia and France,
and after that had been done to make her final effort
against England, to seize Belgium and the northern
coast of France, and ruin us by the possession of those
coasts, after weakening her continental neighbours so
that they could not, even if they still desired it, give
us any assistance. Some people even suggest that if
we failed to help them against Germany, Russia and
France might in their resentment have been not in-
disposed to see England also crushed. And therefore
the argument is that we ought to regard the horrible
war of 1914 not only as inevitable, but also as on the
whole a fortunate thing. Now, if our Ministers thought
that the Rulers of Germany entertained a project of
this kind, then they must have felt that the danger
confronting us was the most serious to which we have
been exposed in all history. If the greatest military
Power in the world were in possession of the Channel
ports of France and Belgium, and resolved upon our
destruction, we should be in a more serious position

than even in the Napoleonic times. True that we should be fighting on our native element, the sea, with all our men available for defence in our own country, but still the risk would be immense. The course of events in the Balkans in 1912–13 must have proved to Ministers that a quarrel between Russia and Austria might quite likely break out in those regions and involve Germany and France according to treaty and so lead to a European war.

In this perplexity the proper constitutional course was clear. It was not to hold inconclusive conclaves of selected Ministers and Foreign Office officials who neither could nor would face responsibility and come to decisions till the hurricane upon us left them no choice. The constitutional and proper course was to go straight to the House of Commons as soon as the danger became clear. It would not have been difficult to lay the situation before the House without giving any justifiable cause of offence to any foreign Power, and in any case candour was required by our own safety. Ministers might have said to the House that they desired peace above all things, and would never make or support any attack upon Germany, and would give the fullest assurances to that effect, but that the conditions in the Balkans and the unrest in Europe made it necessary to recognize that possibly war might arise between the Central Powers on the one side against France and Russia on the other side, and that if the Central Powers should overwhelm France and Russia in that conflict, a most serious situation would arise for this country. Belgium and the French coast might be mastered by the greatest military Power in the world, and our very existence thereby threatened.

It was therefore necessary, they might have said, for us all to take counsel and determine whether or not we should make an open defensive Alliance with France and Russia on conditions which should most abundantly secure the Central Powers against any fear of aggression, or what other precautions we should take for our own security. This was the open and manly course, and it would have helped to clear away the cloud of suspicion that was poisoning international relations on the Continent. For the good faith and enormous power of this country has always been well known, and a definite pronouncement of policy with the approval of the House of Commons carries enormous weight. It would also have prevented us being caught by surprise and unprepared, and decisions could have been taken even by timid Ministers when supported by an ascertained public opinion. So far as human judgment can foresee, the war would not have come if this had been done, for it would have been known that the force of Great Britain would have been against the aggressors.

Instead of that we found ourselves on a sudden plunged into war. We could not have been more completely surprised. General Mahon, who was attached to the War Office and whose duty it was to tour the country and expedite by every possible means the supplies of ammunition, says in his letter to *The Times*, published on 10th June 1919, that he found the cupboard bare, or nearly so. He says, "To create out of nothing, or next to nothing, the prodigious require-
" ments of an immense army was a task almost super-
" human in its difficulty. No politician of them all
" who feared to place the armed forces on a proper

" footing had thought of accumulating reserves of
" guns, rifles, or ammunition sufficient to enable rapid
" expansion of strength if such became necessary,
" and we are told that they knew it would be necessary.
" When the time came there was nothing to start on.
" No machinery, in many cases no raw material, no
" men accustomed to the work, for of these latter vast
" numbers had sought other employment owing to the
" pre-war policy." Ministers who contemplated taking
part in continental warfare ought to have made provision for that contingency. But the root of the
whole trouble was their secretiveness before the war,
both as regards the dangers we might have to encounter
and the policy they were pursuing with resources
wholly inadequate for the enterprises they had in
view. If it were not for the necessity of preventing a
like catastrophe from recurring again, every one would
try to forget these deplorable reminiscences, now that
the danger is over. But it is necessary to remember
these things in order to prevent the same trouble from
overtaking us again.

A mere dialectical discussion of what would or
might have happened under conditions which never
arose would indeed be unprofitable and inconclusive.
But it must be useful, in view of our future relations
with Germany, that we should try to realize the forces
and traditions which actuated their Government and
people in years preceding the war, and will undoubtedly
affect the policy they may pursue in years to come.
People continually say in England that not only the
Hohenzollerns and the military caste but the whole
population of Germany, with few exceptions, had for
many years favoured an aggressive foreign policy and

longed for war in order to obtain a complete supremacy over free nations and subject Europe to their will. This is unquestionably true of the military caste, and even more true of the Professors and teaching classes, with many honourable exceptions, and a part of the Press, but it is not true of the great mass of the German people. On the best materials available the more rational view is, not that the German nation as a whole consists of seventy million devils incarnate, but that they, like most other nations, consist in the main of men and women whose chief concern in life is to earn their own living and decently maintain their families. They have been brought up to unquestioning obedience and have been deprived by electioneering devices of the power of governing themselves, as we understand self-government. It is true that they have ordinarily been very tame in their submission to their masters and very blameworthy in allowing their affairs to be managed for them by the unscrupulous men and under the skilfully organized system which has led them to ruin. Those men indeed deserve punishment, all the more that they have endeavoured to corrupt the masses under their control by systematic appeals to national vanity and greed and selfishness in every shape. Those are the men who ordered the inhuman treatment of women and children, who tortured prisoners and fired on their own troops from the rear. It would be a sorry business to judge by that type of " military aristocrat " the soldier who obeyed orders on pain of instant death, however we may be convinced that our own men would have faced death rather than do what the Germans were ordered to do. A short and summary sketch of the way in which the German Government became able to inflict upon the world the tragedy of 1914, and to use its population in that task until flesh and blood would stand it no longer, will enable us to estimate what kind of people we have to deal with in the future. We have seen a great and powerful and industrious nation persuaded or compelled to devote its whole energies and strength for nearly five years to the most devilish work of all time, to the destruction of other nations and of the accumulated treasures bequeathed by former generations, with a thoroughness and ferocity hitherto unknown in history. There never has been a change of national character so rapid and complete as that from the old kindliness and sentimentalism and idealism of Germany fifty years ago to what we have seen in these later days. Perhaps one ought rather say, to that which alone we have been allowed to see in these later days. It is worth while to search for the causes of this astonishing metamorphosis, and that is what is here attempted.

Throughout modern history Germany has been governed on patriarchal lines by a number of hereditary Rulers who mostly managed their principalities, large and small, as if they were patrimonial estates. Notably the Prussian dominions were governed in this way by the Hohenzollerns. Promises of self-government were made by these autocrats in times of difficulty and evaded when the danger was over, and though they made war upon their neighbours occasionally, with little regard to justice, and also upon one another, yet the safety of Europe was not in real danger from German ambitions so long as that country was disunited. On the other hand, the same disunion which made them feeble for attack made them also feeble for self-defence. They lay between France on the West and Russia on the East. It would be a falsification of history to deny that for many years, under the Bourbons, France repeatedly attacked one or other of the German States without adequate justification, and French monarchical ambition was a source of danger to them under both Louis XIV and Louis XV. Then Prussia and Austria most unwarrantably invaded France when the Bourbons had been dethroned by the Revolution of 1789. After, and indeed because of that, the Napoleonic tyranny succeeded to power. The tables were turned, and for twenty years almost every State in Germany was compelled to submit to the French yoke and underwent immense slaughter. Russia as well as Great Britain supported Germany in that long Napoleonic war, but Russia had in former years been herself a constant danger to Germany on her eastern frontier. When Napoleon was defeated and dethroned after Waterloo, the German people reverted to their old servitude under their old Kings and Princes. They obtained some little measure of self-government then and in subsequent years, and from time to time made efforts to obtain freedom. But what hindered their efforts more than anything else was the fact that geographically they were situated between France and Russia, from both of whom they had suffered in the past. German patriotism from 1815 onwards was deeply interested in procuring the unification of their country under some central government which should enable them to defend themselves both on the East and on the West.

So far as the people were concerned, they wished for unity in order to get security. Princes were unwilling to secure unity by a surrender of any part of the authority which they had inherited in their several dominions. A wiser and more resolute people would have succeeded in spite of the Princes, but the Germans were not politically wise or resolute. They were docile and unenterprising. They had been in mediæval fetters for generations. The Prussian Government ably and skilfully administered their country from the point of view of material progress but was military in its spirit, and the population allowed themselves to forget the proverbial dangers of autocratic control in the prosperity and security which it enabled them to enjoy. That was a terrible fault, for which they have been terribly punished, but a fault different in kind from the guilt of their military masters, who deliberately designed war in order to subjugate other nations.

* * *

In 1848 began a series of events which were destined to produce many though not sufficient changes. In that stupendous Revolutionary year an immense effort was made by many of the peoples of Europe to secure for themselves some measure of freedom in place of the mediæval conditions which had been riveted on them after the overthrow of Napoleon Bonaparte. Paris gave the signal of Revolution in 1848 by expelling Louis Philippe and setting up a Republic. Spain, Austria, Hungary, Holland, Rome, and other Italian cities, even Switzerland, had their insurrections, some of which, unorganized and ill directed though they were, seemed at one time to be on the road

to success. If they had succeeded, most of the wars
which have made Europe miserable in the last seventy
years, would have been avoided. They failed, and then
feudalism regained the upper hand. Nowhere was
this movement of revolution more formidable than in
Germany, and particularly in Berlin. The King of
Prussia was threatened in his palace, his troops withdrawn from the city under popular pressure after a
collision with the mob, and the Crown Prince, who
afterwards become Kaiser Wilhelm I, was in 1848
obliged to fly for refuge in England. It seemed as if
the Hohenzollern dynasty might be expelled, and in
any case that self-government would have been established seventy years ago in place of autocracy in
Germany.

* * *

At that moment a really great man of action,
Bismarck, began to make himself felt in Prussia.
Whatever else he may have been, he was a man.
The whole system of Parliamentary Government was
odious to him. He laid his hopes for the future of his
country in a strong Monarchy and a strong Army, with
a subordinate and skilfully gerrymandered Assembly
to criticize and recommend but not to control executive
action either at home or abroad. Bismarck saw that
Germany, with its scores of sovereign Princes, united
in a tedious and impotent Diet at Frankfort under the
Presidency of Austria, could not be an effective fighting
force, or even an effective force for legitimate self-
defence. He wanted union in Germany, but that
Prussia and not Austria should be the supreme power.
He felt bitterly the wrongs that France had inflicted
on his country in past times, and was resolved to make

Germany strong enough to defy that danger in future.
In this last wish all Germany agreed with him. The
Union of Germany, the exclusion from it of Austria,
the defeat of France — these were his chief aims.
The Army was to be his instrument, and the King to
be his tool. For that and other reasons he wished
to keep all executive power in the King's hands, independent of Parliament. Before Bismarck reached
power by becoming a Minister in 1862, Napoleon III
had seated himself on the throne of France by per-
fidious violence, and the restlessness of that feeble
usurper made it all the more easy for Prussia to justify
autocracy and strong armaments. France under the
Second Empire was a standing menace, by no fault
of her own, to all Europe.

* * *

Bismarck's career is well known. From 1848 to
1862 he had been the centre of a constant resistance
offered by the agrarian and military parties in Prussia
to the popular demand for Parliamentary Government.
When in 1862 he became Chief Minister the state of
the Monarchy in Prussia seemed desperate. A vast
majority demanded military reforms which would
have diminished the Army, and obstinately refused
supplies. The King, who would under no circumstances
allow interference with the Army or admit of Parliamentary control, had written out his abdication and
meant to proclaim it. Then Bismarck undertook to
govern without or even against Prussia's Parliament.
He faced the Lower House and defied them, denying
them any control of policy and claiming the right to
levy taxes without their consent on the scale which

had prevailed in the former year. He ran the risk of losing his head, relying upon the support of the King and the devotion of the Army to their Sovereign. How long this dangerous dictatorship would have lasted without civil war may be doubted. Serious foreign complications, to a large extent of Bismarck's own creation, first modified and in the end extinguished the internal difficulties of Prussia. Three victorious wars between 1862 and 1871 restored domestic harmony and at the same time raised Prussia to a height of power which her most zealous patriots hardly thought she could ever attain. It is an old device to divert attention from domestic grievances by fomenting foreign wars. Very likely that was one of Bismarck's reasons for embroiling his country in war. It was not his only reason. He aimed at making Prussia dominant in Germany and a really great Power.

＊　　＊　　＊

Under his management in 1864 Prussia, with Austria, whom Bismarck had induced to co-operate with him, declared war against Denmark. It is true that Denmark had put herself in the wrong. She had incorporated in her Kingdom two Provinces, Schleswig and Holstein, of which the King was the Sovereign Prince, but not Sovereign in his capacity as King of Denmark. And Holstein had been for long a German principality, represented as such at the Germanic Diet. All kinds of disputes arose as to the true title to these Provinces. Certainly neither Prussia nor Austria could claim to be the legitimate sovereigns. But Bismarck, as he quite frankly admits, intended from the first to obtain both these Provinces for

Prussia, and he eventually did so by the war of 1864. He coolly told the King of Prussia that his predecessors had added Provinces to the Kingdom, and that he ought to follow their example. Two years later in 1866 a war broke out between Prussia and Austria relating to the division of the provinces which they had conquered, Schleswig and Holstein. Austria must certainly share the blame of this war. She entertained the most complete confidence in victory. But in about two months her forces and those of her South German allies—Saxony, Bavaria, Würtemberg, and other States—were signally defeated. As a result of this triumph, Austria ceased to be the first State in Germany, and ceased even to be within the sphere of German States. For the Diet was dissolved and a North German Confederation formed with Prussia at its head, while the other German States were practically constrained to make military conventions with Prussia, subordinating themselves to her authority. Prussia also obtained Schleswig and Holstein and considerable other territories in Germany which she annexed on the ground that they had fought against her in the war.

* * *

Nothing remained except to settle accounts with France. These immense accessions to German territory aroused the jealousy of Napoleon III. After that usurper had in vain attempted to get " compensation " in Belgium or on the Rhine, and finally in Luxemburg, in order to support his tottering throne, an occasion of quarrel arose between France and Prussia in 1870, in regard to the threatened elevation of a Hohenzollern Prince to the throne of Spain. This quarrel would have been settled, and was in everyone's opinion in fact settled, by the withdrawal of the Hohenzollern candidate, largely at the instance of the King of Prussia. Unfortunately the recklessness of the French Government and the pretensions of the Parisian Press led to a further demand by France for guarantees by Prussia against a renewal of any such candidature, and the tone of the French Foreign Minister became inexcusably arrogant. Some authorities erroneously maintain that Bismarck had not originally intended to provoke France on this occasion. In any case he seized the opportunity. He had hated France all his life, and expected an attack some day from Napoleon III. He deeply resented the tone of the Press and the Foreign Office in France, and resolved to bring the quarrel to a head. His ingenious perversion of the famous Ems telegram roused France to fury, as indeed Bismarck intended, and made peace impossible. When that war was over, Napoleon III had been dethroned, the whole of Germany excepting Austria had been united in one Empire and had become by far the most powerful State on the Continent of Europe. One capital blunder marred the triumph, because it left behind the seeds of future war. The military advisers of the Prussian King, seconded by unreflecting patriotism, insisted upon the annexation of Alsace-Lorraine. Bismarck disapproved, at all events of so large a spoliation. The soldiers insisted, and this marked a signal advance in the control of Prussian policy by military men. Seldom in history have results so great and apparently so permanent been obtained in so short a· time. Seven or eight years sufficed to obliterate a most formidable con-

17

stitutional crisis, to unify Germany (a task which had
baffled many generations), to obtain the unquestioned
supremacy of Prussia in that long distracted country,
to gain great extensions of territory, and to destroy
the power of France. These results had been obtained,
to use Bismarck's phrase, by blood and iron. They
tended to foster an arrogant military spirit in a nation
which had known in the past more humiliations than
victories. And his victories were due to the Army.
That made the Army popular and greatly increased
the authority of its Chiefs.

*   *   *

In Bismarck's opinion there were two solid institutions in his country on which all others rested—the
Crown and the Army. He had relied on them and
owed his successes to that reliance. His legacy to
the succeeding generation was that they too should
rely, not on self-government, but on a strong Monarchy
and a strong Army. But that was not the only warning
he bequeathed. He declared in his old age that it
had always been his ideal after establishing German
unity " to win the confidence not only of the smaller
" European States but also of the Great Powers, and
" to convince them that German policy will be just
" and peaceful now that it has repaired the *injuria*
" *temporum*, the disintegration of the nation." He
foresaw the danger of military leaders dictating policy
instead of confining themselves to their professional
sphere. Indeed, he had himself suffered from their
interference even in 1866 and in 1870, when his power
was at its height, and often complained of the mischief
it caused. Moltke's love of combat and delight in
battles and " keen desire to put in practice his military

" and strategic tastes and ability " were noted and
deplored by Bismarck. They had caused him incon-
venience. " Even victorious wars," he says, " cannot
" be justified unless they are forced on one, and one
" cannot foresee the cards of Providence far enough
" ahead to anticipate historical developments according
" to one's own calculation. It is natural that in the
" staff of the Army not only younger active officers
" but likewise experienced strategists should feel the
" need of turning to account the efficiency of the
" troops led by them and their own capacity to lead
" and of making them prominent in history. It
" would be a matter of regret if this effect of the
" military spirit did not exist in the Army.   The
" task of keeping its results within such limits as the
" nation's need of peace can justly claim is the duty of
" the political, not the military, heads of the State.
" That at the time of the Luxemburg question during
" the crisis of 1875 invented [so said Bismarck] by
" Gortchakoff and France, and even down to the most
" recent times the Staff and its leaders have allowed
" themselves to be led astray and to endanger peace
" lies in the very spirit of the institution which I would
" not forgo.   It becomes dangerous only under a
" Monarch whose policy lacks sense of proportion and
" power to resist one-sided and constitutionally
" unjustifiable influences." So said Bismarck in his
old age, and though his own practice had not always
conformed to these principles there can be no doubt
that the principles themselves are sound, so far as
they restrict the interference of soldiers in policy.

* * *

It is impossible to put more clearly the dangers of

military ascendancy in Germany, and no one knew
the ground better than Bismarck. One Power alone,
namely the Sovereign, could prevent the Army Leaders
from enforcing a regime of pure violence. If the
Sovereign lost his head or proved feeble enough
to let the soldiers direct foreign affairs or decide on
war, then Europe could not rely on a durable peace.
Bismarck was no saint, and it was his own policy that
had mainly helped to make the Prussian Monarchy
triumph over democratic forces in Germany and to
exalt military influences. But when he had unified
Germany, and removed, as he thought, the danger
from France, he wished for European peace and saw
what threatened it. A volatile and versatile Sovereign
under pressure from military zealots and surrounded
by Ministers of his own choice, who were clerks rather
than independent statesmen, fulfilled exactly the
conditions which the great Founder of the German
Empire had apprehended. So long as those conditions
lasted there was danger. They were not, however,
necessarily permanent conditions, and there was always
the chance or even the probability that the Kaiser
would be in favour of peace.

In 1888 Kaiser Wilhelm the Second succeeded to
the throne, at the age of twenty-nine, after a strict
military education and with an enormously exaggerated
sense of his own ability and importance. Bismarck
was still at the head of affairs, old and self-willed but
with vast experience and unrivalled skill in the conduct
of diplomacy. He had enemies, notably among the
Army Leaders. The new Kaiser had flatterers, also
in the Army as elsewhere. " I will give the old man
" six months as a breathing space and then I will

"rule myself," the Kaiser is reported to have said. In March 1890 he summarily demanded the old Chancellor's resignation, and selected in his place a series of inconsiderable men, no one of whom showed independence.

* * *

Mr. Hammer in an able volume entitled *William the Second* has traced the record of the Kaiser's reign. Industrious and devoted to the aggrandizement of Germany he certainly was. Wise he never has been, though for a long time he desired to avoid war. His first step in foreign policy was a grave blunder. Bismarck knew and recognized the danger in which Germany stood from the possibility of an alliance between France and Russia. It had been his nightmare. And though he executed various Treaties with Austria-Hungary and aimed at a close intimacy with that Power, he always contrived also to keep on good terms with Russia by means of Treaties and understandings. When he resigned in 1890, his agreement with Russia, which secured the neutrality of the latter, required renewal. The new Kaiser did not renew it or provide any substitute. Bismarck prophesied that this would lead to an alliance between Russia and France. In 1896 it did lead to that result. But by far the most important feature in the Kaiser's new system was his ceaseless exaltation of the Army at the expense of the Civil Power. It was the danger which Bismarck had foreseen. No really powerful figure in civil life appeared to exercise that control of military ambitions which Bismarck had pronounced to be necessary. The Kaiser devoted himself to the

perfection of his formidable instrument and to the
organization of Germany as a military machine. At
times he spoke of that machine as the only element
in the State that he could fully trust. He spared no
pains to organize industries as well, but always with
an eye to their military usefulness. Presently he
established also a very powerful Navy. It is probable
that the Kaiser intended to retain these instruments
in his own control, and thought he could control them.
It had always been the tradition of the Prussian Army
to support and obey their Sovereign, and, though in
the hour of victory, as in 1871, the strategical claims of
the Army unhappily had weight, military men had not
theretofore dictated policy. That was for the Sovereign
and his Ministers, if he chose to regard them. But
the Kaiser Wilhelm II became in effect his own
Minister in 1890, and it was impossible that he should
so constantly and emphatically associate himself with
the Army and treat it as by far the most important
element in the State without coming under the powerful Prussian military influences which were always
favourable to aggressive and violent courses. He
had misgivings and did for long endeavour to resist
a bellicose policy; but just as water will wear out
stone, so the continuous pressure of the Army Chiefs
wore down the resistance of a Sovereign who was by
no means adamantine. Nothing can be less true
than that the Kaiser followed Bismarck's policy.
Bismarck would never have submitted to military
dictation. The Kaiser did.

It would be an injustice to say that the Kaiser
throughout designed the embroilment of Europe in
war. He continually disclaimed that purpose, and

was often the means of preserving peace. But he was a fanatic, possessed with the belief that his Kingship was an ordinance of God and himself almost inspired. And above all he lacked the firmness and sagacity which alone could keep the military elements within their proper sphere. It was due very largely to him that the military caste in Germany grew more and more formidable till it became a power by itself strong enough to overbear all opposition.

*　　*　　*

The Kaiser has never been able to hold his tongue. His numerous utterances from the very commencement of his reign would form a curious volume. A few specimens may illustrate his singular frame of mind and the attitude he adopted toward Europe as the man chosen of God, with a sword in one hand and an olive branch in the other. Ten million men in arms, or capable of bearing arms, made it necessary to take him seriously. How seriously and how strangely he took himself his own language enables us to discern with an accuracy unattainable in the case of most Sovereigns.

In 1888, a few months after his accession, he said :
" I am well aware that the public at large, particularly
" in foreign countries, credit me with ambitions and
" warlike thoughts. May God keep me from such
" criminal folly."

" We would rather see our eighteen Army Corps
" and our whole population of forty-two million perish
" on the field of battle than give up a single stone of
" what my grandfather and Prince Frederic Charles
" have won in fight " (1888).

" We (Hohenzollerns) regard ourselves as chosen by
" God to govern and guide the people over whom we
" are appointed to rule " (1890).

Addressing the Generals, the Kaiser said that the
Social Democrats were a gang of men not worthy to
bear the name of Germans, and if the nation did
not repudiate them " you (the Generals) must arm
" yourselves against the traitorous crew and lead a
" campaign which shall rid us of such creatures "
(1895).

" My aim is above all the maintenance of peace "
(1891).

Addressing Naval Recruits, the Kaiser said in 1895 :
" The gracious God and I have heard your vow. . . .
" Just as I, your Emperor and Ruler, devote all my
" actions and aspirations to the Fatherland, so are
" you also obliged to devote the whole of your lives
" to me " (1895).

This old Emperor (Wilhelm I), said the Kaiser,
had " raised for us Princes an altar which it is our
" duty to keep holy, the altar of Monarchy by Divine
" Right, monarchy with its heavy duties, its incessant
" abiding labour and pains, its awful responsibility
" to the Creator alone, a responsibility from which
" no human being, no Minister, no representative
" assembly, no nation is able to deliver the Prince "
(1897).

When Germany sent a naval expedition to China
in 1897 under Prince Henry, the Kaiser thus publicly
addressed the Prince : " Should anyone attempt
" to affront us or to infringe our lawful rights, then
" do you strike out with your mailed fist." In
answer to which the Prince promised " to proclaim

" the Gospel of your Majesty's exalted person "
(1897).

Next year, on a visit to Sultan Abdul Hamid's
dominions (the man who ordered the Bulgarian and
Armenian massacres), the Kaiser declared that the
Sultan and the three hundred millions of Moham-
medans throughout the world who honour him as
their spiritual chief may rest assured that at all times
the German Emperor will be their friend (1898).

The well-known Kruger telegram intimating that
Germany would have been ready to help the Boers
on the occasion of the Jameson Raid, though extremely
offensive, was the work of the German Government,
and it is now believed that the Kaiser personally
did not like sending it. Yet he did send it.

In 1900 a German expedition was sent out to China
to help in suppressing the Boxer Riots. The Kaiser,
infuriated by the news that the German Ambassador
had been murdered in Pekin, addressed the troops
as follows : " When you come in contact with the
" enemy strike him down. Quarter is not to be
" given. Prisoners are not to be made. Whoever
" falls into your hands will be at your mercy. Just
" as a thousand years ago the Huns, under the leader-
" ship of Attila, gained a reputation by which they
" still live in historical tradition, so may the German
" name be known in such a fashion in China that no
" Chinaman will ever again dare to look askance at
" a German. The blessing of the Lord be upon you "
(1900).

A few more sentences, taken at random from the
Kaiser's numerous allocutions, may illustrate his
peculiar views. " We (Germans) are the salt of the

" earth." " There is but one law, and that is my
" will." " Nothing must henceforth be settled in
" the world without the intervention of Germany and
" the German Kaiser." " I shall not rest until I
" have brought my fleet to the same standard as my
" Army." " The trident ought to be in our fist."
And, addressing the Army in 1914, he said : " You are
" the chosen people. The spirit of the Lord has de-
" scended on me because I am the German Kaiser.
" I am the instrument of the Most High."

In 1908 was published in the *Daily Telegraph* the
famous interview of the Kaiser with an interviewer,
in which he proclaimed his friendliness to England and
said with truth that he had refused to allow the Boer
delegates to enter Germany during the Boer War,
but that the German people did not share in that
friendliness. The indiscretion of this publication,
coming on the top of his numerous preceding irresponsible utterances, caused immense indignation in
Germany, and the German Chancellor was obliged to
promise in the Reichstag that the Kaiser would in
future be more guarded in his speeches. There can
be no doubt that the constitutional movement in
Germany was much strengthened by this incident
in 1908, but the Chancellor who gave the promise
was soon afterwards removed from office.

The glory of the Hohenzollerns, support of the Army,
and the special alliance existing between God and both
of them are almost the only things on which this
singular being was always consistent. No wonder
that his sanity was at times suspected.

His constant professions of a love for peace have
been stigmatized as pure hypocrisy. It may be so.

In an emotional impulsive nature possessed by fixed ideas as to his mission on earth and a confidence in himself which nearly overstepped the limits of reason, it is not always easy to say whether a man is sincere or not. But, without attempting to enter upon the record of all this man actually did, which is the true touchstone, it is noteworthy that M. Jules Cambon, French Ambassador in Berlin, a man of rare penetration with unsurpassed opportunities of forming a sound judgment, thought in November 1913 that the Kaiser had exerted " on many critical occasions " his personal influence in favour of peace." [1] On the same occasion, however, M. Cambon warns his Government that " the Kaiser is becoming used to an " order of ideas which were formerly repugnant to " him, and that, to borrow from him a phrase which " he likes to use, we must keep our powder dry."

* * *

On the whole this man seems for many years to have thought he could keep the military party in control. Possibly he tried to make them run straight also, which was a difficult task in a country permeated by the traditions of Frederic the Great. He failed, largely from weakness of character. Many crimes are due to that failing, and the Kaiser's crimes among them. Possibly also he was insane. Possibly from a suspicion of that kind, his Ministers kept back from him a good deal that happened, as he has himself stated.

This appears to be, upon the best available information, the sound view. The Kaiser was expressing his

[1] French Yellow Book, No. 6.

own real opinion when he spoke in favour of peace, and he acted upon it on many critical occasions. But he had exalted the Army and stimulated what is called Imperialism not only by language which could not fail to intensify an unwholesome national vanity but also by encouraging aggressive organizations like the Navy League, and accustoming the public to shows and reviews and the celebration of anniversaries, almost every one· of which was associated with the idea of war and conquest. In this way his own spirit tended to inflame fanaticism in others who did not see, as he sometimes saw, the value of peace. A powerful party in the Army and out of it, supported by the teaching class, which took its inspiration and derived its emoluments from the same source, grew up to alarming proportions, ready to draw the sword at a moment's notice, and penetrated with the idea that greatness consists in exercising dominion, and that brute force is the proper ruling power in this world. When the hour of trial came in the summer of 1914 the· Kaiser, upon whose decision everything still rested, had been weakened in his love of peace by the demon he himself had called into being. He still made some tardy efforts, as the narrative already given shows, to prevent war, but they were half-hearted at the beginning because he thought his Army invincible. When he realized the terrible danger, he made more efforts, which might have succeeded. A strong man would have suspended a declaration of war, though it would have exposed him to a groundless charge of cowardice from the fire-eating caste which dominated him. But he was not a strong man, and he could not resist the Army Leaders who had fastened

their will upon him. Statements have been publicly
made which, from the very nature of them, do not
admit of complete authentication, but are nevertheless
very probably true. It is said that General Moltke,
Chief of the German General Staff, returned home
from the Council Room on the critical day in 1914
worn out by the efforts he had made in order to
get the Kaiser's assent to the step which brought
on the war, and even that, when the Kaiser signed
the ultimatum to Russia he said, addressing the
Generals, that it was they who ought to have signed
it, not himself, and he hoped they would not live
to repent of it.

* * *

We have the means of forming some opinion of
the disposition prevalent in Germany among the
military chiefs and also among sections of the
governing classes from two books published shortly
before the war. One of them was written by
General Bernhardi and the other by Prince von
Buelow.

General Bernhardi has often been cited in this
country. He is a German officer of no particular
distinction, and it is said that his utterances did not
receive much attention in his own country. Certainly
he is in no sense a representative of the ordinary public.
But what he says is characteristic of a military school
which was undoubtedly very powerful there, and
merely gives cynical expression to doctrines which
many people now tell us were widely held in Germany.
He says that the German people are pacific because
they are good natured and do not desire to be disturbed
in their commercial pursuits, and then proceeds in his

book to disabuse them of this supposed folly. The
desire for peace, he thinks, has made most nations
anæmic. War is a biological necessity of the first
importance. The law of struggle prevails in the
world, and for this maxim he appeals to the Darwinian
theory as he understands it. A growing people like
the Germans must obtain territory by war, which is
a moral necessity. "An intellectual and vigorous
" nature can experience no worse destiny than to be
" lulled into a Phæacian existence by the undisputed
" enjoyment of peace." The General seems to be
conscious that these opinions somewhat violently
conflict with what has usually been understood to
be the teaching of Christianity.   Accordingly we are
told by the General that " Christian morality is personal
" and social and in its nature cannot be political."
" Arbitration Treaties," proceeds the General, "must
" be peculiarly detrimental to an aspiring people
" which has not yet reached its political and national
" zenith and is bent on expanding its power in order
" to play its part honourably in the civilized world."
The corollaries of this neo-Christian creed are obvious
and unequivocally asserted. The cessation of war
would check real progress, thinks the General. The
highest moral duty of a State is to increase its power.
Cunning and deception are justifiable between States
when in a state of latent war. So says Bernhardi.
And then come the practical applications. It is the
duty of Germany to check the onrush of Slavism.
Germany will need colonies under her own flag. It
was, he says, chiefly Germany's own fault that she
did not assert herself till too late when the partition
of the globe was long concluded, and now what they

want must be fought for. France is always bent upon
revenge for her loss of Alsace-Lorraine. Russia aims
at supremacy in the Balkans and a free entrance
into the Mediterranean. Panslavism is hard at work.
It was an unpardonable error for England not to
support the southern States of America in their seces-
sion fifty or sixty years ago. The Dominions will
sever their connection with England. A pacific
agreement between England and Germany is out of
the question. England will not agree to Germany
enlarging her Colonial power and having free opportunity for commercial and industrial competition.
Germany must square accounts with France and
support Italy and Turkey and make the small Powers
feel that she is their strongest protector. She must
get colonies, and he asks whether the subsisting
Treaties about the neutrality of Belgium and the
Congo are to be regarded as still operative. Finally,
no people, in General Bernhardi's opinion, is so little
qualified as the German to direct their own destinies.
And so, we must infer, they are to be directed by
their rulers to a destiny in which they will have a
chance of gaining the whole world with a certainty
of losing their own soul and a very good prospect
for many of them of losing their lives also.

This book is here cited, not because it is an official
work, which it is not, but because it shows the spirit
which underlay militarism in Prussia and was put into
action as soon as the soldiers had overborne the feeble
resisting power of the Kaiser. It seems to be scarcely
possible to believe that so wicked and absurd a theory
of life could be entertained by a great nation generally,
however it might commend itself to sections of the

community, but undoubtedly the Professors in many
cases taught this spirit.

* * *

The other book to which attention must be called
is of a different order. It is Prince von Buelow's
Imperial Germany. This gentleman must be considered very seriously. He was German Foreign
Secretary from 1897 to 1899, and then German Chancellor from 1899 to 1909. It was he who advised or
acquiesced in the foreign policy of Germany during
those critical years in which the cautious and conservative attitude of Prince Bismarck's later career was
changed into a feverish restlessness which alarmed
all Europe. It is not without significance that in
1909 Prince von Buelow was deprived of office and
replaced by Dr. Bethmann-Hollweg, who, according to
every reliable account, did try to establish friendly
relations with Great Britain, and, as we have seen,
did try too late to avert this war. Quite likely Bethmann-Hollweg might have accomplished both these
objects if he had been allowed a free hand. However,
it is with Prince von Buelow and his book that we are
now concerned. If he is telling the truth we here
get at the secret springs of action in official Berlin
during a vital period of ten years. What he says is
illuminating.

The Prince, after the interregnum of a few nonen-
tities, succeeded Bismarck in the direction of foreign
affairs. He was not himself a very great force. He
thought that the unification of Germany, which
Bismarck had accomplished, was only the beginning of
a new era. The German population had increased
from forty-one millions in 1871 to a vastly greater

figure. (In 1916 it was sixty-eight millions or there-
about.) Emigration, which had been very high, had
dwindled to quite small numbers. There was much
more employment. The foreign trade of Germany
had become the second in the world and was rapidly
approaching that of Great Britain. For that reason
a Navy, he thought, became necessary, and in 1897
the first great German Navy Bill was passed with its
rather ominous preamble. The Prince prides himself
on the skill with which from 1897 onwards he contrived to build the German Fleet without quarrelling
with England. For he thinks that the true source
of British hostility was the great development of
German industry, and apparently does not doubt
that we should have liked an excuse for destroying
the German Fleet in embryo. He refused to join
France in hostile measures against England during
the Boer War, because in his opinion the French would
never really forget their humiliation in 1871 and would
leave Germany in the lurch, face to face with the
British Fleet. He quotes Mr. Lee, M.P., and the
Daily Chronicle, which was then the organ of " Liberal
Imperialism," in attempting to show that we had
contemplated stifling the German Fleet *in ovo,* and that
we regretted not having done so. Germany wanted
to reach out into the wide world, as " a transition
to world politics," and King Edward VII, according
to the Prince, tried to encircle Germany by a series
of ententes with Spain, France, Italy, and even
Austria. Of this he does not give proofs, and in another passage he says that Germany has been en-
circled for a thousand years by her geographical
position between Latins and Slavs, which latter

18

statement is geographically true. He is proud of the
intervention of Germany " in shining armour," to
support the Austrian annexation of Bosnia-Herze-
govina in 1908, and thinks that incident put an end
to King Edward's encircling policy. Germany wished,
he says, for an organized and independent Turkey,
and wished also for friendship with England, but
the Prince feared that an alliance with England would
have this danger that it might lead to Germany
having to fight against Russia. Commerce Colonies
and a powerful Fleet to protect them are the objects
set out by the Prince, and he does not in the least
conceal his desire for German influence being extended
in " world politics," or his belief that Great Britain
was very jealous of German prosperity and very ready
to use means, however unscrupulous, in order to arrest
it. But he shares Bernhardi's opinion of the in-
capacity of Germans to manage their own affairs,
being a good Imperialist, and quotes with gusto one
of the German Ministers who, after saying to him that
Germans were the most learned of nations and the
best soldiers, that they had done much in science and
art, were the greatest philosophers and poets and
musicians, and the greatest in industrial developments,
proceeded with the remark : " How can you wonder
" that we are political asses ? there must be a weak
" point somewhere."   It never seems to have occurred
to Prince Buelow that if his countrymen were half as
gifted as he represents, and gifted they undoubtedly
are, they might possibly have discovered, had they
been admitted to a control of their own political
affairs, some wiser course than that of creating irritation all the world over, when they were so conspicu-

ously prosperous. Germany has incurred the hatred of nearly every nation. There must be something very wrong somewhere. We maintain in England that the something wrong was the fact that German policy was directed by an impulsive almost fanatical Sovereign on the dictation of an aristocratic military caste.

* * *

From other sources we know that from early days in the reign of Kaiser Wilhelm II protests were made in Germany, increasing in weight and volume as years went by, against the irresponsibility of the Kaiser and the Ministers he appointed of his own will, and against the language he used in regard to foreign affairs. Equally strong resentment was felt against the overbearing attitude which German officers under his patronage adopted toward the civil population. These protests received immense sympathy in Germany, especially in 1905 and 1908, notwithstanding the ubiquitous and carefully organized bureaucratic system which prevailed everywhere. At the time of the Zabern incident, very shortly before the war, this feeling was intense. How powerful this undercurrent was may best be tested in the votes recorded for Social Democratic candidates at elections for the Reichstag. Social Democrats were frowned upon and denounced by the Kaiser and by the " re- spectable " section of the community, and therefore were not very likely to attract support from the influential classes. But they were all in favour of peace and against militarism. The number of Social Democratic votes increased from 1,400,000 in 1890 to 2,108,000 in 1898, and to 4,400,000 in 1912. Indeed,

the fear of Democratization in Germany is stated in
the French Yellow Book, No. 5, to be one of the causes
which inclined their upper classes toward a policy of
war. It is quite true that the Prussian, and in a
lesser degree the German, people have been sedulously
trained in obedience to military traditions, and to
unquestioning confidence in their bureaucratic Government. Their schools and universities methodically
set out to create that type of character. If it had
not been for this training a system of Government
so meddlesome and a policy so full of danger not only
to freedom but also to peace could not have been
endured so long by an educated people. They were
prospering beyond all expectation. Why should we
be so certain that the people at large wished to embark on war which must put all their future in danger.
·What had they to gain by it ?

* * *

The danger lay in the spirit which pervaded the
Military classes. President Wilson said truly of the
latter that " these men never regarded nations as
" peoples of men, women, and children of like blood
" and frame as themselves for whom Governments
" existed and in whom Governments had their life.
" They regarded them merely as serviceable organiza-
" tions which they could either by force or intrigue
" bend or corrupt to their own purpose." It would
be a mistake to take for granted that nearly 70,000,000
of men and women in Germany would permanently
endure a system of military control such as that which
President Wilson describes. Mr. Bonar Law was very
likely accurate when he said that if war could have
been avoided for ten or fifteen years it might have

been avoided altogether. A little time was the thing
wanted.

Bismarck, in deprecating what is called " preventive war," said that we cannot see in advance
" the cards of Providence." He meant the same thing
that Wellington expressed in observing that if war
must come sooner or later, " let it come later." Very
likely it would not come at all. That is what those
two great men meant. There are many chances in
human affairs ; many expectations which seem at the
moment certain of fulfilment are in the end utterly
disconcerted. We have an illustration before our
eyes. In the third year of this war a Revolution
broke out in Russia. The new Russian Government
at once disclaimed all ideas of conquest and proclaimed
its love of peace even in the midst of war, and the
later excesses of Bolshevism do not alter the significance
of this fact. It has been known for many years that
Russia was full of combustible materials. There have
been several unsuccessful attempts there at Revolution of late years. The Government of the Czars
lived on the brink of a volcano under an autocracy
tempered by assassination, sustained by a secret
police more unprincipled and wicked than would be
believed. Suppose that this war had been averted
for the moment, and that a Revolution had then
supervened in Russia, as was indeed very likely in
quite a short time, there would have been an end of
Servian nationalist agitation directed against Austria.
At all events it could not have led to a European
war. There would also have been an end of France's
duty to support her Russian ally against Germany.
The Balkans could not then have led to a European

war. We could have come to terms with Germany
as regards Asia Minor : in fact, we did come to terms
with her on that subject in 1913 under a hitherto
unpublished agreement initialed both by the Russians
and ourselves, it is said. The whole train of causes
which brought about the tragedy of August 1914
would have been dissolved by a Russian Revolution,
and would have ceased to be sources of danger for the
future so far as the general peace of Europe was
concerned. Nor could the Alsace-Lorraine difficulty
have produced trouble. No one will pretend that
France would have been aggressive when deprived of
Russian support, considering that she was devoted to
peace even when she had that support. Had the
Russian Revolution come, war would not have come.

*   *   *

We are here dealing with the " cards of Providence,"
the contingencies which were obscure. A Revolution
in Russia might have come, the democratization of
Germany might have come, or, at all events, a per-
ception of the immense danger involved in a continuance of Imperialist policy.

Again, the Emperor of Austria was nearly ninety
years old when the war broke out. If that crisis had
been overcome he would have been succeeded very
soon by the man who did succeed him very soon after,
and who from the first did his utmost to procure peace.
Without the certainty of Austrian co-operation even
the military madmen who forced on the war would
not have succeeded, probably they would not have
wished, to bring Germany single-handed into a conflict with France and Russia. Quite likely there
were other arrows in the quiver of Fate, unknown to

and unseen by us. War might have come later, or it might not. Among the gifts in Pandora's box there might even have been the replacement by more capable men of the Ministers, who in fact guided all nations into the horror. We might have seen wiser Ministers in the various countries concerned who would have guided the world towards peace. We might have had next time, if this crisis had been tided over, some Minister in Germany who would not consent to give Austria a free hand or bow the knee to the General Staff, someone in Russia who would have allowed another forty-eight hours before mobilizing, someone in France like Jaurès who would have told Russia roundly that France would not help her if she mobilized prematurely. Any one of these contingencies would have made all the difference next time if only there could have been a next time, with plain language and competent men, instead of some hundreds of hesitating telegrams followed by a blind furious rush into " an Abyss so deep " and vast that Echo's self will not make answer " there."

We can only conjecture what might have happened if this war had been averted. But we know what in fact did happen. In reality this war was precipitated by the absorbing ambitions of the Army Leaders in Germany which had been encouraged by the Kaiser, and by his want of character and courage to resist their importunity, not by the deliberate wish or with the approval of the German people themselves, as President Wilson said. The real remedy before 1914 was the overthrow of the autocracy. That has been now effected, but at the cost of many millions of human lives and of suffering among men, women, and children, almost all over the world, which cannot ever be forgotten and must darken the lives of generations to come. That autocracy was to blame for the war. Whatever judgment may be passed on the ambitions of Servia, or on the blind obstinacy of Austria, or the premature mobilization of Russia in a difficult position, or on the errors of judgment on the part of any other Government, nothing can obscure the fact that at any moment till the actual fighting commenced, the men in power at Berlin could without risk either of damage or dishonour have prevented a single drop of blood being spilt, and that they designedly preferred war. Every other nation would have welcomed peace at the end. We must not lighten the burden of guilt on these men by distributing it over seventy millions of subject peoples. There is much reason for believing that the German people themselves would before long have insisted upon obtaining self-government, and even for believing that the apprehension of thus losing their power was the decisive consideration which led the military authorities to determine upon war in 1914, so as to avoid domestic reforms.

This point of view is elaborated, not for the purpose of further embittering the legitimate and already uncontrollable indignation of all right-minded people against the men who have outraged nature by plotting this war, and conducting it with infamy, nor with the purpose of excusing the German people from heavy blame. The purpose is to discriminate. The German people, apart from the actual criminals, are heavily to blame for not displacing, if need be, by a Revolution

before the war, the military system which exposed
themselves and all Europe to danger, for allowing
themselves to be flattered and fooled, and for not
protesting effectively during the war against the
manner in which it was carried on. No doubt the
individual penalty for such protests might have been
death, and they had not the moral courage to face
the risk. National vanity and want of moral courage
are grave faults, but they are less than wilful crime,
and are such that a nation, like an individual, who is
guilty of them may be allowed to retrieve his character. If the German people are ready to make such
reparation as they can for the past, and to live peaceably for the future, they may succeed in retrieving
their character. It is more to their own interest
than to that of anyone else that they should do so.

Mr. Gerard, in his profoundly interesting book
My Four Years in Germany, lays the blame for this
war on the military aristocracy, and says that the mass
of the Germans, in consenting to the great sacrifice
entailed by their enormous preparation for war,
were actuated by fear. " I am convinced that the
" fear of war, induced by an hereditary instinct,
" caused the mass of the Germans to become the
" tools and dupes of those who played upon this very
" fear in order to create a military autocracy." Their
history explains this hereditary instinct in Mr. Gerard's
opinion. Long ago their Thirty Years War left
Germany almost a desert, with a population reduced
from thirty millions to four millions. They were
reduced to cannibalism and polygamy, and wolves
scoured hundreds of square miles. In the eighteenth
century one-tenth of their population perished through

the wars of Frederic the Great. Then followed their struggle against the French Revolution, and against the tyranny of Napoleon, which lasted during more than twenty years of continual carnage. After that came Bismarck's three wars of 1864, 1866, and 1870. These campaigns were conducted with extraordinary military ability and succeeded by a period of un-exampled commercial prosperity. All the credit of this result was of course claimed by the Hohenzollerns and the military caste which supported them. In this way, by controlling the Press and the whole system of education, by the distribution of titles or decorations to the middle classes, with schemes for pensions and sick pay for workmen, and various gerrymandering devices to prevent the franchise from being used with effect, the military caste con-trived to reserve foreign policy in their own hands. There was reality in the popular hereditary instinct which made the masses fear war. France, whom they had wronged, was on their western frontier; and Russia, whom they dreaded, was on the east. They were taught to regard their military system as the only means of averting these dangers, and had not the sagacity or moral courage to perceive that the domestic was greater than the foreign peril.

Mr. Gerard, who was the American Ambassador to Germany from 1913 till 1917, had rare opportunities of forming an opinion. He gives a full account of the German Constitution, and shows how the control of policy was usurped by soldiers. He also describes the famous Zabern affair of 1913-4 which exhibited in its crudest form the cowardly insolence of German aristocratic officers toward the people. There had

been many instances, he tells us, where officers having
a slight dispute with civilians instantly cut the civilian
down. One such instance occurred in the Zabern
case. The offending officer was not punished, but
when the business came before the Reichstag a vote of
censure on the Government was passed by 293 votes
against 54 even in ·that carefully gerrymandered
Assembly. The Chancellor, however, refused to resign,
and declared that the choice or dismissal of Ministers
did not concern the Reichstag, but was for the Kaiser
alone. At the close of the proceedings, instead of the
customary cheers for the Sovereign, some of the
members hissed. Mr. Gerard says that " the move-
" ment against militarism, culminating in the Zabern
" vote, warned the Government and military people
" that the mass of Germans were coming to their
" senses and were preparing to shake off the bogy of
" militarism and fear which had roosted too long on
" their shoulders." He also says: " To my mind
" the course (? cause) which really determined the
" Emperor and the ruling class for war was the atti-
" tude of the whole people in the Zabern affair, and
" their evident and growing dislike of militarism."
What happened at the close of the session of the
Reichstag " indicated a new spirit of resistance to auto-
" cracy, and autocracy saw that if it was to keep its
" hold upon Germany it must lead that nation into
" a short and successful war." Mr. Gerard truly says
that " this is no new trick of a ruling and aristocratic
" class." The Prussian military camarilla may have
a private war god of their own " with whom they
" believe they have a gentleman's working agree-
" ment," but " the world does not believe that a free

"Germany will needlessly make war, believe in war "for war's sake, or take up the profession of arms "as a national industry." Certainly after our experience we cannot afford to run risks, but all this makes us reflect when we are told that the German nation as a whole desired war, and would have insisted on it later if not in 1914. They now see, it is to be hoped, that the war has been neither short nor successful.

This matter is of such vital importance, especially with regard to the future, that this chapter ought not to conclude without a reference to the extremely interesting interview with Lord Milner published in the *Evening Standard* of 17th October 1918. Stating in brief Lord Milner's argument the interviewer says:

"It is a serious mistake, Lord Milner thinks, to "imagine that the German people are in love with "militarism. They have submitted to it partly "from security, partly owing to the glamour of its "hitherto unbroken success. But especially of late "years, until it was submerged by the war, there was "a rising tide of revolt against the Junker and the "Jackboot. Lord Milner was in Germany at the time "of the Zabern incident, and then the people were "so incensed that a revolt against the brutality of the "system was with difficulty restrained. The German "people tolerated Imperialism and militarism, be-"cause these forces had bound together several "puny and helpless States that had been the sport of "greater Powers into one united whole, and given their "peoples prestige, prosperity, and the feeling of "strength."

We may differ from Lord Milner in other things, but

he knows Germany.   He is anxious to hasten the day when the utter wreckage of the Prussian military machine is demonstrated before the very eyes of the German people.   And that has now been done.   Such is the people with whom we have to live in this world for the future.   They have been the instruments of their own militarist party, and must also be numbered among its victims.   With the militarists no reconciliation is possible, but, unless some ultimate reconciliation can be effected with the people, the prospect of lasting peace in Europe is not bright.

CHAPTER XI

REMEDIES

THE object of every sane man must be to attain security, so far as it is possible, against the recurrence of a tragedy such as this war has proved. For this purpose two things are needed above all others. In the first place, we must place the management of our own foreign affairs under strict and effective Parliamentary control. The British Empire at all events ought not again to be plunged at a few hours' notice into a war arising out of a train of policy, however well intended, pursued behind a veil. In the second place, we must do everything in our power to procure continuous and concerted action among different States in order to forestall differences and to remove them if they arise by means of that concerted action. This is what people have in mind when they speak about a League of Nations.

Let us begin with the first of these requisites, the establishment of real national control over our own foreign policy, including therein a full share of control by the Dominions and Dependencies of the Crown. Sometimes the widespread desire for a change of this kind has been crudely expressed in a demand for the abolition of secret diplomacy. Mr. Asquith says it is quite impracticable that all international negotiations shall be conducted in public. No doubt negotiation would often be impossible if secrecy were never allowed. What can be done is to prevent the knot of men who control foreign affairs and those in their confidence from taking advantage of this need of secrecy in the actual handling of negotiation so as to constitute themselves the autocratic dictators of policy. The policy and the purpose of negotiations must be known to and approved by the nation. The actual handling of them may be left to Ministers under proper Parliamentary supervision. And no treaties or engagements ought to be valid without the consent of the nation's representatives. That it has become absolutely necessary to make this change has been abundantly proved by experience.

* * *

The foregoing pages furnish the first illustration of this necessity. A series of difficulties were known to exist in Europe, many among them of long standing. These were the things which begot alarms and provided the fuel that fed dynastic and military ambitions. Prominent among them were the feud between France and Germany which centred in Alsace-Lorraine, and the antagonism between Austria and Russia which centred in the Balkans. But nearly all the nations had either grievances or ambitions. Now British policy had no share in bringing about these continental quarrels, and our chief territorial concern in Europe was that Belgium should remain a perfectly neutral State. As for the other international antagonisms on the Continent, it certainly had been for a couple of generations the generally accepted view that British lives and fortunes ought not to be sacrificed either to procure Alsace-Lorraine for France, or to restore the Kingdom of Poland, or to procure Italia Irredenta for Italy, or to break up the Austrian Empire for the benefit of the Czechs and Slovacks, or, in short, to act the part of Don Quixote in setting right the wrongs of the world, however much we might sympathize with injured peoples. It was the general belief, whether right or wrong, that we could do as much and more good by not committing ourselves to vast military operations on the Continent, but keeping a perfectly free hand so as to act as we thought right if a crisis should arise. That was the basis on which our estimates were framed. And as it is beyond doubt a constitutional maxim, that foreign policy is to be conducted on lines known to be acceptable in Parliament, so also it follows as a corollary of that maxim that any new departure of a serious order in the aims of the Foreign Office should be taken with the approval of Parliament. Now what happened before this war was in reality a gradual and subtle new departure which was not made known to Parliament but in substance denied. Our entente with France was openly commenced in 1904 by Lord Lansdowne, not as an exclusive friendship but as a friendship to be followed by similar arrangements with other nations. Lord Lansdowne publicly announced this intention, and his treaty with France in 1904 expressly stipulated that we were bound only to give diplomatic support to France on particular subjects. After 1904 this entente gradually changed its character till in 1914 it had become practically a defensive Alliance with

France against Germany. But the Ministers who knew all that had happened did not see and did not think that it had so changed its character as we must in justice infer from the express statements they made in Parliament. And in this way became possible the unique scene in the House of Commons on 3rd August 1914, when Sir Edward Grey, on the very eve of war, elaborately affirmed that the House was perfectly free to decide for peace or war, and then told it of dealings and communications between this country and France which in most men's minds led to quite an opposite conclusion. Indeed he told it that our honour would be soiled and our interests imperilled if we did not go to war. If some machinery had existed by which Parliament could have, through a Committee, retained control of what was happening in good time, would not that Committee have done one of two things? Would it not either have prevented an honourable obligation being contracted at all toward France, or have insisted on adequate military preparations to meet the danger.

Still more recent illustrations may be given of the dangers that attend clandestine transactions in foreign affairs. Secret treaties involving enormous and unprecedented schemes of conquest all over the world were undertaken by our Government during the war itself.

We came into this war not as principals in any quarrel of our own, but as accessories in the third degree. First, Russia was drawn in because of Servia. Next, France was drawn in because of Russia. Last of all, on 2nd August 1914, we came in because of our obligations to France. A month afterwards, on 7th

19

September 1914, our Government signed a Treaty, which was made public, with France and Russia, stipulating that neither we nor these Powers were to conclude peace separately during the present war, and the three Governments agreed publicly "that "when terms of peace come to be discussed no one "of the Allies will demand terms of peace without "the previous agreement of each of the other Allies." Now the later words just cited were equally vital with the earlier words. While none of the Allied Powers was to make peace separately, so also none of them was to demand terms of peace without the previous consent of all the others, so that no one could either leave the others in the lurch or hinder the conclusion of peace by even asking for terms in their own interest till all the others had agreed to them. This was the two-sided agreement which was published at the time, and its effect was to reassure people that we should not be obliged to go on fighting in order to satisfy the ambitions of other nations which we might not think in the circumstances reasonable. None of the Allies was to desert the Allies by making a separate peace, but then none of them was to delay the making of a common peace by advancing any demand for terms unless it had been approved by all.

*　*　*

After this Treaty of September 1914 had been published, Mr. Asquith, then Prime Minister, made a speech in which he used these words: "We shall "never sheathe the sword, which we have not lightly "drawn, until Belgium—and I will add Servia— "recovers in full measure all and more than all which

" she has sacrificed, until France is adequately secured
" against the menace of aggression, until the rights of
" the smaller nationalities of Europe are placed upon
" an unassailable foundation, and until the military
" domination of Prussia is wholly and finally de-
" stroyed." This sentence Mr. Asquith subsequently
described as " clear, direct, explicit, and emphatic
language." In reality it is language that may cover
almost anything. For everyone may decide for himself what will satisfy a promise to give " more than
all " they have sacrificed to Belgium and Servia, how
France is to be " adequately secured against the
menace of aggression," how the rights of small nationalities are to be made " unassailable," and in what
way the military domination of Prussia is to be
" wholly and finally destroyed." But, though the
phrasing was a little rhetorical, unsophisticated people
thought it all meant that full reparation and security
were to be obtained for small nationalities, that
France was to be freed from aggression, and Prussia
no longer allowed to play the part of a military bully
in Europe. Those were unselfish and lofty ideals.

*   *   *

This language of Mr. Asquith just cited was repeatedly reaffirmed by himself and others for years
after it was first used. The uninitiated would hardly
suppose that it could be meant to cover vast changes
in the map of Europe, Asia, and Africa. Everyone
will remember how in 1914, 1915, and 1916 official
and unofficial orators, together with a great portion of
the Press, represented the then Government as men
who, having most reluctantly entered upon war,

were pursuing it for the noblest of human ideals—
the rescue of small nationalities, the right of peoples
to be governed according to their own desires, the
overthrow of brutal military despotism, and the preservation of human liberty. It was quite true that
every single one of these elementary principles had
been and was being violated by the military masters of
Germany. That story is too well known to need
repetition. But it is also true that while this was
being said our Ministers had on the anvil at the same
time a series of engagements with our Allies, undisclosed to the public, which committed us to schemes
of territorial conquest on an unprecedented scale for
the increase of our own and our Allies' dominions,
often at the expense of small nationalities all over
the world. No doubt Mr. Asquith's vague phrases
were elastic enough to cover that or almost anything
else. Still, the fact remains. In public we were given
to understand that none of the Allies would demand
terms of peace, without the prior consent of the others,
while in private that consent was given beforehand to
demands involving a vast scheme of world-wide conquest, and a considerable disregard of the wishes of
small nationalities.

It is right to say at once that our Ministers made
these engagements under great pressure from Allied
nations, and under circumstances that put them in a
cruel dilemma. The Central Powers were exhibiting
immense strength on land and greatly outnumbering
our slender divisions of half-trained and half-equipped
soldiers. America had not come into the struggle.
It was greatly desired that the armed assistance of
Italy and Rumania and other neutral Powers should

be obtained, and that the continuance of Russian support should be secured. These Powers fixed the price of their support, and His Majesty's Ministers were not in a favourable position for bargaining. They thought that the military support they were thus purchasing must be bought even at the price demanded for it, and if the thing was to be done it had to be done without publicity. All this does not justify the law which allows Ministers to make such far-reaching engagements in the dark. On the contrary, it furnishes an additional illustration of the necessity for abolishing that law. But it does greatly affect the way in which the action of these particular Ministers should be regarded.

* * *

The secret was well kept for two or three years. But in November 1917 the Russian Revolutionary Government published a number of private official documents which they had discovered in the archives of St. Petersburg. They have been printed in this country by various journals, and published in a small volume by Mr. Seymour Cocks, and their effect may be here summarized.

On 19th February to 4th March 1915 the Russian Foreign Minister handed to the French and British Ambassadors a memorandum of the following territories which Russia desired to acquire " as a result of the present war." The territories were Constantinople, the western coast of the Bosphorus, the Sea of Marmora, the Dardanelles, Southern Thrace as far as the Enos-Midia line, the coast of Asia Minor between the Bosphorus and the river Sakaria, and a point on the Gulf of Ismid to be defined later, the islands in the Sea of Marmora, and the islands of Imbros and Tenedos. "Both the French and the British Govern-"ments expressed their readiness to agree to our "wishes, provided the war is won and provided a "number of claims made by France and England "both in the Ottoman Empire and in other places "are satisfied." This memorandum then proceeds to say what those French and English claims were.

THE FRENCH AND ENGLISH DEMANDS

As far as Turkey is concerned they were, put briefly, Constantinople to be a free port, and a free passage to be given through the Straits to merchant ships. The rights of England and France in Asiatic Turkey are to be defined and recognized (as they in fact were later on). The sacred Mohammedan places are to be protected, and Arabia to be under an independent Mohammedan Sovereign. The neutral zone in Persia is to be in the English sphere of influence.

The Russian Government recognized these demands in general as satisfactory, but made several reservations which need not be further examined.

THE ITALIAN DEMANDS

On the entrance of Italy into the war in 1915, that Government agreed to the Russian demands, " provided " the war ended in the successful realization of Italian " claims in general, and in the East in particular." We shall see presently what these Italian claims were.

FURTHER RUSSIAN DEMANDS

On 11th March 1917 the Russian Ambassador at Paris telegraphed that France " recognizes for Russia " full freedom in the arrangement of her western " frontiers." (This seems to mean that Russia might annex whatever portion of Germany or Austria-Hungary she might think fit.)

On 9th March 1916 the Russian Foreign Minister sent a telegram to the Russian Ambassador in Paris directing him in regard to a then impending Conference that the political agreements made between the Allies during the war must not be subjected to any revision. " In general . . . we are ready to leave to France and " England full freedom to fix the western frontiers of " Germany, and that we count upon the Allies leaving " to us in turn full freedom to fix our frontiers against " Germany and Austria-Hungary. It is above all " necessary to demand that the Polish Question should " be excluded from the subjects of international " negotiation, and that all attempts to place Poland's " future under the guarantee and control of the Powers " should be prevented." This document then refers to Sweden, Norway, and Rumania. As to China, it says : " The question of driving the Germans out of " the Chinese market is of very great importance," but must be postponed till Japan can have a representative present ; but France and England may meantime be consulted. (It is difficult to reconcile the Russian attitude as regards Poland with our expressions of anxiety for the freedom of oppressed nationalities. The Czars have oppressed Poland for generations.)

FURTHER RUSSIAN AND FRENCH DEMANDS

On 30th January (12th February) 1917 the Russian Foreign Minister informs the Russian Ambassador that M. Doumerque (French Ambassador in St. Petersburg) had informed the Czar of France's wish to get Alsace-Lorraine at the end of the war and also " a " special position in the Saar Valley, and to bring " about the detachment from Germany of the terri- " tories west of the Rhine and their reorganization " in such a way that in future the Rhine may form " a permanent strategic obstacle to any German " advance." The Czar was pleased to express his approval in principle of this proposal. Accordingly the Russian Foreign Minister expresses his wish that an Agreement by exchange of Notes should take place on this subject and desires that if Russia agrees to the unrestricted right of France and England to fix Germany's western frontiers so Russia is to have an assurance of freedom of action in fixing Germany's future frontier on the west. (This means on the Russian western frontier.)

DEMANDS OF RUMANIA

A Report of General Polivanov as to Rumania, among the papers published by the Revolutionists at St. Petersburg, and dated 7th/20th November 1916, deals with Rumania's entry into the war and the promises by which she was induced to take that step after remaining neutral for two years.

It explains how Rumania was at first neutral, but shifting between different inclinations—a wish not to come in too late for the partition of Austria-Hungary, and a wish to earn as much as possible at the expense of the belligerents. At first, according to this Report, she favoured our enemies and had obtained very favourable commercial agreements with Germany and Austria-Hungary. Then in 1916, on the Russian successes under Brusilov, she inclined to the Entente Powers. The Russian Chief of the Staff thought Rumanian neutrality preferable to her intervention, but later on General Alexeiev adopted the view of the Allies, " who looked upon Rumania's entry as a decisive " blow for Austria-Hungary and as the nearing of the " war's end." So in August 1916 an agreement was signed with Rumania (who it was signed by is not stated) assigning to her Bukovina and all Transylvania. " The events which followed," says this Report, " showed how greatly our Allies were mistaken, and " how they overvalued Rumania's entry." In fact, Rumania was in a brief time utterly overthrown. And then Polivanov points out that the collapse of Rumania's plans as a Great Power " is not particularly " opposed to Russia's interests." What secret diplomacy meant in Russia may be further seen in a telegram from the Russian Minister in Stockholm dated 18th August 1917, saying that the Russian Chargé d'Affaires in Madrid announces that it is " intended as though in " error to open on occasion the Swedish courier's bag." The Russian Minister begs that this may not be done, because it would put the new Swedish Cabinet against Russia. Good faith is not mentioned.

On 24th September 1917 the Russian Foreign Minister sends a telegram to the Russian Chargé d'Affaires in Paris, which is also communicated to

London and Rome, saying that the publication of the
agreements concluded during the war, especially of the
Rumanian and Italian Treaties, " is regarded by our
" Allies as undesirable." He then says that " on the
" part of Russia no obstacles will be placed in the
" way of publishing all agreements published " (query
made) " before or during the war in the event of the
" other Allies who are parties to them consenting.
" Regarding the question of Asia Minor agreements
" I will communicate to you my views in a special
" supplementary telegram."

NEGOTIATIONS WITH GREECE

There is among the St. Petersburg documents a
document cited as a " Confidential memorandum,
exact source not indicated." It refers to Greece, and
includes statements that on 22nd November 1914
Russia, England, and France promised to Greece the
southern portion of Albania, except Valona, if Greece
would immediately enter the war in aid of Servia.
In reply, Venizelos asked that Rumania should
guarantee Greece against an attack by Bulgaria, and
as this guarantee was not given, Greece did not help
Servia, though she was already bound by Treaty to do
so. Other negotiations in March and April 1915 are
also recorded in which the Russian, British, and
French Governments are said to have offered to Greece,
as an inducement to her helping Servia, important
territorial acquisitions on the coast of Asia Minor and
other territories. But she demanded a guarantee of
her integrity, and failing that remained neutral for
the time.

We may now come to the

DEMANDS OF ITALY

A Treaty, this time with Italy, was signed on 20th
April 1915 by Sir Edward Grey and the Ambassadors
of France and Russia on behalf of Great Britain,
France, and Russia. Those three Powers received
from Italy an undertaking to enter the war actively
within a month at latest, and in return declared their
full agreement with the memorandum presented to
them by the Italian Government. This memorandum
required large territorial annexations to be added to
Italy in the future Treaty of peace. If Signor Salandra,
who became Italian Foreign Minister in October 1914,
is a correct interpreter of his country's policy, the
terms in which he described it are as follows : " What
" is needed is . . . a freedom from all preconceptions
" and prejudices, and from every sentiment except that
" of sacred egoism (*sacro egoismo*) for Italy." The
memorandum was framed strictly in this spirit. Italy
was to receive the Trentino, the whole of Southern Tyrol
as far as the Brenner, Trieste and its surroundings,
the County of Gorizia and Gradisca, Istria as far as
the Quarvero and the Istrian islands, the province of
Dalmatia in its present extent, including certain
specified places and valleys, all the islands north and
west of the Dalmatian coast, with other specified
islands. Provision is then made for the neutraliza-
tion of a considerable extent of coast on the Adriatic
and all the islands not assigned to Italy. It is also
provided that districts on the Adriatic shall be included in the territory of Croatia, Servia, and Monte-

negro, together with certain islands and some ports. Italy is also to obtain Valona and the island of Sasero and other territory. If she obtains Trentino, Istria, Dalmatia, the Adriatic islands, and the Gulf of Valona, and in the event of a small autonomous and neutralized State being formed in Albania, Italy agrees not to oppose the possible desire of France, Great Britain, and Russia to partition the northern and southern districts of Albania between Montenegro, Servia, and Greece; Italy is to have the right of conducting the foreign relations of Albania, and to have all the islands of the Dodecannese at present occupied by her. These islands are inhabited almost entirely by Greeks. France, Great Britain, and Russia recognize the right of Italy to take over, when Turkey is broken up, a portion equal to theirs in the Mediterranean, namely, in that part which borders on the province of Adalia. " In the same way regard must be had " for the interests of Italy even in the event of.the " Powers maintaining for a further period of time the " inviolability of Asiatic Turkey, and merely pro- " ceeding to map out spheres of interest among them- " selves." Italy is also to receive a military contri- bution, and in the event of an extension of the French and British Colonial possessions in Africa, at the expense of Germany, the right of Italy to demand for herself compensations in Africa is admitted. The 15th Article of this memorandum states that " France, " Great Britain, and Russia undertake to support " Italy in so far as she does not permit the representa- " tives of the Holy See to take diplomatic action " with regard to the conclusion of peace and the " regulation of questions connected with the war."

The last Article stipulated that " the present Treaty
" is to be kept secret." Sir E. Grey signed this
Treaty in its entirety. The effect of this Treaty
with Italy would be to place under the Italian Crown
considerable districts inhabited mainly or even exclusively by Germans, Slavs, Albanians, and Greeks,
without consulting any of them about their destiny.
There is very little regard for the rights of small
nationalities, especially the Southern Slavs and Albania.

The dates of these agreements, so far as they are
indicated, deserve notice. Those which may be called
the master agreements and which determined the
broad lines of policy, namely, the adoption in the war
of projects of conquest, were made in 1914, or the
first three or four months of 1915. The others seem
to have been consequential upon a policy already
accepted, from which it may. have been too late to
depart. When once you begin partitioning a considerable part of the globe in concert with Allies, the
process tends to become progressive. Indeed, promises of territorial aggrandizement to one of the
Allies may necessitate, as a corollary, similar promises
to others also.

Finally, agreement was attained between · Great
Britain, France, and Russia in regard to the parti-
tion of Asiatic Turkey. Britain was to have Southern
Mesopotamia with Bagdad, and two ports in Syria.
France was to have Syria, Adana, Vilayet, and Western
Kurdistan. Russia was to have, in addition to
Constantinople, Trebizond, Erzeroum, Bitlis, Van,
and territory in Southern Kurdistan. In other words,
Turkey was to be completely broken up.

Moreover, it seems probable from the peep which

the Revolutionary Russian Government has already given us, by publishing these documents, that there must have been more agreements or understandings of a similar kind, relating to the aggrandizement of Servia, Rumania, Montenegro, and Japan, the contemplated break-up of Turkey and Austria-Hungary, and the future of the German Colonies in all directions, to many if not all of which our own Government would naturally be a party. We are not told if it was so. Notably it will have been observed that very little beyond indications can be found in these documents about the projected annexations in Europe at the expense of Germany. Russia desired a free hand in fixing the boundaries between herself and her neighbours, namely, Germany and Austria-Hungary. Did she get it? It would seem that she did, though it is not certain. She wished that the Polish Question should be excluded from negotiation. Was it excluded? We all know the history of Poland's extinction in the past. If ever a nation rightfully struggled to be free, it was Poland. Russia was willing that England and France should settle the western boundary of Germany, which includes the questions of Alsace-Lorraine and the frontier of the Rhine, so much disputed in past times. Did England and France come to any agreement fixing the western boundary of Germany? We have not been told, but it looks as if something of the kind was done. Lord R. Cecil said in the House of Commons on 24th July 1917 that " it will be for the French to say what they desire " there (Alsace-Lorraine) and for this country to back " up the French in what they desire. I will not go " through all the others of our Allies—there are a

" good many of them—but the principle [to stand by
" our Allies] will be equally true in the case of all
" and particularly in the case of Servia." This appears
to mean that as regards Alsace-Lorraine we were bound
to fight, and France was to say what we are to fight
for. Were we also in any way committed to procure
for France the Rhine boundary? That seems uncertain and on the whole unlikely. It has already
been pointed out that the concealment of these Treaties
in order to obtain military support at a difficult time
was a very different thing from the other gratuitous
concealments practised by Ministers in their earlier
career. Nevertheless the Treaties did not produce the
results expected of them. Russia fell out of the
fighting, and neither Italy nor Rumania were able to
render the conclusive assistance which it was hoped
would end the war. And in other ways these transactions proved unsatisfactory. It was not wholesome
that while our people were stimulated to unparalleled
exertions by a parade of lofty motives there should be
at the same time in existence agreements of this kind,
of which no public mention could be made, and from
which little has resulted except the right of foreign
Powers to demand their fulfilment on our part. They
are of so wide a scope that if they are to be fulfilled
the manhood of this country might be occupied for
years of warfare in enforcing them. And that brings
us to the true lesson of these proceedings. So long as
officials can bind this country by subterranean engagements of this kind, it will be possible for the British
people to be diverted from their peaceful industry and
required as legionaries to spill their blood all over the
world in satisfying the ambitions and settling the

quarrels of other people, without being so'much as consulted on the policy for which they are to sacrifice their
lives. They might be employed in making Southern
Slavs or Greeks or Tyrolese submit to Italian con-
querors, or in readjusting the map all over the earth.
We must at all hazards deprive our Ministers of powers
so formidable.

*　　*　　*

It can hardly be doubted that the discovery of the
schemes of conquest indicated in these secret agreements was a most powerful weapon in the hands of
the German and Austrian and Turkish Governments
for the purpose of inducing their people to endure
the enormous sacrifices that fell upon them. Our
promises were priceless to our enemies. Nations
that believe they are defending their own country
will endure to the last. Were not the terms included in these documents the chief weapons of
the military party in Germany to support their
contention that they were fighting a defensive war?
Dr. Michaelis certainly so employed them in the
Reichstag on 20th August 1917. They must have
fortified the morale of their troops and led them to
believe that they had no choice except to fight on.

We shall learn about these things hereafter. They
are, however, directly relevant to the momentary
purpose. The present purpose is to establish that
we are not in a practical sense a self-governing country
at all in regard to foreign affairs so long as Parliament
does not exercise a real control over the proceedings
of those who manage our foreign affairs. We are
liable to be committed to enter upon a war and then

to alter the whole character of the war and make
peace more difficult, without Parliament having
knowledge or effective control, though the very
existence of the British Empire is thereby put in
jeopardy.

* * *

It is very possible that these projected annexations,
if they could have been attained without prolonging
the war and were desired by the inhabitants of the
countries concerned, might be in themselves salutary.
Some of them certainly were. But that is not the
point. The point is this. In public we were told
that none of the Allies would claim any condition of
peace without the consent of their Allies, and that
the objects of the war were fine ideals, freedom, the
protection of small nationalities, and the defeat of a
cruel military bully. In private the consent of our
Government was given beforehand to vast schemes of
territorial annexation in which great districts were to
be distributed among Great Powers, including ourselves, with no stipulation for consulting the wishes
of the populations concerned, but simply by the
right of conquest. In this way our enemies, who
knew of and published these arrangements, were
provided with the best of all stimulants for prolonging
the war, and no one can say how much the advent
of peace was thereby retarded. When we learn the
whole truth about the peace proposals of the Central
Powers in 1916, 1917, and 1918, which were at the
time denounced as Peace Traps by the Press that
really dictated the Ministerial policy in those days,
we shall be in a position to judge how far these secret
treaties were responsible for continuing the slaughter.

20

The claims of Italy under the Italian Treaty were reported to have caused difficulties with the Southern Slavs when peace terms were discussed at Paris, and indeed to have poisoned the atmosphere of the Conference.

It is said that all this was necessary in order to induce France, Russia, Italy, Rumania, and other countries to enter or to continue in the war. We ought not to assume it in view of the lofty aims which these nations have themselves proclaimed as the reasons of their intervention. But even if it were so, we came in as auxiliaries, not as principals, in the quarrel, and our Ministers owed a duty to the people of this country. No doubt they thought their own action necessary and wise, but they took the risk of thereby making the war interminable, except after a conflict so long as to bring Allies as well as enemies face to face with Revolution, Anarchy, and Famine, and they imperilled the very existence of the British Empire, unknown to Parliament. No one has a right to do that. When America came into the war and turned the tide of victory their statesmen were too wise to join in these secret treaties. Indeed, their Constitution did not admit of their doing so. What would have happened if America had not come in no human being can say. Yet there was little prospect of America coming in when we made the treaties. We ought to have as much control over our own executive Ministers as America has over hers. No one ever ventured to ask the American Government to sign these Treaties, because everyone must have known that the Senate would have refused its assent. No one would have asked the British Government for its assent to them if there had been an independent authority behind our Ministers who would have had to debate in public, and who possessed the power of either refusing approval or affixing conditions. Our whole future as a nation depends on our obtaining effective control over foreign as well as domestic policy.

＊　＊　＊

If it be true that the existence of these secret agreements were an important ingredient in causing the prolongation of the war, as seems probable, and even assuming that it was prudent to make them on this particular occasion, yet surely these things prove the necessity of some more effective control by Parliament over foreign affairs.

It is said that Ministers hold office subject to the consent of the House of Commons, which is true, and that the Cabinet exercises control over the conduct of foreign affairs, which ought to be true, but is of limited truth in practice. Since the recent institution of a separate War Cabinet even the theory for a time disappeared during the war. Ministers of standing and ability are always charged with the administration of laborious Departments, and this, added to the exacting requirements of their Parliamentary duties, to say nothing of their constituencies, leaves very little spare time. They are in alliance with their colleagues in a common service covering all affairs of State. They necessarily expect to be told of anything serious in foreign affairs. The rule has always of course been that if any serious question arises, or anything that may have serious consequences, any Minister directly concerned shall inform his colleagues, who have to share the responsibility with him. There are grave

defects in this system. Sir Edward Grey's speech
on 3rd August 1914 in the House of Commons shows
that a Minister can in practice withhold important
information. His colleagues may not suspect, and
the House of Commons may not suspect. Those who
in the end pay with lives and money for the blunders
of diplomacy are the people, and they are represented
by the House of Commons. That House has no
instrument of its own to check those blunders. It is
not natural to suppose that Ministers will distrust
one another or suspect that something is being concealed from them by one of their own trusted colleagues,
for a Cabinet could not work except on terms of mutual
confidence. The House of Commons, having taken
out of the hands of the Sovereign and entrusted to
Ministers the exercise of the Royal Prerogative in
respect of Treaty-making and binding the people by
pledges towards other nations, ought to go further
and insist on a more direct supervision and some more
immediate power of its own.

In the old days the House of Commons found it
necessary to check the Sovereign by interposing the
Minister. A Minister who acts in the dark and chooses
his own instruments and his own advisers may be as
dangerous as an unconstitutional·Sovereign.

*   *   *

How, then, are we to procure a system which shall
secure us for the future from the risk of having all
that we possess placed at the mercy of a few men who
may prove to be injudicious or may suppose that
vital matters are so unimportant that they may be
kept secret, or who may believe that they need no
advice or direction from Parliament ? All these

things may happen, and we cannot afford to let men
play the part of Bismarck at our expense, even if
we are quite sure that they possess the qualities of
that great man. The mischief is inopportune and
uncontrolled secrecy. We must have a method
which admits of prompt and decisive action when it
is needed, which will prevent policies and engagements
of all kinds on the part of this country being undertaken without their consequences being fully realized
or fully provided for, and which shall prevent Ministers
from drifting through negotiations into a catastrophe
either because they have already compromised their
own freedom of action, or because they cannot appreciate what they have themselves done.

*   *   *

In America the difficulty of reconciling effective
action with popular control has been met by en-
trusting to the Senate the power of disallowing treaties,
and thus bestowing upon it a special authority in
regard to diplomacy which it uses through the medium
of a Foreign Affairs Committee. In Lord Bryce's
work on the American Constitution we are told that it
is usually the best policy for the Executive to be in
constant communication with that Committee, and
to keep it informed of the progress of any pending
negotiation. Lord Bryce also says that the Senate,
through its right of confirming or rejecting engagements with foreign powers, secures a general control
over foreign policy. The Senate frequently partici-
pates in negotiations. It would obviously be very
difficult under such a system for undesirable relations
to grow up imperceptibly between the United States
and any other country of such a kind as to make war

unavoidable. Lord Bryce thinks that this control
of foreign policy by the Senate "goes far to meet
" that terrible difficulty which a Democracy, or indeed
" any free government, finds in dealing with foreign
" policy," namely, the difficulty of drawing a line
between the conveniences and inconveniences of
secrecy in international dealings.

Cut-and-dried plans in regard to the composition
and authority of the Foreign Affairs Committee which
Parliament should be urged to establish would be
premature even if they were appropriate in this
inquiry. The principle is the important thing. It
must suffice to say that the need of a more effective
control of foreign policy by Parliament itself, with
the co-operation of the Empire, is the first great lesson
we ought to learn from our frightful experiences.
If this be done through a Committee, which is obviously
the most natural way, then that body ought not to
have the power of giving directions or of interfering
on its own authority with the work of the Foreign
Office, but it ought to have the power of requiring the
fullest information of seeing all documents and discussing with the Secretary of State all questions of
policy. If they thought it necessary, such a Committee might report to Parliament, and at once check
in this way any false step. These duties would undoubtedly be delicate and difficult, and therefore
ought to be entrusted to quite a small number of
men, carefully chosen, enough to keep the Foreign
Office under supervision.

* * *

We must hope, though we cannot enforce it, that
other nations also will put an end to this pestilent

system of concealment which has done so much harm. They have suffered from it like ourselves. It can hardly be out of place in this connection to look back a little and point out how large a part secret treaties and secret diplomacy have played for a long time past in European policy, and how disastrous have been the results. Illustrations had better be taken chronologically and with reference to all Continental nations. The following is quite an incomplete enumeration of some among these underground arrangements during the last sixty or seventy years. Students of history will perceive in each of them the gravity of the consequences to which they gave rise. Space does not admit of anything beyond bare allusion.

In 1858 Napoleon III was induced by Cavour secretly to promise French assistance in a war against Austria, in return for a promise that Savoy and Nice should be ceded to France. The first term led to the war of 1859. The price of the latter condition was Italian hatred of France for a good many years. France resented this promise, but was powerless, because she was governed at that time by the incompetent and unscrupulous despotism of Napoleon III.

In 1864 the first serious suggestion to Prussia that she should take Schleswig-Holstein for herself came secretly from Napoleon III. It sealed the fate of Schleswig-Holstein, and brought about, at all events in part, the war of 1864.

In 1866, at the outbreak of the war between Austria and Prussia, Napoleon III secretly concluded a treaty with Austria, holding out to her the prospect of recovering Silesia from the Prussians in return for a cession of Venetia to Italy. The promise was dis-

covered, and this alienated Prussia from France.
In the same year—1866—Napoleon III secretly demanded from Prussia the cession to France of the
Rhenish Palatinate belonging to Bavaria, together
with other German territory. This demand proved
a godsend to Bismarck, because he was able (also
secretly) to inform Bavaria of it, and of her danger
from Napoleonic ambition. In this way the Prussian
Minister was enabled to conclude three more secret
treaties in the same year, namely, the treaties by
which Bavaria, Würtemberg, and Baden agreed to
place their armies and all military arrangements, in
case of war, under the control of the King of Prussia.
This sealed the fate of France in the Franco-Prussian
War. If these treaties had been known to the
French Government in 1870 they would probably
have averted war, for the war of 1870 was in part due
to the folly of the French Government, which was
unaware that it would have all Germany against it.

In 1867 Bismarck, on behalf of Prussia, made a secret
compact with France, one article of which stated that
Prussia would not object to the annexation of Belgium
by France.

In the earlier part of 1870 secret negotiations were
proceeding between France and Austria with a view
to a joint invasion of North Germany, with the
assistance of Italy if it could be procured. And
this negotiation, though never reduced to an actual
treaty, seemed likely to end in an agreement when the
war of 1870 between Prussia and France broke out.
It is probable that Bismarck knew of it, and this may
explain his anxiety to bring on the Franco-German
War at once in 1870. In the same year Bismarck in

another way contributed to that war by clandestine instigation of the Hohenzollern candidature for the throne of Spain, and that was the question on which France and Prussia quarrelled. That candidature directly led to the war of 1870.

In 1872, or a little later, Germany made a secret compact with Austria to secure for the latter some territory in the Balkans to compensate her for her losses of 1859 and 1866. This furthered the union of the Central Powers, and very likely had much to do with the annexation of Bosnia and Herzegovina by the Austrians in 1908, and the consequent quarrel with Servia in 1914.

In 1878, just before the Berlin Congress, Great Britain made a secret treaty with Russia, agreeing on the terms which should supersede the Treaty of San Stefano, and very soon afterwards made another secret convention relative to Cyprus with Turkey, both of which very crucially affected the Treaty of Berlin itself and hindered a settlement of the Balkans. The unrest in the Balkans was one of the main causes that led to the Great War of 1914.

In 1879 Germany and Austria came to a secret agreement for common defence if either of them should be attacked by Russia. This was an important stage in cementing the friendship of Germany and Austria, and has influenced European policy now for many years.

From 1879 onwards there was a perfect spider's web of diplomatic arrangements and intrigues between Russia and the various Balkan States, with counteracting arrangements on the part of Austria and Germany, nearly all of them undisclosed.

In 1890 there were rumours of secret agreements between Germany and Belgium to facilitate the passage of German troops through Belgian territory to attack France, and also rumours of agreements between France and Russia for defensive common action against Germany. Whether all these things were more than mere gossip seems uncertain. Uncertainty is a powerful factor in producing warlike combinations. Europe was being gradually educated in the methods of underground diplomacy.

In 1896 the famous Treaty between France and Russia was signed which forced France into the Great War of 1914 as the ally of Russia and brought about our intervention also through France.

The Paris *Figaro* published in 1904 official documents purporting to prove that Russia declared her readiness to support France in arms if she went to war with Great Britain in connection with the Fashoda affair of 1898. The Fashoda incident was not very far from producing war, but that was averted.

It has become known since this war began that in the same year, 1904, Germany endeavoured secretly to get an agreement with Russia and France which was to have been used against Great Britain. It is known as the Treaty of Bjorke, and is described in Dr. Dillon's *Eclipse of Russia*. The Czar for the moment agreed and then receded. France refused her consent.

Our own private dealings with France since 1904 have already been the subject of full criticism in these pages, though it is quite possible that some of them are still unknown.

Particulars on these subjects will be found in Mr.

Holland Rose's important volume called *The Development of the European Nations, 1870-1900,* which gives a profoundly interesting history of this period. Few indeed are the European wars during the last hundred years in regard to which, if their origins are closely investigated, you do not encounter the stench of dishonest diplomacy working behind the scenes. It is not often completely discovered even after the lapse of many years, because there is a convention between the different Foreign Offices that communications between them are not to be made public without the assent of both. It is easy in ordinary times for one of them, if pressed by inconvenient inquiries at home, to contrive that the other shall object and so avert disclosure.

* * *

Probably not one man or woman out of a hundred in any one of the great nations of Europe, possibly not one in a thousand, desired this or any war. They were occupied in peaceful industry and thinking of their own and their families' welfare, willing indeed to make sacrifices for their country, but desirous of peace. Yet by the action of some among their rulers they have all been repeatedly precipitated into horrible conflicts and obliged to undergo indescribable sufferings. Europe really ought to mean those hundreds of millions of peace-loving people. It is for them and for the still more pitiable millions of smaller nationalities that human government exists, to keep order among them and enable them to live tolerable lives during the few years which are allowed to them on this earth. Instead of that, vast parts of the Continent have been converted periodically into a hell, full of murder, massacre, starvation, sorrow, and hatred. Able, courageous, broad-minded men are very rarely to be found under such a system as prevails in Foreign Offices. It was said long ago that, internationally speaking, Europe is simply a number of wicked old gentlemen wearing decorations. Certainly it is true that in and before 1914 the Foreign Offices of the various European States had contrived to exclude almost entirely every popular or Parliamentary influence from control over foreign affairs by keeping knowledge, which is power, in their own possession. They were so profoundly convinced of their own supreme ability as to regard any interference from outside almost in the light of a desecration. Recent experience has taught the nations to think very differently of diplomatists, and they cannot be allowed to throw dust in the eyes of the public any longer. Not a single one of the men who had real power was wise enough and strong enough to arrest the military demon that was about to bring upon us all the most awful catastrophe in human history. And after this war had commenced, though very many of them from motives either of fear or of humanity desired to see it ended, they had so committed themselves to one another or were so distrustful of each others' private intentions for the future that they could not close the conflict for the origin of which they had been themselves responsible. Meanwhile the guiltless peoples were destroyed.

*　　*　　*

Enough has been said to indicate the first great lesson of the war, namely, the persistent danger of the system of secret diplomacy as hitherto tolerated

and abused in this and other countries. So far as
this country is concerned, the remedy is in our own
hands.

The second great lesson of the war is that hitherto
there has been no effective method, hardly even the
pretence of a method, for bringing the nations of the
earth together with a view to preventing dangerous
disputes from arising, and settling them without
bloodshed when they have arisen. Mr. Lowes Dickinson has written instructively on what he calls European
Anarchy. The description is apt and just.

The Peace Conference at Paris has already agreed
to the principles of a League of Nations. Naturally
they have been much criticized. But they contain
the root of the matter. The peace of mankind is
recognized as the common interest of mankind, and
not as the private province of a number of busybodies
scheming to outwit one another, or of any individual
Power. All the nations within the League are to unite
in watching, warning, and defeating any attempt at
aggression or inhumanity, to insist on arbitration and
mediation, and to enforce their will by combined
economic and, if need be, military pressure. That
ought to suffice.

The aim of this proposal is to make war impossible
for the future. Its chief Architect has been President
Wilson, whose efforts in this supreme cause will place
him alongside of the greatest figures in history. Our
own countrymen will recall with gratitude the efforts
of Lord R. Cecil in the same direction, and of General
Smuts who fought against us twenty years ago in the
South African War and has since requited the wrong
then done to his country by rendering splendid service

to the British Empire both in the field and at the Council table. That is indeed true greatness.

Whether any League of Nations will succeed or not must depend upon the spirit in which it is worked. If there are defects in its machinery, they can be repaired in the light of experience. But the spirit is everything. Experience has proved to all nations that men dealing in private with great subjects cannot in any Department be trusted with uncontrolled power. Even the work of a man of genius like Bismarck, after being vaunted as a masterpiece for fifty years, has ended in utter discomfiture and disgrace. It might have lasted a little longer if there had been a little wisdom among Bismarck's successors; but it was born in injustice, and structures of that kind have a way of coming to a ruinous end, especially when they fall into incompetent hands, as in time they always do.

Secrecy, surprise, and the want of any effective organization among peace-loving nations for a concerted remonstrance or warning were the main factors that enabled the military commanders who controlled Germany to rush on the war of 1914. Any international arrangement which will provide for publicity, delay, and concerted protest against aggression would make the repetition of that outrage almost inconceivable because almost certain to fail. The circumstances of Europe are very favourable for President Wilson's enterprise. Austria-Hungary has ceased to exist. Bulgaria is reduced to impotence. Turkey is doomed to be driven out of Europe. Germany will be obliged to make a definite choice. When that people learns, as it can from its own soldiers and seamen, what was done in Belgium and France and

Servia and Rumania, and learns how their own German Ambassador encouraged and steadily refused to take any step for preventing the deliberate massacre of nearly a million guiltless Armenians—men, women, and children of all ages—by the Turks, without reckoning submarine murders at sea and their leaders' conduct toward defenceless prisoners; when they learn all this they will be put to the choice—either of unequivocally condemning these things and renouncing for ever the men and the methods that made them possible, or of accepting responsibility in the face of the world. For these things are undeniable and indefensible, and the only course for a self-respecting nation is to repudiate the iniquities that have been perpetrated in its name.

But the success of this League of Nations will depend upon the spirit in which it is supported and administered. There are many reasons for expecting that this will be loyal and trustworthy. We all have in our hearts the terrible memory of the last four or five years. We have seen national friendships contracted almost spontaneously. We have seen the dangers of disunion in industrial as well as foreign affairs. Want of confidence does as much harm in the one sphere as in the other. And, if we miss this opportunity of uniting the honest nations in a common bond, they may drift asunder and leave us face to face with another European war when time has passed. If it ever comes, that next war will be even more destructive than this has been. The most noticeable feature of the fighting now ended has been the degree to which noncombatants, particularly women and children, have been made to suffer. This has aggravated the horrors of warfare in a way hitherto without precedent. And if the increased resources of science were sedulously utilized during the years ahead of us in multiplying devices for the destruction of mankind, such as poisoning sources of water with the bacilli of diseases and the employment of deadly fumes, still longer ranges for projectiles, more powerful mines, submarines, and aeroplanes, whole populations would be liable to extirpation with little chance of defence even by the odious method of reprisals. Under such conditions life itself would be scarcely tolerable to mankind. But most nations already detest war, and now that they will all have the power of controlling their own destinies we may reasonably expect that they will welcome any honourable means of diminishing its probability. That is what makes the prospects of a League of Nations hopeful, and the longer it lasts the more effective it is likely to become. We have had ample opportunities of seeing what is the outcome of European Anarchy. Hitherto throughout history wars have arisen chiefly because the Rulers of nations have quarrelled about their ambitions and have been clever enough to make their peoples fight in order to attain the Rulers' purposes. The peoples have now discovered the truth, and are not likely to let themselves be treated as mere food for powder in the future. But reconciliation must come before the League can really succeed, and the prospect of this seems to be daily becoming more remote. Seven million young men have already been killed, and twenty million disabled, many of them permanently disabled. We have dealt a knock-out blow to all our enemies. Yet the secular hatreds which have infested Europe for centuries remain unappeased, and unhappily, perhaps inevitably, the terms imposed on Germany and, so far as we know, projected for Austria-Hungary, Turkey, and Bulgaria, bid fair to add a new crop of hatreds no less implacable than the old. Up to the present time the last state of Europe is worse than the first. It always has been so and always will be so where Imperialism gets the upper hand.

In this country there is no fear of Ministers bringing us into war through projects of ambition. The days for that have long gone by. But though we cannot expect of them that they will be heroes or sages, they must possess certain homely qualities—candour, courage, and common sense—or this nation may have to undergo its terrible experiences all over again.

APPENDIX

SIR E. GREY'S SPEECH ON 3RD AUGUST 1914

LAST week I stated that we were working for peace not only for this country, but to preserve the peace of Europe. To-day events move so rapidly that it is exceedingly difficult to state with technical accuracy the actual state of affairs, but it is clear that the peace of Europe cannot be preserved. Russia and Germany, at any rate, have declared war upon each other.

Before I proceed to state the position of His Majesty's Government, I would like to clear the ground so that, before I come to state to the House what our attitude is with regard to the present crisis, the House may know exactly under what obligations the Government is, or the House can be said to be, in coming to a decision on the matter. First of all let me say, very shortly, that we have consistently worked with a single mind, with all the earnestness in our power, to preserve peace. The House may be satisfied on that point. We have always done it. During these last years, as far as His Majesty's Government are concerned, we would have no difficulty in proving that we have done so. Throughout the Balkan crisis, by general admission, we worked for peace. The co-operation of the Great Powers of Europe was successful in working for peace in the Balkan crisis. It is true that some of the Powers had great difficulty in adjusting their points of view. It took much time and labour and discussion before they could settle their differences, but peace was secured, because peace was their main object, and they were willing to give time and trouble rather than accentuate differences rapidly.

In the present crisis, it has not been possible to secure the peace of Europe ; because there has been little time, and there has been a disposition—at any rate in some quarters on which I will not dwell—to force things rapidly to an issue, at any rate, to the risk of peace, and, as we now know, the result of that is that the policy of peace, as far as the Great Powers generally are concerned, is in danger. I do not want to dwell on that, and to comment on it, and to say where the blame seems to us to lie, which Powers were most in favour of peace, which were most disposed to risk or endanger peace, because I would like the House to approach this crisis in which we are now, from the point of view of British interests, British honour, and British obligations, free from all passion as to why peace has not been preserved.

We shall publish Papers as soon as we can regarding what took place last week when we were working for peace ; and when those Papers are published, I have no doubt that to every human being they will make it clear how strenuous and genuine and whole-hearted our efforts for peace were, and that they will enable people to form their own judgment as to what forces were at work which operated against peace.

I come first, now, to the question of British obligations. I have assured the House—and the Prime Minister has assured the House more than once—that if any crisis such as this arose, we should come before the House of Commons and be able to say to the House that it was free to decide what the British attitude should be, that we would have no secret engagement which we should spring upon the House, and tell the House that, because we had entered into that engagement, there was an obligation of honour upon the country. I will deal with that point to clear the ground first.

There have been in Europe two diplomatic groups, the Triple Alliance and what came to be called the "Triple Entente," for some years past. The Triple Entente was not an Alliance—it was a Diplomatic Group. The House will remember that in 1908 there was a crisis, also a Balkan crisis, originating in the annexation of Bosnia and Herzegovina. The Russian Minister, M. Isvolsky, came to London, or happened to come to London, because his visit was planned before the crisis broke out. I told him definitely then, this being a Balkan crisis, a Balkan affair, I did not consider that public opinion in this country would justify us in promising to give anything more than diplomatic support. More was never asked from us, more was never given, and more was never promised.

In this present crisis, up till yesterday, we have also given no promise of anything more than diplomatic support—up till yesterday no promise of more than diplomatic support. Now I must make this question of obligation clear to the House. I must go back to the first Moroccan crisis of 1906. That was the time of the Algeciras Conference, and it came at a time of very great difficulty to His Majesty's Government when a General Election was in progress, and Ministers were scattered over the country, and I—spending three days a week in my constituency and three days at the Foreign Office—was asked the question whether if that crisis developed into war between France and Germany we would give armed support. I said then that I could promise nothing to any foreign Power unless it was subsequently to receive the whole-hearted support of public opinion here if the occasion arose. I said, in my opinion, if the war was forced upon France, then on the question of Morocco—a question which had just been the subject of agreement between this country and France, an agreement exceedingly popular on both sides—that if out of that agreement war was forced on France at that time, in my view public opinion in this country would have rallied to the material support of France.

I gave no promise, but I expressed that opinion during the crisis, as far as I remember, almost in the same words, to the French Ambassador and the German Ambassador at the time. I made no promise, and I used no threats; but I expressed that opinion. That position was accepted by the French Government, but they said to me at the time—and I think very reasonably—"If you think it possible that the public opinion of Great Britain might, should a sudden crisis arise, justify you in giving to France the armed support which you cannot promise in advance, you will not be able to give that support, even if you wish to give it, when the time comes, unless some " conversations have already taken place between naval and military experts." There was force in that. I agreed to it, and authorized those conversations to take place, but on the distinct understanding that nothing which passed between military or naval experts should bind either Government or restrict in any way their freedom to make a decision as to whether or not they would give that support when the time arose.

As I have told the House, upon that occasion a General Election was in prospect. I had to take the responsibility of doing that without the Cabinet. It could not be summoned. An answer had to be given. I consulted Sir Henry Campbell-Bannerman, the Prime Minister; I consulted, I remember, Lord Haldane, who was then Secretary of State for War, and the present Prime Minister, who was then Chancellor of the Exchequer. That was the most I could do, and they authorized that on the distinct understanding that it left the hands of the Government free whenever the crisis arose. The fact that conversations between military and naval experts took place was later on—I think much later on, because that crisis passed, and the thing ceased to be of importance—but later on it was brought to the knowledge of the Cabinet.

The Agadir crisis came—another Morocco crisis—and throughout that I took precisely the same line that had been taken in 1906. But subsequently, in 1912, after discussion and consideration in the Cabinet it was decided that we ought to have a definite understanding in writing which was to be only in the form of an unofficial letter, that these conversations which took place were not binding upon the freedom of either Government; and on the 22nd of November 1912, I wrote to the French Ambassador the letter which I will now read to the House, and I received from him a letter in similar terms in reply. The letter which I have to read to the House is this, and it will be known to the public now as the record that, whatever took place between military and naval experts, they were not binding engagements upon the Government :—

" MY DEAR AMBASSADOR,—From time to time in recent years the French and British naval and military experts have consulted together. It has always been

understood that such consultation does not restrict the
freedom of either Government to decide at any future
time whether or not to assist the other by armed force.
We have agreed that consultation between experts is
not and ought not to be regarded as an engagement
that commits either Government to action in a contingency that has not yet arisen and may never arise.
The disposition, for instance, of the French and British
Fleets respectively at the present moment is not based
upon an engagement to co-operate in war.

" You have, however, pointed out that, if either
Government had grave reason to expect an unprovoked
attack by a third Power, it might become essential to
know whether it could in that event depend upon the
armed assistance of the other.

" I agree that, if either Government had grave reason
to expect an unprovoked attack by a third Power, or
something that threatened the general peace, it should
immediately discuss with the other whether both
Governments should act together to prevent aggression
and to preserve peace, and, if so, what measures they
would be prepared to take in common."

That is the starting point for the Government with
regard to the present crisis. I think it makes it clear that
what the Prime Minister and I said to the House of
Commons was perfectly justified, and that, as regards our
freedom to decide in a crisis what our line should be,
whether we should intervene or whether we should abstain,
the Government remained perfectly free and, *a fortiori*,
the House of Commons remains perfectly free. That I
say to clear the ground from the point of view of obligation. I think it was due to prove our good faith to the
House of Commons that I should give that full information to the House now, and say what I think is obvious
from the letter I have just read, that we do not construe
anything which has previously taken place in our diplomatic relations with other Powers in this matter as restrict-
ing the freedom of the Government to decide what attitude
they should take now, or restrict the freedom of the House
of Commons to decide what their attitude should be.

Well, Sir, I will go further, and I will say this : The

situation in the present crisis is not precisely the same
as it was in the Morocco question. In the Morocco
question it was primarily a dispute which concerned
France—a dispute which concerned France and France
primarily — a dispute, as it seemed to us, affecting
France, out of an agreement subsisting between us
and France, and published to the whole world, in
which we engaged to give France diplomatic support.
No doubt we were pledged to give nothing but diplomatic
support ; we were, at any rate, pledged by a definite
public agreement to stand with France diplomatically in
that question.

The present crisis has originated differently. It has
not originated with regard to Morocco. It has not
originated as regards anything with which we had a
special agreement with France ; it has not originated with
anything which primarily concerned France. It has
originated in a dispute between Austria and Servia. I
can say this with the most absolute confidence—no Government and no country has less desire to be involved in war
over a dispute with Austria and Servia than the Government and the country of France. They are involved in it
because of their obligation of honour under a definite
alliance with Russia. Well, it is only fair to say to the
House that that obligation of honour cannot apply in the
same way to us. We are not parties to the Franco-Russian
Alliance. We do not even know the terms of that Alliance.
So far I have, I think, faithfully and completely cleared
the ground with regard to the question of obligation.

I now come to what we think the situation requires of
us. For many years we have had a long-standing friendship with France. [An Hon. Member : "And with
Germany ! "] I remember well the feeling in the House—
and my own feeling—for I spoke on the subject, I think,
when the late Government made their agreement with
France—the warm and cordial feeling resulting from the
fact that these two nations, who had had perpetual differences in the past, had cleared these differences away. I
remember saying, I think, that it seemed to me that some
benign influence had been at work to produce the cordial
atmosphere that had made that possible. But how far
that friendship entails obligation—it has been a friendship

between the nations and ratified by the nations—how far that entails an obligation let every man look into his own heart, and his own feelings, and construe the extent of the obligation for himself. I construe it myself as I feel it, but I do not wish to urge upon anyone else more than their feelings dictate as to what they should feel about the obligation. The House, individually and collectively, may judge for itself. I speak my personal view, and I have given the House my own feeling in the matter.

The French fleet is now in the Mediterranean, and the Northern and Western Coasts of France are absolutely undefended. The French fleet being concentrated in the Mediterranean, the situation is very different from what it used to be, because the friendship which has grown up between the two countries has given them a sense of security that there was nothing to be feared from us.

The French coasts are absolutely undefended. The French fleet is in the Mediterranean, and has for some years been concentrated there because of the feeling of confidence and friendship which has existed between the two countries. My own feeling is that if a foreign fleet engaged in a war which France had not sought, and in which she had not been the aggressor, came down the English Channel and bombarded and battered the undefended coasts of France, we could not stand aside and see this going on practically within sight of our eyes, with our arms folded, looking on dispassionately, doing nothing ! I believe that would be the feeling of this country. There are times when one feels that if these circumstances actually did arise, it would be a feeling which would spread with irresistible force throughout the land.

But I also want to look at the matter without sentiment, and from the point of view of British interests, and it is on that that I am going to base and justify what I am presently going to say to the House. If we say nothing at this moment, what is France to do with her fleet in the Mediterranean ? If she leaves it there, with no statement from us as to what we will do, she leaves her Northern and Western Coasts absolutely undefended, at the mercy of a German fleet coming down the Channel, to do as it pleases in a war which is a war of life and death between them. If we say nothing, it may be that the French fleet is withdrawn from the Mediterranean. We are in the presence of a European conflagration; can anybody set limits to the consequences that may arise out of it? Let us assume that to-day we stand aside in an attitude of neutrality, saying, "No, we cannot undertake and engage to help either party in this conflict." Let us suppose the French fleet is withdrawn from the Mediterranean; and let us assume that the consequences—which are already tremendous in what has happened in Europe even to countries which are at peace—in fact, equally whether countries are at peace or at war—let us assume that out of that come consequences unforeseen, which make it necessary at a sudden moment that, in defence of vital British interests, we should go to war : and let us assume —which is quite possible—that Italy, who is now neutral —[Hon. Members : "Hear, hear !"]—because, as I understand, she considers that this war is an aggressive war, and the Triple Alliance being a defensive alliance her obligation did not arise—let us assume that consequences which are not yet foreseen—and which perfectly legitimately consulting her own interests—make Italy depart from her attitude of neutrality at a time when we are forced in defence of vital British interests ourselves to fight, what then will be the position in the Mediterranean ? It might be that at some critical moment those consequences would be forced upon us because our trade routes in the Mediterranean might be vital to this country.

Nobody can say that in the course of the next few weeks there is any particular trade route the keeping open of which may not be vital to this country. What will be our position then ? We have not kept a fleet in the Mediterranean which is equal to dealing alone with a combination of other fleets in the Mediterranean. It would be the very moment when we could not detach more ships to the Mediterranean, and we might have exposed this country from our negative attitude at the present moment to the most appalling risk. I say that from the point of view of British interests. We feel strongly that France was entitled to know—and to know at once !—whether or not in the event of attack upon her unprotected Northern and Western Coasts she could depend upon British support. In that emergency, and in these compelling circumstances, yesterday afternoon I gave to the French Ambassador the following statement :—

" I am authorized to give an assurance that if the German fleet comes into the Channel or through the North Sea to undertake hostile operations against the French coasts or shipping, the British Fleet will give all the protection in its power. This assurance is, of course, subject to the policy of His Majesty's Government receiving the support of Parliament, and must not be taken as binding His Majesty's Government to take any action until the above contingency of action by the German fleet takes place."

I read that to the House, not as a declaration of war on our part, not as entailing immediate aggressive action on our part, but as binding us to take aggressive action should that contingency arise. Things move very hurriedly from hour to hour. Fresh news comes in, and I cannot give this in any very formal way ; but I understand that the German Government would be prepared, if we would pledge ourselves to neutrality, to agree that its fleet would not attack the Northern Coast of France. I have only heard that shortly before I came to the House, but it is far too narrow an engagement for us. And, Sir, there is the more serious consideration—becoming more serious every hour—there is the question of the neutrality of Belgium.

I shall have to put before the House at some length what is our position in regard to Belgium. The governing factor is the Treaty of 1839, but this is a Treaty with a history—a history accumulated since. In 1870, when there was war between France and Germany, the question of the neutrality of Belgium arose, and various things were said. Amongst other things, Prince Bismarck gave an assurance to Belgium that, confirming his verbal assurance, he gave in writing a declaration which he said was superfluous in reference to the Treaty in existence— that the German Confederation and its allies would respect the neutrality of Belgium, it being always understood that

that neutrality would be respected by the other belligerent Powers. That is valuable as a recognition in 1870 on the part of Germany of the sacredness of these Treaty rights.

What was our attitude? The people who laid down the attitude of the British Government were Lord Granville in the House of Lords, and Mr. Gladstone in the House of Commons. Lord Granville, on the 8th of August 1870, used these words. He said :—

" We might have explained to the country and to foreign nations that we did not think this country was bound either morally or internationally or that its interests were concerned in the maintenance of the neutrality of Belgium, though this course might have had some conveniences, though it might have been easy to adhere to it, though it might have saved us from some immediate danger, it is a course which Her Majesty's Government thought it impossible to adopt in the name of the country with any due regard to the country's honour or to the country's interests."

Mr. Gladstone spoke as follows two days later :—

" There is, I admit, the obligation of the Treaty. It is not necessary, nor would time permit me, to enter into the complicated question of the nature of the obligations of that Treaty ; but I am not able to subscribe to the doctrine of those who have held in this House what plainly amounts to an assertion, that the simple fact of the existence of a guarantee is binding on every party to it, irrespectively altogether of the particular position in which it may find itself at the time when the occasion for acting on the guarantee arises. The great authorities upon foreign policy to whom I have been accustomed to listen, such as Lord Aberdeen and Lord Palmerston, never to my knowledge took that rigid and, if I may venture to say so, that impracticable view of the guarantee. The circumstance that there is already an existing guarantee in force is of necessity an important fact, and a weighty element in the case to which we are bound to give full and ample consideration. There is also this further consideration, the force of which we must all feel most deeply, and that is, the common interests against the unmeasured aggrandisement of any Power whatever."

The Treaty is an old Treaty—1839—and that was the view taken of it in 1870. It is one of those Treaties which are founded, not only on consideration for Belgium, which benefits under the Treaty, but in the interests of those who guarantee the neutrality of Belgium. The honour and interests are, at least, as strong to-day as in 1870, and we cannot take a more narrow view or a less serious view of our obligations, and of the importance of those obligations, than was taken by Mr. Gladstone's Government in 1870.

I will read to the House what took place last week on this subject. When mobilization was beginning, I knew that this question must be a most important element in our policy—a most important subject for the House of Commons. I telegraphed at the same time in similar terms to both Paris and Berlin to say that it was essential for us to know whether the French and German Governments respectively were prepared to undertake an engagement to respect the neutrality of Belgium. These are the replies. I got from the French Government this reply :—

" The French Government are resolved to respect the neutrality of Belgium, and it would only be in the event of some other Power violating that neutrality that France might find herself under the necessity, in order to assure the defence of her security, to act otherwise. This assurance has been given several times. The President of the Republic spoke of it to the King of the Belgians, and the French Minister at Brussels has spontaneously renewed the assurance to the Belgian Minister of Foreign Affairs to-day."

From the German Government the reply was :—

" The Secretary of State for Foreign Affairs could not possibly give an answer before consulting the Emperor and the Imperial Chancellor."

Sir Edward Goschen, to whom I had said it was important to have an answer soon, said he hoped the answer would

not be too long delayed. The German Minister for
Foreign Affairs then gave Sir Edward Goschen to understand that he rather doubted whether they could answer
at all, as any reply they might give could not fail, in the
event of war, to have the undesirable effect of disclosing,
to a certain extent, part of their plan of campaign. I
telegraphed at the same time to Brussels to the Belgian
Government, and I got the following reply from Sir Francis
Villiers :—

"The Minister for Foreign Affairs thanks me for the
communication, and replies that Belgium will, to the
utmost of her power, maintain neutrality, and expects
and desires other Powers to observe and uphold it. He
begged me to add that the relations between Belgium
and the neighbouring Powers were excellent, and there
was no reason to suspect their intentions, but that the
Belgian Government believe, in the case of violation,
they were in a position to defend the neutrality of their
country."

It now appears from the news I have received to-day—
which has come quite recently, and I am not yet quite
sure how far it has reached me in an accurate form—that
an ultimatum has been given to Belgium by Germany,
the object of which was to offer Belgium friendly relations
with Germany on condition that she would facilitate the
passage of German troops through Belgium. Well, Sir,
until one has these things absolutely definitely, up to the
last moment, I do not wish to say all that one would say
if one were in a position to give the House full, complete,
and absolute information upon the point. We were
sounded in the course of last week as to whether if a
guarantee were given that, after the war, Belgium integrity
would be preserved that would content us. We replied
that we could not bargain away whatever interests or
obligations we had in Belgian neutrality.

Shortly before I reached the House I was informed that
the following telegram had been received from the King
of the Belgians by our King—King George :—

"Remembering the numerous proofs of your Majesty's
friendship and that of your predecessors, and the friendly

attitude of England in 1870, and the proof of friendship she has just given us again, I make a supreme appeal
to the Diplomatic intervention of your Majesty's Government to safeguard the integrity of Belgium."

Diplomatic intervention took place last week on our part.
What can diplomatic intervention do now ? We have
great and vital interests in the independence—and integrity
is the least part—of Belgium. If Belgium is compelled
to submit to allow her neutrality to be violated, of course
the situation is clear. Even if by agreement she admitted the violation of her neutrality, it is clear she could
only do so under duress. The smaller States in that
region of Europe ask but one thing. Their one desire is
that they should be left alone and independent. The
one thing they fear is, I think, not so much that their
integrity but that their independence should be interfered
with. If in this war which is before Europe the neutrality
of one of those countries is violated, if the troops of one
of the combatants violate its neutrality and no action be
taken to resent it, at the end of the war, whatever the
integrity may be, the independence will be gone.
I have one further quotation from Mr. Gladstone as to
what he thought about the independence of Belgium. It
will be found in " Hansard," vol. 203, p. 1787. I have not
had time to read the whole speech and verify the context,
but the thing seems to me so clear that no context could
make any difference to the meaning of it. Mr. Gladstone
said :—

" We have an interest in the independence of Belgium
which is wider than that which we may have in the
literal operation of the guarantee. It is found in the
answer to the question whether, under the circumstances
of the case, this country, endowed as it is with influence
and power, would quietly stand by and witness the per-
petration of the direst crime that ever stained the pages
of history, and thus become participators in the sin."

No, Sir, if it be the case that there has been anything
in the nature of an ultimatum to Belgium, asking her to
compromise or violate her neutrality, whatever may have
been offered to her in return, her independence is gone if

that holds. If her independence goes, the independence of Holland will follow. I ask the House, from the point of view of British interests, to consider what may be at stake. If France is beaten in a struggle of life and death, beaten to her knees, loses her position as a Great Power, becomes subordinate to the will and power of one greater than herself—consequences which I do not anticipate, because I am sure that France has the power to defend herself with all the energy and ability and patriotism which she has shown so often—still, if that were to happen, and if Belgium fell under the same dominating influence, and then Holland, and then Denmark, then would not Mr. Gladstone's words come true, that just opposite to us there would be a common interest against the unmeasured aggrandizement of any Power?

It may be said, I suppose, that we might stand aside, husband our strength, and that whatever happened in the course of this war, at the end of it intervene with effect to put things right, and to adjust them to our own point of view. If, in a crisis like this, we run away from those obligations of honour and interest as regards the Belgian Treaty, I doubt whether, whatever material force we might have at the end, it would be of very much value in face of the respect that we should have lost. And do not believe, whether a Great Power stands outside this war or not, it is going to be in a position at the end of it to exert its superior strength. For us, with a powerful Fleet, which we believe able to protect our commerce, to protect our shores, and to protect our interests, if we are engaged in war, we shall suffer but little more than we shall suffer even if we stand aside.

We are going to suffer, I am afraid, terribly in this war whether we are in it or whether we stand aside. Foreign trade is going to stop, not because the trade routes are closed, but because there is no trade at the other end. Continental nations engaged in war—all their populations, all their energies, all their wealth, engaged in a desperate struggle—they cannot carry on the trade with us that they are carrying on in times of peace, whether we are parties to the war or whether we are not. I do not believe for a moment, that at the end of this war, even if we stood aside and remained aside, we should be in a position, a material position, to use our force decisively to undo what had happened in the course of the war, to prevent the whole of the West of Europe opposite to us—if that had been the result of the war—falling under the domination of a single Power, and I am quite sure that our moral position would be such as to have lost us all respect. I can only say that I have put the question of Belgium somewhat hypothetically, because I am not yet sure of all the facts, but, if the facts turn out to be as they have reached us at present, it is quite clear that there is an obligation on this country to do its utmost to prevent the consequences to which those facts will lead if they are undisputed.

I have read to the House the only engagements that we have yet taken definitely with regard to the use of force. I think it is due to the House to say that we have taken no engagement yet with regard to sending an Expeditionary armed force out of the country. Mobilization of the Fleet has taken place ; mobilization of the Army is taking place ; but we have as yet taken no engagement, because I do feel that in the case of a European conflagration such as this, unprecedented, with our enormous responsibilities in India and other parts of the Empire, or in countries in British occupation, with all the unknown factors, we must take very carefully into consideration the use which we make of sending an Expeditionary Force out of the country until we know how we stand. One thing I would say.

The one bright spot in the whole of this terrible situation is Ireland. The general feeling throughout Ireland—and I would like this to be clearly understood abroad—does not make the Irish question a consideration which we feel we have now to take into account. I have told the House how far we have at present gone in commitments and the conditions which influence our policy, and I have put to the House and dwelt at length upon how vital is the condition of the neutrality of Belgium.

What other policy is there before the House ? There is but one way in which the Government could make certain at the present moment of keeping outside this war, and that would be that it should immediately issue

22

a proclamation of unconditional neutrality.   We cannot do
that.   We have made the commitment to France that I
have read to the House which prevents us from doing
that.   We have got the consideration of Belgium which
prevents us also from any unconditional neutrality, and,
without those conditions absolutely satisfied and satisfactory, we are bound not to shrink from proceeding to
the use of all the forces in our power.   If we did take that
line by saying, " We will have nothing whatever to do with
this matter " under no conditions—the Belgian Treaty
obligations, the possible position in the Mediterranean,
with damage to British interests, and what may happen
to France from our failure to support France—if we were
to say that all those things mattered nothing, were as
nothing, and to say we would stand aside, we should, I
believe, sacrifice our respect and good name and reputation
before the world, and should not escape the most serious
and grave economic consequences.

My object has been to explain the view of the Government, and to place before the House the issue and the
choice.   I do not for a moment conceal, after what I have
said, and after the information, incomplete as it is, that I
have given to the House with regard to Belgium, that
we must be prepared, and we are prepared, for the consequences of having to use all the strength we have at any
moment—we know not how soon—to defend ourselves
and to take our part.   We know, if the facts all be as I
have stated them, though I have announced no intending
aggressive action on our part, no final decision to resort
to force at a moment's notice, until we know the whole of
the case, that the use of it may be forced upon us.   As
far as the forces of the Crown are concerned, we are ready.
I believe the Prime Minister and my right hon. friend
the First Lord of the Admiralty have no doubt whatever
that the readiness and the efficiency of those forces were
never at a higher mark than they are to-day, and never
was there a time when confidence was more justified in
the power of the Navy to protect our commerce and to
protect our shores.   The thought is with us always of the
suffering and misery entailed from which no country in
Europe will escape abstention, and from which no neutrality
will save us.   The amount of harm that can be done by an

enemy ship to our trade is infinitesimal, compared with
the amount of harm that must be done by the economic
condition that is caused on the Continent.

The most awful responsibility is resting upon the
Government in deciding what to advise the House of
Commons to do. We have disclosed our mind to the
House of Commons. We have disclosed the issue, the
information which we have, and made clear to the House
I trust, that we are prepared to face that situation, and that
should it develop, as probably it may develop, we will
face it. We worked for peace up to the last moment, and
beyond the last moment. How hard, how persistently, and
how earnestly we strove for peace last week, the House will
see from the Papers that will be before it.

But that is over, as far as the peace of Europe is concerned. We are now face to face with a situation and all
the consequences which it may yet have to unfold. We
believe that we shall have the support of the House at
large in proceeding to whatever the consequences may
be and whatever measures may be forced upon us by the
development of facts or action taken by others. I believe
the country, so quickly has the situation been forced upon
it, has not had time to realize the issue. It perhaps is
still thinking of the quarrel between Austria and Servia,
and not the complications of this matter which have
grown out of the quarrel between Austria and Servia.
Russia and Germany we know are at war. We do not yet
know officially that Austria, the ally whom Germany is to
support, is yet at war with Russia. We know that a
good deal has been happening on the French frontier.
We do not know that the German Ambassador has left
Paris.

The situation has developed so rapidly that technically
as regards the condition of the war, it is most difficult to
describe what has actually happened. I wanted to bring
out the underlying issues which would affect our own
conduct, and our own policy, and to put them clearly.
I have put the vital parts before the House, and if, as
seems not improbable, we are forced, and rapidly forced,
to take our stand upon those issues, then I believe, when
the country realizes what is at stake, what the real issues
are, the magnitude of the impending dangers in the West

of Europe, which I have endeavoured to describe to the House, we shall be supported throughout, not only by the House of Commons, but by the determination, the resolution, the courage, and the endurance of the whole country.

PRINTED BY MORRISON AND GIBB LTD., EDINBURGH

A SELECTION OF BOOKS PUBLISHED BY METHUEN AND CO. LTD. LONDON 36 ESSEX STREET W.C. 2

CONTENTS

A SELECTION OF

MESSRS. METHUEN'S
PUBLICATIONS

In this Catalogue the order is according to authors.

Colonial Editions are published of all Messrs. METHUEN'S Novels issued at a price above 4s. net, and similar editions are published of some works of General Literature. Colonial Editions are only for circulation in the British Colonies and India.

All books marked net are not subject to discount, and cannot be bought at less than the published price. Books not marked net are subject to the discount which the bookseller allows.

The prices in this Catalogue are liable to alteration without previous notice.

Messrs. METHUEN'S books are kept in stock by all good booksellers. If there is any difficulty in seeing copies, Messrs. Methuen will be very glad to have early information, and specimen copies of any books will be sent on receipt of the published price *plus* postage for net books, and of the published price for ordinary books.

This Catalogue contains only a selection of the more important books published by Messrs. Methuen. A complete catalogue of their publications may be obtained on application.

Andrewes (Lancelot). PRECES PRIVATAE. Translated and edited, with Notes, by F. E. BRIGHTMAN. *Cr. 8vo. 7s. 6d. net.*

Aristotle. THE ETHICS. Edited, with an Introduction and Notes, by JOHN BURNET. *Demy 8vo. 15s. net.*

Atkinson (T. D.). ENGLISH ARCHITECTURE. Illustrated. *Fourth Edition. Fcap. 8vo. 6s. net.*

A GLOSSARY OF TERMS USED IN ENGLISH ARCHITECTURE. Illustrated. *Second Edition. Fcap. 8vo. 6s. net.*

Atteridge (A. H.). FAMOUS LAND FIGHTS. Illustrated. *Cr. 8vo. 7s. 6d. net.*

Baggally (W. Wortley). TELEPATHY: GENUINE AND FRAUDULENT. *Cr. 8vo. 3s. 6d. net.*

Bain (F. W.). A DIGIT OF THE MOON: A HINDOO LOVE STORY. *Twelfth Edition. Fcap. 8vo. 5s. net.*

THE DESCENT OF THE SUN: A CYCLE OF BIRTH. *Seventh Edition. Fcap. 8vo. 5s. net.*

A HEIFER OF THE DAWN. *Ninth Edition. Fcap. 8vo. 5s. net.*

IN THE GREAT GOD'S HAIR. *Sixth Edition. Fcap. 8vo. 5s. net.*

A DRAUGHT OF THE BLUE. *Sixth Edition. Fcap. 8vo. 5s. net.*

AN ESSENCE OF THE DUSK. *Fourth Edition. Fcap. 8vo. 5s. net.*

AN INCARNATION OF THE SNOW. *Fourth Edition. Fcap. 8vo. 5s. net.*

A MINE OF FAULTS. *Fourth Edition. Fcap. 8vo. 5s. net.*

THE ASHES OF A GOD. *Second Edition. Fcap. 8vo. 5s. net.*

BUBBLES OF THE FOAM. *Second Edition. Fcap. 4to. 7s. 6d. net. Also Fcap. 8vo. 5s. net.*

A SYRUP OF THE BEES. *Fcap. 4to. 7s. 6d. net. Also Fcap. 8vo. 5s. net.*

THE LIVERY OF EVE. *Second Edition. Fcap. 4to. 7s. 6d. net. Also Fcap. 8vo. 5s. net.*

AN ECHO OF THE SPHERES. Rescued from Oblivion by F. W. BAIN. *Wide Demy 8vo. 10s. 6d. net.*

Balfour (Graham). THE LIFE OF ROBERT LOUIS STEVENSON. *Fifteenth Edition. In one Volume. Cr. 8vo. Buckram, 7s. 6d. net.*

Baring (Hon. Maurice). LANDMARKS IN RUSSIAN LITERATURE. *Third Edition. Cr. 8vo. 7s. 6d. net.*

THE RUSSIAN PEOPLE. *Second Edition. Demy 8vo. 15s. net.*

A YEAR IN RUSSIA. *Cr. 8vo. 7s. 6d. net.*

Baring-Gould (S.) THE TRAGEDY OF THE CÆSARS: A STUDY OF THE CHARACTERS OF THE CÆSARS OF THE JULIAN AND CLAUDIAN HOUSES. Illustrated. *Seventh Edition. Royal 8vo. 15s. net.*

A BOOK OF CORNWALL. Illustrated. *Third Edition. Cr. 8vo. 7s. 6d. net.*

A BOOK OF DARTMOOR. Illustrated. *Third Edition. Cr. 8vo. 7s. 6d. net.*

A BOOK OF DEVON. Illustrated. *Third Edition. Cr. 8vo. 7s. 6d. net.*

Baring-Gould (S.) and Sheppard (H. F.). A GARLAND OF COUNTRY SONG. English Folk Songs with their Traditional Melodies. *Demy 4to. 7s. 6d. net.*

Baring-Gould (S.), Sheppard (H. F.), and Bussell (F. W.). SONGS OF THE WEST. Folk Songs of Devon and Cornwall. Collected from the Mouths of the People. New and Revised Edition, under the musical editorship of CECIL J. SHARP. *Second Edition. Large Imperial 8vo. 7s. 6d. net.*

Barker (E.). GREEK POLITICAL THEORY: PLATO AND HIS PREDECESSORS. *Demy 8vo. 14s. net.*

Bastable (C. F.). THE COMMERCE OF NATIONS. *Eighth Edition. Cr. 8vo. 5s. net.*

Beckford (Peter). THOUGHTS ON HUNTING. Edited by J. OTHO PAGET. Illustrated. *Third Edition. Demy 8vo. 7s. 6d. net.*

Belloc (H.). PARIS. Illustrated. *Third Edition. Cr. 8vo. 7s. 6d. net.*

HILLS AND THE SEA. *Ninth Edition. Fcap. 8vo. 6s. net.*

ON NOTHING AND KINDRED SUBJECTS. *Fourth Edition. Fcap. 8vo. 6s. net.*

ON EVERYTHING. *Fourth Edition. Fcap. 8vo. 6s. net.*

ON SOMETHING. *Third Edition. Fcap. 8vo. 6s. net.*

FIRST AND LAST. *Second Edition. Fcap. 8vo. 6s. net.*

THIS AND THAT AND THE OTHER. *Second Edition. Fcap. 8vo. 6s. net.*

MARIE ANTOINETTE. Illustrated. *Fourth Edition. Demy 8vo. 18s. net.*

THE PYRENEES. Illustrated. *Second Edition. Demy 8vo. 10s. 6d. net.*

Bennett (Arnold). THE TRUTH ABOUT AN AUTHOR. *Fcap. 8vo. 5s. net.*

Bennett (W. H.). A PRIMER OF THE BIBLE. *Fifth Edition. Cr. 8vo. 4s. net.*

Bennett (W. H.) and Adeney (W. F.). A BIBLICAL INTRODUCTION. With a concise Bibliography. *Sixth Edition. Cr. 8vo. 8s. 6d. net. Also in Two Volumes. Cr. 8vo. Each 5s. net.*

Berriman (Algernon E.). AVIATION. Illustrated. *Second Edition. Cr. 8vo. 12s. 6d. net.*

MOTORING. Illustrated. *Demy 8vo. 12s. 6d. net.*

Bicknell (Ethel E.). PARIS AND HER TREASURES. Illustrated. *Fcap. 8vo. Round corners. 6s. net.*

Blake (William). ILLUSTRATIONS OF THE BOOK OF JOB. With a General Introduction by LAURENCE BINYON. Illustrated. *Quarto. £1 1s. net.*

Bloemfontein (Bishop of). ARA CŒLI: AN ESSAY IN MYSTICAL THEOLOGY. *Seventh Edition. Cr. 8vo. 5s. net.*

FAITH AND EXPERIENCE. *Third Edition. Cr. 8vo. 5s. net.*

THE CULT OF THE PASSING MOMENT. *Fourth Edition. Cr. 8vo. 5s. net.*

THE ENGLISH CHURCH AND RE-UNION. *Cr. 8vo. 5s. net.*

Brabant (F. G.). RAMBLES IN SUSSEX. Illustrated. *Cr. 8vo. 7s. 6d. net.*

Braid (James). ADVANCED GOLF. Illustrated. *Eighth Edition. Demy 8vo. 12s. 6d. net.*

Bulley (M. H.). ANCIENT AND MEDIEVAL ART. Illustrated. *Cr. 8vo. 7s. 6d. net.*

Carlyle (Thomas). THE FRENCH REVOLUTION. Edited by C. R. L. FLETCHER. *Three Volumes. Cr. 8vo. 18s. net.*

THE LETTERS AND SPEECHES OF OLIVER CROMWELL. With an Introduction by C. H. FIRTH, and Notes and Appendices by S. C. LOMAS. *Three Volumes. Demy 8vo. 18s. net.*

Chambers (Mrs. Lambert). LAWN TENNIS FOR LADIES. Illustrated. *Second Edition. Cr. 8vo. 5s. net.*

Chesterton (G. K.). CHARLES DICKENS. With two Portraits in Photogravure. *Eighth Edition. Cr. 8vo. 7s. 6d. net.*

THE BALLAD OF THE WHITE HORSE. *Fifth Edition. 6s. net.*

ALL THINGS CONSIDERED. *Tenth Edition. Fcap. 8vo. 6s. net.*

TREMENDOUS TRIFLES. *Fifth Edition. Fcap. 8vo. 6s. net.*

ALARMS AND DISCURSIONS. *Second Edition. Fcap. 8vo. 6s. net.*

A MISCELLANY OF MEN. *Second Edition. Fcap. 8vo. 6s. net.*

WINE, WATER, AND SONG. *Ninth Edition. Fcap. 8vo. 1s. 6d. net.*

Clausen (George). ROYAL ACADEMY LECTURES ON PAINTING. Illustrated. *Cr. 8vo. 7s. 6d. net.*

Clephan (R. Coltman). THE TOURNAMENT: Its Periods and Phases. With Preface by CHAS. J. FFOULKES. Illustrated. *Royal 4to. £2 2s. net.*

Clutton-Brock (A.). THOUGHTS ON THE WAR. *Ninth Edition. Fcap. 8vo. 1s. 6d. net.*

WHAT IS THE KINGDOM OF HEAVEN? *Cr. 8vo. 5s. net.*

Conrad (Joseph). THE MIRROR OF THE SEA: Memories and Impressions. *Fcap. 8vo. 5s. net.*

Coulton (G. G.). CHAUCER AND HIS ENGLAND. Illustrated. *Second Edition. Demy 8vo. 12s. 6d. net.*

Cowper (William). POEMS. Edited, with an Introduction and Notes, by J. C. BAILEY. Illustrated. *Demy 8vo. 12s. 6d. net.*

Cox (J. C.). RAMBLES IN SURREY. Illustrated. *Second Edition. Cr. 8vo. 7s. 6d. net.*

RAMBLES IN KENT. Illustrated. *Cr. 8vo. 7s. 6d. net.*

Dalton (Hugh). WITH BRITISH GUNS IN ITALY. Illustrated. *Cr. 8vo. 8s. 6d. net.*

Davis (H. W. C.). ENGLAND UNDER THE NORMANS AND ANGEVINS: 1066-1272. *Fifth Edition. Demy 8vo. 12s. 6d. net.*

Day (Harry A.), F.R.H.S. SPADECRAFT: OR, HOW TO BE GARDENER. *Second Edition. Cr. 8vo. 2s. net.*

VEGECULTURE: HOW TO GROW VEGETABLES, SALADS, AND HERBS IN TOWN AND COUNTRY. *Second Edition. Cr. 8vo. 2s. net.*

THE FOOD-PRODUCING GARDEN. *Cr. 8vo. 2s. net.*

Dearmer (Mabel). A CHILD'S LIFE OF CHRIST. Illustrated. *Fourth Edition. Large Cr. 8vo. 6s. net.*

Dickinson (Mrs. G. L.). THE GREEK VIEW OF LIFE. *Eleventh Edition. Cr. 8vo. 5s. net.*

Ditchfield (P. H.). THE VILLAGE CHURCH. *Second Edition. Illustrated. Cr. 8vo. 6s. net.*

THE ENGLAND OF SHAKESPEARE. Illustrated. *Cr. 8vo. 6s. net.*

Dowden (J.). FURTHER STUDIES IN THE PRAYER BOOK. *Cr. 8vo. 6s. net.*

Durham (The Earl of). THE REPORT ON CANADA. With an Introductory Note. *Second Edition. Demy 8vo. 7s. 6d. net.*

Egerton (H. E.). A SHORT HISTORY OF BRITISH COLONIAL POLICY. *Fifth Edition. Demy 8vo. 10s. 6d. net.*

'Etienne.' A NAVAL LIEUTENANT, 1914-1918. Illustrated. *Cr. 8vo. 8s. 6d. net.*

Fairbrother (W. H.). THE PHILOSOPHY OF T. H. GREEN. *Second Edition. Cr. 8vo. 5s. net.*

ffoulkes (Charles). THE ARMOURER AND HIS CRAFT. Illustrated. *Royal 4to. £2 2s. net.*

DECORATIVE IRONWORK. From the XIth to the XVIIIth Century. Illustrated. *Royal 4to. £2 2s. net.*

Firth (C. H.). CROMWELL'S ARMY. A History of the English Soldier during the Civil Wars, the Commonwealth, and the Protectorate. Illustrated. *Second Edition. Cr. 8vo. 7s. 6d. net.*

Fisher (H. A. L.). THE REPUBLICAN TRADITION IN EUROPE. *Cr. 8vo. 7s. 6d. net.*

FitzGerald (Edward). THE RUBÁIYÁT OF OMAR KHAYYÁM. Printed from the Fifth and last Edition. With a Commentary by H. M. BATSON, and a Biographical Introduction by E. D. ROSS. *Cr. 8vo. 7s. 6d. net.*

Fyleman (Rose). FAIRIES AND CHIMNEYS. *Fcap. 8vo. Fourth Edition. 3s. 6d. net.*

Garstin (Crosby). THE MUD-LARKS AGAIN. *Fcap. 8vo.* 3*s.* 6*d. net.*

Gibbins (H. de B.). INDUSTRY IN ENGLAND: HISTORICAL OUT-LINES. With Maps and Plans. *Ninth Edition. Demy 8vo.* 12*s.* 6*d. net.*

THE INDUSTRIAL HISTORY OF ENGLAND. With 5 Maps and a Plan. *Twenty-sixth Edition. Cr. 8vo.* 5*s.*

Gibbon (Edward). THE DECLINE AND FALL OF THE ROMAN EMPIRE. Edited, with Notes, Appendices, and Maps, by J. B. BURY. Illustrated. *Seven Volumes. Demy 8vo.* Illustrated. *Each* 12*s.* 6*d. net. Also in Seven Volumes. Cr. 8vo. Each* 7*s.* 6*d. net.*

Gladstone (W. Ewart). GLADSTONE'S SPEECHES: DESCRIPTIVE INDEX AND BIBLIOGRAPHY. Edited by A. TILNEY BAS-SETT. With a Preface by VISCOUNT BRYCE, O.M. *Demy 8vo.* 12*s.* 6*d. net.*

Glover (T. R.). THE CONFLICT OF RELIGIONS IN THE EARLY ROMAN EMPIRE. *Seventh Edition. Demy 8vo.* 10*s.* 6*d. net.*

POETS AND PURITANS. *Second Edition. Demy 8vo.* 10*s.* 6*d. net.*

FROM PERICLES TO PHILIP. *Second Edition. Demy 8vo.* 10*s.* 6*d. net.*

VIRGIL. *Third Edition. Demy 8vo.* 10*s.* 6*d. net.*

THE CHRISTIAN TRADITION AND ITS VERIFICATION. (The Angus Lecture for '1912.) *Second Edition. Cr. 8vo.* 6*s. net.*

Grahame (Kenneth). THE WIND IN THE WILLOWS. *Eighth Edition. Cr. 8vo.* 7*s.* 6*d. net.*

Griffin (W. Hall) and Minchin (H. C.). THE LIFE OF ROBERT BROWNING. Illustrated. *Second Edition. Demy 8vo.* 12*s.* 6*d. net.*

Haig (K. G.). HEALTH THROUGH DIET. *Fourth Edition. Cr. 8vo.* 6*s. net.*

Hale (J. R.). FAMOUS SEA FIGHTS: FROM SALAMIS TO TSU-SHIMA. Illustrated. *Third Edition. Cr. 8vo.* 7*s.* 6*d. net.*

Hall (H. R.). THE ANCIENT HISTORY OF THE NEAR EAST FROM THE EARLIEST TIMES TO THE BATTLE OF SALAMIS. Illustrated. *Fourth Edition. Demy 8vo.* 16*s. net.*

Hannay (D.). A SHORT HISTORY OF THE ROYAL NAVY. Vol. I., 1217-1688. *Second Edition.* Vol. II., 1689-1815. *Demy 8vo. Each* 10*s.* 6*d. net.*

Harker (Alfred). THE NATURAL HIS-TORY OF IGNEOUS ROCKS. With 112 Diagrams and 2 Plates. *Demy 8vo.* 15*s. net.*

Harper (Charles G.). THE 'AUTOCAR' ROAD-BOOK. With Maps. *Four Volumes. Cr. 8vo. Each* 8*s.* 6*d. net.*

I.—SOUTH OF THE THAMES.

II.—NORTH AND SOUTH WALES AND WEST MIDLANDS.

III.—EAST ANGLIA AND EAST MIDLANDS.

IV.—THE NORTH OF ENGLAND AND SOUTH OF SCOTLAND.

Hassall (Arthur). THE LIFE OF NAPOLEON. Illustrated. *Demy 8vo.* 10*s.* 6*d. net.*

Henley (W. E.). ENGLISH LYRICS: CHAUCER TO POE. *Second Edition. Cr. 8vo.* 6*s. net.*

Hill (George Francis). ONE HUNDRED MASTERPIECES OF SCULPTURE. Illustrated. *Demy 8vo.* 12*s.* 6*d. net.*

Hobhouse (L. T.). THE THEORY OF KNOWLEDGE. *Second Edition. Demy 8vo.* 15*s. net.*

Hobson (J. A.). INTERNATIONAL TRADE: AN APPLICATION OF ECONOMIC THEORY. *Cr. 8vo.* 5*s. net.*

PROBLEMS OF POVERTY: AN INQUIRY INTO THE INDUSTRIAL CONDITION OF THE POOR. *Eighth Edition. Cr. 8vo.* 5*s. net.*

THE PROBLEM OF THE UN-EMPLOYED: AN INQUIRY AND AN ECONOMIC POLICY. *Sixth Edition. Cr. 8vo.* 5*s. net.*

GOLD, PRICES AND WAGES: WITH AN EXAMINATION OF THE QUANTITY THEORY. *Second Edition. Cr. 8vo.* 5*s. net.*

Hodgson (Mrs. W.). HOW TO IDENTIFY OLD CHINESE PORCELAIN. Illus-trated. *Third Edition. Post 8vo.* 7*s.* 6*d. net.*

Holdsworth (W. S.). A HISTORY OF ENGLISH LAW. *Four Volumes. Vols. I., II., III. Each Second Edition. Demy 8vo. Each* 15*s. net.*

Hutt (C. W.). CROWLEY'S HYGIENE OF SCHOOL LIFE. Illustrated. *Second and Revised Edition. Cr. 8vo.* 6*s. net.*

Hutton (Edward). THE CITIES OF UMBRIA. Illustrated. *Fifth Edition. Cr. 8vo. 7s. 6d. net.*
THE CITIES OF LOMBARDY. Illustrated. *Cr. 8vo. 7s. 6d. net.*
THE CITIES OF ROMAGNA AND THE MARCHES. Illustrated. *Cr. 8vo. 7s. 6d. net.*
FLORENCE AND NORTHERN TUSCANY, WITH GENOA. Illustrated. *Third Edition. Cr. 8vo. 7s. 6d. net.*
SIENA AND SOUTHERN TUSCANY. Illustrated. *Second Edition. Cr. 8vo. 7s. 6d. net.*
VENICE AND VENETIA. Illustrated. *Cr. 8vo. 7s. 6d. net.*
NAPLES AND SOUTHERN ITALY. Illustrated. *Cr. 8vo. 7s. 6d. net.*
ROME. Illustrated. *Third Edition. Cr. 8vo. 7s. 6d. net.*
COUNTRY WALKS ABOUT FLORENCE. Illustrated. *Second Edition. Fcap. 8vo. 6s. net.*
THE CITIES OF SPAIN. Illustrated. *Fifth Edition. Cr. 8vo. 7s. 6d. net.*

Ibsen (Henrik). BRAND. A Dramatic Poem, translated by WILLIAM WILSON. *Fourth Edition. Cr. 8vo. 5s. net.*

Inge (W. R.). CHRISTIAN MYSTICISM. (The Bampton Lectures of 1899.) *Fourth Edition. Cr. 8vo. 7s. 6d. net.*

Innes (A. D.). A HISTORY OF THE BRITISH IN INDIA. With Maps and Plans. *Second Edition. Cr. 8vo. 7s. 6d. net.*
ENGLAND UNDER THE TUDORS. With Maps. *Fifth Edition. Demy 8vo. 12s. 6d. net.*

Innes (Mary). SCHOOLS OF PAINTING. Illustrated. *Third Edition. Cr. 8vo. 8s. net.*

Jenks (E.). AN OUTLINE OF ENGLISH LOCAL GOVERNMENT. *Third Edition.* Revised by R. C. K. ENSOR. *Cr. 8vo. 5s. net.*
A SHORT HISTORY OF ENGLISH LAW: FROM THE EARLIEST TIMES TO THE END OF THE YEAR 1911. *Demy 8vo. 10s. 6d. net.*

Johnston (Sir H. H.). BRITISH CENTRAL AFRICA. Illustrated. *Third Edition. Cr. 4to. 18s. net.*
THE NEGRO IN THE NEW WORLD. Illustrated. *Crown 4to. £1 1s. net.*

Julian (Lady) of Norwich. REVELATIONS OF DIVINE LOVE. Edited by GRACE WARRACK. *Sixth Edition. Cr. 8vo. 5s. net.*

Keats (John). POEMS. Edited, with Introduction and Notes, by E. de SÉLINCOURT. With a Frontispiece in Photogravure. *Third Edition. Demy 8vo. 10s. 6d. net.*

Keble (John). THE CHRISTIAN YEAR. With an Introduction and Notes by W. LOCK. Illustrated. *Third Edition. Fcap. 8vo. 5s. net.*

Kelynack (T. N.), M.D., M.R.C.P. THE DRINK PROBLEM OF TO-DAY IN ITS MEDICO-SOCIOLOGICAL ASPECTS. *Second and Revised Edition. Demy 8vo. 10s. 6d. net.*

Kidd (Benjamin). THE SCIENCE OF POWER. *Eighth Edition. Cr. 8vo. 7s. 6d. net.*

Kipling (Rudyard). BARRACK - ROOM BALLADS. *180th Thousand. Cr. 8vo. Buckram, 7s. 6d. net. Also Fcap. 8vo. Cloth, 6s. net; leather, 7s. 6d. net.* Also a Service Edition. *Two Volumes. Square fcap. 8vo. Each 3s. net.*
THE SEVEN SEAS. *140th Thousand. Cr. 8vo. Buckram, 7s. 6d. net. Also Fcap. 8vo. Cloth, 6s. net; leather, 7s. 6d. net.* Also a Service Edition. *Two Volumes. Square fcap. 8vo. Each 3s. net.*
THE FIVE NATIONS. *120th Thousand. Cr. 8vo. Buckram, 7s. 6d. net. Also Fcap. 8vo. Cloth, 6s. net; leather, 7s. 6d. net.* Also a Service Edition. *Two Volumes. Square fcap. 8vo. Each 3s. net.*
THE YEARS BETWEEN. *Cr. 8vo. Buckram, 7s. 6d. net. Also on thin paper. Fcap. 8vo. Blue cloth, 6s. net; Limp lambskin, 7s. 6d. net.* Also a Service Edition. *Two volumes. Square fcap. 8vo. Each 3s. net.*
DEPARTMENTAL DITTIES. *84th Thousand. Cr. 8vo. Buckram, 7s. 6d. net. Also Fcap. 8vo. Cloth, 6s. net; leather, 7s. 6d. net.* Also a Service Edition. *Two Volumes. Square fcap. 8vo. Each 3s. net.*
HYMN BEFORE ACTION. Illuminated. *Fcap. 4to. 1s. 6d. net.*
RECESSIONAL. Illuminated. *Fcap. 4to. 1s. 6d. net.*
TWENTY POEMS FROM RUDYARD KIPLING. *360th Thousand. Fcap. 8vo. 1s. net.*

Lamb (Charles and Mary). THE COMPLETE WORKS. Edited by E. V. LUCAS. *A New and Revised Edition in Six Volumes. With Frontispieces. Fcap. 8vo. Each 6s. net.*
The volumes are:—
I. MISCELLANEOUS PROSE. II. ELIA AND THE LAST ESSAYS OF ELIA. III. BOOKS FOR CHILDREN. IV. PLAYS AND POEMS. V. and VI. LETTERS.

Lane-Poole (Stanley). A HISTORY OF
EGYPT IN THE MIDDLE AGES.
Illustrated. *Second Edition, Revised.* Cr.
8vo. 9s. net.

Lankester (Sir Ray). SCIENCE FROM
AN EASY CHAIR. Illustrated. *Eighth
Edition.* Cr. 8vo. 7s. 6d. net.
SCIENCE FROM AN EASY CHAIR.
Second Series. Illustrated. *First Edition.*
Cr. 8vo. 7s. 6d. net.
DIVERSIONS OF A NATURALIST.
Illustrated. *Second Edition.* Cr. 8vo.
7s. 6d. net.

Lewis (Edward). EDWARD CARPEN-
TER : AN EXPOSITION AND AN APPRECIA-
TION. *Second Edition.* Cr. 8vo. 6s. net.

Lock (Walter). ST. PAUL, THE
MASTER BUILDER. *Third Edition.*
Cr. 8vo. 5s. net.
THE BIBLE AND CHRISTIAN LIFE.
Cr. 8vo. 6s. net.

Lodge (Sir Oliver). MAN AND THE
UNIVERSE : A STUDY OF THE INFLUENCE
OF THE ADVANCE IN SCIENTIFIC KNOW-
LEDGE UPON OUR UNDERSTANDING OF
CHRISTIANITY. *Ninth Edition. Crown 8vo.*
7s. 6d. net.
THE SURVIVAL OF MAN : A STUDY IN
UNRECOGNISED HUMAN FACULTY. *Seventh
Edition.* Cr. 8vo. 7s. 6d. net.
MODERN PROBLEMS. *Cr. 8vo.* 7s. 6d.
net.
RAYMOND ; OR, LIFE AND DEATH. Illus-
trated. *Eleventh Edition. Demy 8vo.* 15s.
net.
THE WAR AND AFTER : SHORT CHAP-
TERS ON SUBJECTS OF SERIOUS PRACTICAL
IMPORT FOR THE AVERAGE CITIZEN IN A.D.
1915 ONWARDS. *Eighth Edition. Fcap.*
8vo. 2s. net.

Loreburn (Earl). CAPTURE AT SEA.
Second Edition. Cr. 8vo. 2s. 6d. net.
HOW THE WAR CAME. With a Map.
Cr. 8vo. 7s. 6d. net.

Lorimer (George Horace). LETTERS
FROM A SELF-MADE MERCHANT
TO HIS SON. Illustrated. *Twenty-
fourth Edition.* Cr. 8vo. 6s. net.
OLD GORGON GRAHAM. Illustrated.
Second Edition. Cr. 8vo. 6s. net.

Lorimer (Norma). BY THE WATERS
OF EGYPT. Illustrated. *Third Edition.*
Cr. 8vo. 7s. 6d. net.

Lucas (E. V.). THE LIFE OF CHARLES
LAMB. Illustrated. *Sixth Edition. Demy
8vo.* 10s. 6d. net.

A WANDERER IN HOLLAND. Illus-
trated. *Sixteenth Edition.* Cr. 8vo. 8s. 6d.
net.
A WANDERER IN LONDON. Illus-
trated. *Eighteenth Edition, Revised.* Cr.
8vo. 8s. 6d. net.
LONDON REVISITED. Illustrated. *Third
Edition.* Cr. 8vo. 8s. 6d. net.
A WANDERER IN PARIS. Illustrated.
Thirteenth Edition. Cr. 8vo. 8s. 6d. net.
Also Fcap. 8vo. 6s. net.
A WANDERER IN FLORENCE. Illus-
trated. *Sixth Edition.* Cr. 8vo. 8s. 6d.
net.
A WANDERER IN VENICE. Illustrated.
Second Edition. Cr. 8vo. 8s. 6d. net.
THE OPEN ROAD : A LITTLE BOOK FOR
WAYFARERS. *Twenty-seventh Edition.*
Fcap. 8vo. 6s. 6d. net. *India Paper,* 7s. 6d.
net.
Also Illustrated. Cr. 4to. 15s. net.
THE FRIENDLY TOWN : A LITTLE BOOK
FOR THE URBANE. *Ninth Edition. Fcap.*
8vo. 6s. net.
FIRESIDE AND SUNSHINE. *Ninth
Edition. Fcap.* 8vo. 6s. net.
CHARACTER AND COMEDY. *Eighth
Edition. Fcap.* 8vo. 6s. net.
THE GENTLEST ART : A CHOICE OF
LETTERS BY ENTERTAINING HANDS.
Tenth Edition. Fcap. 8vo. 6s. net.
THE SECOND POST. *Fifth Edition.*
Fcap. 8vo. 6s. net.
HER INFINITE VARIETY : A FEMININE
PORTRAIT GALLERY. *Eighth Edition.*
Fcap. 8vo. 6s. net.
GOOD COMPANY : A RALLY OF MEN.
Fourth Edition. Fcap. 8vo. 6s. net.
ONE DAY AND ANOTHER. *Seventh
Edition. Fcap.* 8vo. 6s. net.
OLD LAMPS FOR NEW. *Sixth Edition.*
Fcap. 8vo. 6s. net.
LOITERER'S HARVEST. *Third Edition.*
Fcap. 8vo. 6s. net.
CLOUD AND SILVER. *Third Edition.*
Fcap. 8vo. 6s. net.
LISTENER'S LURE : AN OBLIQUE NARRA-
TION. *Twelfth Edition. Fcap.* 8vo. 6s. net.
OVER BEMERTON'S : AN EASY-GOING
CHRONICLE. *Sixteenth Edition.* Fcap.
8vo. 6s. net.
MR. INGLESIDE. *Twelfth Edition.*
Fcap. 8vo. 6s. net.
LONDON LAVENDER. *Twelfth Edition.*
Fcap. 8vo. 6s. net.
LANDMARKS. *Fifth Edition. Fcap.* 8vo.
6s. net.

8   METHUEN AND COMPANY LIMITED

THE BRITISH SCHOOL : An Anecdotal
Guide to the British Painters and
Paintings in the National Gallery.
Fcap. 8vo. 6s. net.

A BOSWELL OF BAGHDAD, AND
OTHER ESSAYS. *Third Edition. Fcap.
8vo. 6s. net.*

'TWIXT EAGLE AND DOVE. *Third
Edition. Fcap. 8vo. 6s. net.*

Lydekker (R.). THE OX AND ITS
KINDRED. Illustrated. *Cr. 8vo. 7s. 6d.
net.*

Macaulay (Lord). CRITICAL AND
HISTORICAL ESSAYS. Edited by F.
C. Montague. *Three Volumes. Cr. 8vo.
18s. net.*

Macdonald (J. R. M.). A HISTORY OF
FRANCE. *Three Volumes. Cr. 8vo.
Each 10s. 6d. net.*

McDougall (William). AN INTRODUC-
TION TO SOCIAL PSYCHOLOGY.
Twelfth Edition. Cr. 8vo. 7s. 6d. net.

BODY AND MIND: A History and a
Defence of Animism. *Fourth Edition.
Demy 8vo. 12s. 6d. net.*

Maeterlinck (Maurice). THE BLUE
BIRD: A Fairy Play in Six Acts.
Translated by Alexander Teixeira de
Mattos. *Fcap. 8vo. 6s. net. Also Fcap.
8vo. 2s. net.* Of the above book Forty-
one Editions in all have been issued.

MARY MAGDALENE: A Play in Three
Acts. Translated by Alexander Teixeira
de Mattos. *Third Edition. Fcap. 8vo.
3s. net. Also Fcap. 8vo. 2s. net.*

DEATH. Translated by Alexander Teixeira de Mattos. *Fourth Edition. Fcap.
8vo. 3s. 6d. net.*

OUR ETERNITY. Translated by Alexander Teixeira de Mattos. *Second
Edition. Fcap. 8vo. 6s. net.*

THE UNKNOWN GUEST. Translated
by Alexander Teixeira de Mattos.
Third Edition. Cr. 8vo. 6s. net.

POEMS. Done into English Verse by
Bernard Miall. *Second Edition. Cr.
8vo. 5s. net.*

THE WRACK OF THE STORM. *Third
Edition. Cr. 8vo. 6s. net.*

THE MIRACLE OF ST. ANTHONY: A
Play in One Act. Translated by Alexander Teixeira de Mattos. *Fcap. 8vo.
3s. 6d. net.*

THE BURGOMASTER OF STILE-
MONDE: A Play in Three Acts.
Translated by Alexander Teixeira de
Mattos. *Fcap. 8vo. 5s. net.*

THE BETROTHAL; or, The Blue
Bird Chooses. Translated by Alexander Teixeira de Mattos. *Fcap. 8vo.
6s. net.*

MOUNTAIN PATHS. Translated by Alexander Teixeira de Mattos. *Fcap. 8vo.
6s. net.*

Mahaffy (J. P.). A HISTORY OF EGYPT
UNDER THE PTOLEMAIC DYNASTY.
Illustrated. *Second Edition. Cr. 8vo. 9s.
net.*

Maitland (F. W.). ROMAN CANON LAW
IN THE CHURCH OF ENGLAND.
Royal 8vo. 10s. 6d. net.

Marett (R. R.). THE THRESHOLD OF
RELIGION. *Third Edition. Cr. 8vo.
7s. 6d. net.*

Marriott (J. A. R.). ENGLAND SINCE
WATERLOO. With Maps. *Second
Edition, Revised. Demy 8vo. 12s. 6d. net.*

Masefield (John). A SAILOR'S GAR-
LAND. Selected and Edited. *Second
Edition. Cr. 8vo. 6s. net.*

Masterman (C. F. G.). TENNYSON
AS A RELIGIOUS TEACHER. *Second
Edition. Cr. 8vo. 7s. 6d. net.*

Medley (D. J.). ORIGINAL ILLUSTRA-
TIONS OF ENGLISH CONSTITU-
TIONAL HISTORY. *Cr. 8vo. 8s. 6d.
net.*

Miles (Eustace). LIFE AFTER LIFE;
or, The Theory of Reincarnation.
Cr. 8vo. 3s. 6d. net.

THE POWER OF CONCENTRATION:
How to Acquire it. *Fifth Edition.
Cr. 8vo. 6s. net.*

PREVENTION AND CURE. *Second
Edition. Crown 8vo. 5s. net.*

Miles (Mrs. Eustace). HEALTH WITH-
OUT MEAT. *Sixth Edition. Fcap. 8vo.
2s. 6d. net.*

Millais (J. G.). THE LIFE AND LET-
TERS OF SIR JOHN EVERETT
MILLAIS. Illustrated. *Third Edition.
Demy 8vo. 12s. 6d. net.*

Milne (J. G.). A HISTORY OF EGYPT
UNDER ROMAN RULE. Illustrated.
Second Edition. Cr. 8vo. 9s. net.

Money (Sir Leo Chiozza). RICHES AND
POVERTY, 1910. *Eleventh Edition.
Demy 8vo. 5s. net.*

Montague (C. E.). DRAMATIC VALUES.
Second Edition. Fcap. 8vo. 5s. net.

Myers (Charles S.). PRESENT-DAY
APPLICATIONS OF PSYCHOLOGY.
Third Edition. Fcap. 8vo. 1s. 3d. net.

Noyes (Alfred). A SALUTE FROM THE
FLEET, AND OTHER POEMS. *Third
Edition. Cr. 8vo. 7s. 6d. net.*
RADA: A BELGIAN CHRISTMAS EVE. Illus-
trated. *Fcap. 8vo. 5s. net.*

Oman (C. W. C.). A HISTORY OF THE
ART OF WAR IN THE MIDDLE
AGES. Illustrated. *Demy 8vo. 15s. net.*
ENGLAND BEFORE THE NORMAN
CONQUEST. With Maps. *Third Edi-
tion, Revised. Demy 8vo. 12s. 6d. net.*

Oxenham (John). BEES IN AMBER: A
LITTLE BOOK OF THOUGHTFUL VERSE.
*118th Thousand. Small Pott 8vo. Paper
1s. 3d. net; Cloth Boards, 2s. net.
Also Illustrated. Fcap. 8vo. 3s. 6d. net.*
ALL'S WELL: A COLLECTION OF WAR
POEMS. *175th Thousand. Small Pott
8vo. Paper, 1s. 3d. net; Cloth Boards,
2s. net.*
THE KING'S HIGH WAY. *120th Thousand.
Small Pott 8vo. 1s. 3d. net; Cloth Boards,
2s. net.*
THE VISION SPLENDID. *100th Thou-
sand. Small Pott 8vo. Paper, 1s. 3d. net;
Cloth Boards, 2s. net.*
THE FIERY CROSS. *80th Thousand.
Small Pott 8vo. Paper, 1s. 3d. net; Cloth
Boards, 2s. net.*
HIGH ALTARS: THE RECORD OF A VISIT
TO THE BATTLEFIELDS OF FRANCE AND
FLANDERS. *40th Thousand. Small Pott
8vo. 1s. 3d. net; Cloth Boards, 2s. net.*
HEARTS COURAGEOUS. *Small Pott
8vo. 1s. 3d net. Cloth Boards, 2s. net.*
ALL CLEAR. *Small Pott 8vo. 1s. 3d. net.
Cloth Boards, 2s. net.*
WINDS OF THE DAWN. *Small Pott 8vo.
2s. net.*

Oxford (M. N.). A HANDBOOK OF
NURSING. *Seventh Edition, Revised.
Cr. 8vo. 5s. net.*

Pakes (W. C. C.). THE SCIENCE OF
HYGIENE. Illustrated. *Second and
Cheaper Edition.* Revised by A. T.
NANKIVELL. *Cr. 8vo. 6s. net.*

Petrie (W. M. Flinders.) A HISTORY
OF EGYPT. Illustrated. *Six Volumes
Cr. 8vo. Each 9s. net.*
VOL. I. FROM THE 1ST TO THE XVITH
DYNASTY. *Eighth Edition.*
VOL. II. THE XVIITH AND XVIIITH
DYNASTIES. *Sixth Edition.*
VOL. III. XIXTH TO XXXTH DYNASTIES.
Second Edition.
VOL. IV. EGYPT UNDER THE PTOLEMAIC
DYNASTY. J. P. MAHAFFY. *Second Edition.*

VOL. V. EGYPT UNDER ROMAN RULE. J. G.
MILNE. *Second Edition.*
VOL. VI. EGYPT IN THE MIDDLE AGES.
STANLEY LANE POOLE. *Second Edition.*
RELIGION AND CONSCIENCE IN
ANCIENT EGYPT. Illustrated. *Cr. 8vo.
5s. net.*
SYRIA AND EGYPT, FROM THE TELL
EL AMARNA LETTERS. *Cr. 8vo.
5s. net.*
EGYPTIAN TALES. Translated from the
Papyri. First Series, ivth to xiith Dynasty.
Illustrated. *Third Edition. Cr. 8vo.
5s. net.*
EGYPTIAN TALES. Translated from the
Papyri. Second Series, xviiith to xixth
Dynasty. Illustrated. *Second Edition.
Cr. 8vo. 5s. net.*

Pollard (Alfred W.). SHAKESPEARE
FOLIOS AND QUARTOS. A Study in
the Bibliography of Shakespeare's Plays,
1594-1685. Illustrated. *Folio. £1 1s. net.*

Porter (G. R.). THE PROGRESS OF
THE NATION. A New Edition. Edited
by F. W. HIRST. *Demy 8vo. £1 1s. net.*

Power (J. O'Connor). THE MAKING OF
AN ORATOR. *Cr. 8vo. 6s. net.*

Price (L. L.). A SHORT HISTORY OF
POLITICAL ECONOMY IN ENGLAND
FROM ADAM SMITH TO ARNOLD
TOYNBEE. *Ninth Edition. Cr. 8vo.
5s. net.*

Rawlings (Gertrude B.). COINS AND
HOW TO KNOW THEM. Illustrated.
Third Edition. Cr. 8vo. 7s. 6d. net.

Regan (C. Tate). THE FRESHWATER
FISHES OF THE BRITISH ISLES.
Illustrated. *Cr. 8vo. 7s. 6d. net.*

Reid (G. Archdall). THE LAWS OF
HEREDITY. *Second Edition. Demy 8vo.
£1 1s. net.*

Robertson (C. Grant). SELECT STAT-
UTES, CASES, AND DOCUMENTS,
1660-1832. *Second Edition, Revised and
Enlarged. Demy 8vo. 15s. net.*
ENGLAND UNDER THE HANOVER-
IANS. Illustrated. *Third Edition. Demy
8vo. 12s. 6d. net.*

Rolle (Richard). THE FIRE OF LOVE
AND THE MENDING OF LIFE.
Edited by FRANCES M. COMPER. *Cr. 8vo.
6s. net.*

Ryley (A. Beresford). OLD PASTE.
Illustrated. *Royal 4to. £2 2s. net.*

'Saki' (H. H. Munro). REGINALD.
Fourth Edition. Fcap. 8vo. 3s. 6d. net.

2

REGINALD IN RUSSIA. *Fcap. 8vo.*
3s. 6d. net.

Schidrowitz (Philip). RUBBER. Illustrated. *Second Edition. Demy 8vo. 15s. net.*

Selous (Edmund). TOMMY SMITH'S ANIMALS. Illustrated. *Sixteenth Edition. Fcap. 8vo. 3s. 6d. net.*

TOMMY SMITH'S OTHER ANIMALS. Illustrated. *Seventh Edition. Fcap. 8vo. 3s. 6d. net.*

TOMMY SMITH AT THE ZOO. Illustrated. *Second Edition. Fcap. 8vo. 2s. 9d.*

TOMMY SMITH AGAIN AT THE ZOO. Illustrated. *Fcap. 8vo. 2s. 9d.*

JACK'S INSECTS. Illustrated. *Cr. 8vo. 6s. net.*

Shakespeare (William). THE FOUR FOLIOS, 1623; 1632; 1664; 1685. Each £4 4s. net, or a complete set, £12 12s. net.

THE POEMS OF WILLIAM SHAKESPEARE. With an Introduction and Notes by GEORGE WYNDHAM. *Demy 8vo. Buckram, 12s. 6d. net.*

Shelley (Percy Bysshe). POEMS. With an Introduction by A. CLUTTON-BROCK and notes by C. D. LOCOCK. *Two Volumes. Demy 8vo. £1 1s. net.*

Sladen (Douglas). SICILY: THE NEW WINTER RESORT. An Encyclopædia of Sicily. With 234 Illustrations, a Map, and a Table of the Railway System of Sicily. *Second Edition, Revised. Cr. 8vo. 7s. 6d. net.*

Sleaser (H. H.). TRADE UNIONISM. *Cr. 8vo. 5s. net.*

Smith (Adam). THE WEALTH OF NATIONS. Edited by EDWIN CANNAN. *Two Volumes. Demy 8vo. £1 5s. net.*

Smith (G. F. Herbert). GEM-STONES AND THEIR DISTINCTIVE CHARACTERS. Illustrated. *Second Edition. Cr. 8vo. 7s. 6d. net.*

Stancliffe. GOLF DO'S AND DONT'S. *Sixth Edition. Fcap. 8vo. 2s. net.*

Stevenson (R. L.). THE LETTERS OF ROBERT LOUIS STEVENSON. Edited by Sir SIDNEY COLVIN. *A New Rearranged Edition in four volumes. Fourth Edition. Fcap. 8vo. Each 6s. net. Leather, each 7s. net.*

Surtees (R. S.). HANDLEY CROSS. Illustrated. *Eighth Edition. Fcap. 8vo. 7s. 6d. net.*

MR. SPONGE'S SPORTING TOUR. Illustrated. *Fourth Edition. Fcap. 8vo. 7s. 6d. net.*

ASK MAMMA; or, THE RICHEST COMMONER IN ENGLAND. Illustrated. *Second Edition. Fcap. 8vo. 7s. 6d. net.*

JORROCKS'S JAUNTS AND JOLLITIES. Illustrated. *Sixth Edition. Fcap. 8vo. 6s. net.*

MR. FACEY ROMFORD'S HOUNDS. Illustrated. *Third Edition. Fcap. 8vo. 7s. 6d. net.*

HAWBUCK GRANGE; or, THE SPORTING ADVENTURES OF THOMAS SCOTT, Esq. Illustrated. *Fcap. 8vo. 6s. net.*

PLAIN OR RINGLETS? Illustrated. *Fcap. 8vo. 7s. 6d. net.*

HILLINGDON HALL. With 12 Coloured Plates by WILDRAKE, HEATH, and JELLICOE. *Fcap. 8vo. 7s. 6d. net.*

Suso (Henry). THE LIFE OF THE BLESSED HENRY SUSO. By HIMSELF. Translated by T. F. KNOX. With an Introduction by DEAN INGE. *Second Edition. Cr. 8vo. 6s. net.*

Swanton (E. W.). FUNGI AND HOW TO KNOW THEM. Illustrated. *Cr. 8vo. 10s. 6d. net.*

BRITISH PLANT-GALLS. *Cr. 8vo. 10s. 6d. net.*

Tabor (Margaret E.). THE SAINTS IN ART. With their Attributes and Symbols Alphabetically Arranged. Illustrated. *Third Edition. Fcap. 8vo. 5s. net.*

Taylor (A. E.). ELEMENTS OF METAPHYSICS. *Fourth Edition. Demy 8vo. 12s. 6d. net.*

Taylor (J. W.). THE COMING OF THE SAINTS. *Second Edition. Cr. 8vo. 6s. net.*

Thomas (Edward). MAURICE MAETERLINCK. Illustrated. *Second Edition. Cr. 8vo. 6s. net.*

A LITERARY PILGRIM IN ENGLAND. Illustrated. *Demy 8vo. 12s. 6d. net.*

Tileston (Mary W.). DAILY STRENGTH FOR DAILY NEEDS. *Twenty-fifth Edition. Medium 16mo. 3s. 6d. net.*

Toynbee (Paget). DANTE ALIGHIERI. His LIFE AND WORKS. With 16 Illustrations. *Fourth and Enlarged Edition. Cr. 8vo. 6s. net.*

Trevelyan (G. M.). ENGLAND UNDER THE STUARTS. With Maps and Plans. *Seventh Edition. Demy 8vo. 12s. 6d. net.*

Triggs (H. Inigo). TOWN PLANNING: PAST, PRESENT, AND POSSIBLE. Illustrated. *Second Edition. Wide Royal 8vo. 16s. net.*

PART II.—A SELECTION OF SERIES

Ancient Cities

General Editor, SIR B. C. A. WINDLE

Cr. 8vo.   6s. net each volume

With Illustrations by E. H. NEW, and other Artists

BRISTOL. Alfred Harvey.

CANTERBURY. J. C. Cox.

CHESTER. Sir B. C. A. Windle.

DUBLIN. S. A. O. Fitzpatrick.

EDINBURGH. M. G. Williamson.

LINCOLN. E. Mansel Sympson.

SHREWSBURY. T. Auden.

WELLS and GLASTONBURY. T. S. Holmes.

The Antiquary's Books

General Editor, J. CHARLES COX

Demy 8vo.   10s. 6d. net each volume

With Numerous Illustrations

ANCIENT PAINTED GLASS IN ENGLAND. Philip Nelson.

ARCHÆOLOGY AND FALSE ANTIQUITIES. R. Munro.

BELLS OF ENGLAND, THE. Canon J. J. Raven. *Second Edition.*

BRASSES OF ENGLAND, THE. Herbert W. Macklin. *Third Edition.*

CASTLES AND WALLED TOWNS OF ENGLAND, THE. A. Harvey.

CELTIC ART IN PAGAN AND CHRISTIAN TIMES. J. Romilly Allen. *Second Edition.*

CHURCHWARDENS' ACCOUNTS. J. C. Cox.

DOMESDAY INQUEST, THE. Adolphus Ballard.

ENGLISH CHURCH FURNITURE. J. C. Cox and A. Harvey. *Second Edition.*

ENGLISH COSTUME. From Prehistoric Times to the End of the Eighteenth Century. George Clinch.

ENGLISH MONASTIC LIFE. Cardinal Gasquet. *Fourth Edition.*

ENGLISH SEALS. J. Harvey Bloom.

FOLK-LORE AS AN HISTORICAL SCIENCE. Sir G. L. Gomme.

GILDS AND COMPANIES OF LONDON, THE. George Unwin.

HERMITS AND ANCHORITES OF ENGLAND, THE. Rotha Mary Clay.

MANOR AND MANORIAL RECORDS, THE. Nathaniel J. Hone. *Second Edition.*

MEDIÆVAL HOSPITALS OF ENGLAND, THE. Rotha Mary Clay.

OLD ENGLISH INSTRUMENTS OF MUSIC. F. W. Galpin. *Second Edition.*

The Antiquary's Books—continued

OLD ENGLISH LIBRARIES. Ernest A. Savage.

OLD SERVICE BOOKS OF THE ENGLISH CHURCH. Christopher Wordsworth, and Henry Littlehales. *Second Edition.*

PARISH LIFE IN MEDIÆVAL ENGLAND. Cardinal Gasquet. *Fourth Edition.*

PARISH REGISTERS OF ENGLAND, THE. J. C. Cox.

REMAINS OF THE PREHISTORIC AGE IN ENGLAND. Sir B. C. A. Windle. *Second Edition.*

ROMAN ERA IN BRITAIN, THE. J. Ward.

ROMANO-BRITISH BUILDINGS AND EARTHWORKS. J. Ward.

ROYAL FORESTS OF ENGLAND, THE. J. C. Cox.

SCHOOLS OF MEDIEVAL ENGLAND, THE. A. F. Leach. *Second Edition.*

SHRINES OF BRITISH SAINTS. J. C. Wall.

The Arden Shakespeare

General Editor—R. H. CASE

Demy 8vo. 6s. net each volume

An edition of Shakespeare in Single Plays; each edited with a full Introduction, Textual Notes, and a Commentary at the foot of the page

ALL'S WELL THAT ENDS WELL.
ANTONY AND CLEOPATRA. *Third Edition.*
AS YOU LIKE IT.
CYMBELINE. *Second Edition.*
COMEDY OF ERRORS, THE.
HAMLET. *Fourth Edition.*
JULIUS CAESAR. *Second Edition.*
KING HENRY IV. PT. I.
KING HENRY V. *Second Edition.*
KING HENRY VI. PT. I.
KING HENRY VI. PT. II.
KING HENRY VI. PT. III
KING HENRY VIII.
KING LEAR. *Second Edition.*
KING RICHARD II.
KING RICHARD III. *Second Edition.*
LIFE AND DEATH OF KING JOHN, THE.
LOVE'S LABOUR'S LOST. *Second Edition.*

MACBETH. *Second Edition.*
MEASURE FOR MEASURE.
MERCHANT OF VENICE, THE. *Fourth Edition.*
MERRY WIVES OF WINDSOR, THE.
MIDSUMMER NIGHT'S DREAM, A.
OTHELLO. *Second Edition.*
PERICLES.
ROMEO AND JULIET. *Second Edition.*
SONNETS AND A LOVER'S COMPLAINT.
TAMING OF THE SHREW, THE.
TEMPEST, THE. *Second Edition.*
TIMON OF ATHENS.
TITUS ANDRONICUS.
TROILUS AND CRESSIDA.
TWELFTH NIGHT. *Third Edition.*
TWO GENTLEMEN OF VERONA, THE.
VENUS AND ADONIS.
WINTER'S TALE, THE.

Classics of Art

Edited by DR. J. H. W. LAING

With numerous Illustrations. Wide Royal 8vo

ART OF THE GREEKS, THE. H. B. Walters. 15s. net.

ART OF THE ROMANS, THE. H. B. Walters. 16s. net.

CHARDIN. H. E. A. Furst. 15s. net.

DONATELLO. Maud Cruttwell. 16s. net.

FLORENTINE SCULPTORS OF THE RENAISSANCE. Wilhelm Bode. Translated by Jessie Haynes. 15s. net.

GEORGE ROMNEY. Arthur B. Chamberlain. 15s. net.

Classes of Art—continued

GHIRLANDAIO. Gerald S. Davies. *Second Edition.* 15s. net.

LAWRENCE. Sir Walter Armstrong. 25s. net.

MICHELANGELO. Gerald S. Davies. 15s. net.

RAPHAEL. A. P. Oppé. 15s. net.

REMBRANDT'S ETCHINGS. A. M. Hind. Two Volumes. 25s. net.

RUBENS. Edward Dillon. 30s. net.

TINTORETTO. Evelyn March Phillipps. 16s. net.

TITIAN. Charles Ricketts. 16s. net.

TURNER'S SKETCHES AND DRAWINGS. A. J. Finberg. *Second Edition.* 15s. net.

VELAZQUEZ. A. de Beruete. 15s. net.

The 'Complete' Series

Fully Illustrated. Demy 8vo

COMPLETE AMATEUR BOXER, THE. J. G. Bohun Lynch. 10s. 6d. net.

COMPLETE ASSOCIATION FOOTBALLER, THE. B. S. Evers and C. E. Hughes-Davies. 10s. 6d. net.

COMPLETE ATHLETIC TRAINER, THE. S. A. Mussabini. 10s. 6d. net.

COMPLETE BILLIARD PLAYER, THE. Charles Roberts. 12s. 6d. net.

COMPLETE COOK, THE. Lilian Whitling. 10s. 6d. net.

COMPLETE CRICKETER, THE. Albert E. Knight. *Second Edition.* 10s. 6d. net.

COMPLETE FOXHUNTER, THE. Charles Richardson. *Second Edition.* 16s. net.

COMPLETE GOLFER, THE. Harry Vardon. *Fifteenth Edition, Revised.* 12s. 6d. net.

COMPLETE HOCKEY-PLAYER, THE. Eustace E. White. *Second Edition.* 10s. 6d. net.

COMPLETE HORSEMAN, THE. W. Scarth Dixon. *Second Edition.* 12s. 6d. net.

COMPLETE JUJITSUAN, THE. W. H. Garrud. 5s. net.

COMPLETE LAWN TENNIS PLAYER, THE. A. Wallis Myers. *Fourth Edition.* 12s. 6d. net.

COMPLETE MOTORIST, THE. Filson Young and W. G. Aston. *Revised Edition.* 10s. 6d. net.

COMPLETE MOUNTAINEER, THE. G. D. Abraham. *Second Edition.* 16s. net.

COMPLETE OARSMAN, THE. R. C. Lehmann. 12s. 6d. net.

COMPLETE PHOTOGRAPHER, THE. R. Child Bayley. *Fifth Edition, Revised.* 12s. 6d. net.

COMPLETE RUGBY FOOTBALLER, ON THE NEW ZEALAND SYSTEM, THE. D. Gallaher and W. J. Stead. *Second Edition.* 12s. 6d. net.

COMPLETE SHOT, THE. G. T. Teasdale-Buckell. *Third Edition.* 16s. net.

COMPLETE SWIMMER, THE. F. Sachs. 10s. 6d. net.

COMPLETE YACHTSMAN, THE. B. Heckstall-Smith and E. du Boulay. *Second Edition, Revised.* 16s. net.

The Connoisseur's Library

With numerous Illustrations. Wide Royal 8vo. 25s. net each volume

ENGLISH COLOURED BOOKS. Martin Hardie.

ENGLISH FURNITURE. F. S. Robinson. *Second Edition.*

ETCHINGS. Sir F. Wedmore. *Second Edition.*

EUROPEAN ENAMELS. Henry H. Cunynghame.

FINE BOOKS. A. W. Pollard.

GLASS. Edward Dillon.

GOLDSMITHS' AND SILVERSMITHS' WORK. Nelson Dawson. *Second Edition.*

ILLUMINATED MANUSCRIPTS. J. A. Herbert. *Second Edition.*

IVORIES. Alfred Maskell.

JEWELLERY. H. Clifford Smith. *Second Edition.*

MEZZOTINTS. Cyril Davenport.

MINIATURES. Dudley Heath.

PORCELAIN. Edward Dillon.

SEALS. Walter de Gray Birch.

WOOD SCULPTURE. Alfred Maskell.

Handbooks of English Church History

Edited by J. H. BURN. *Crown 8vo. 5s. net each volume*

FOUNDATIONS OF THE ENGLISH CHURCH, THE. J. H. Maude.

SAXON CHURCH AND THE NORMAN CONQUEST, THE. C. T. Cruttwell.

MEDIÆVAL CHURCH AND THE PAPACY, THE. A. C. Jennings.

REFORMATION PERIOD, THE. Henry Gee.

STRUGGLE WITH PURITANISM, THE. Bruce Blaxland.

CHURCH OF ENGLAND IN THE EIGHTEENTH CENTURY, THE. Alfred Plummer.

Handbooks of Theology

Demy 8vo

DOCTRINE OF THE INCARNATION, THE. R. L. Ottley. *Fifth Edition. 15s. net.*

HISTORY OF EARLY CHRISTIAN DOCTRINE, A. J. F. Bethune-Baker. *15s. net.*

INTRODUCTION TO THE HISTORY OF RELIGION, AN. F. B. Jevons. *Seventh Edition. 12s. 6d. net.*

INTRODUCTION TO THE HISTORY OF THE CREEDS, AN. A. E. Burn. *12s. 6d. net.*

PHILOSOPHY OF RELIGION IN ENGLAND AND AMERICA, THE. Alfred Caldecott. *12s. 6d. net.*

XXXIX ARTICLES OF THE CHURCH OF ENGLAND, THE. Edited by E. C. S. Gibson. *Ninth Edition. 12s. net.*

Health Series

Fcap. 8vo. 2s. 6d. net

BABY, THE. Arthur Saunders.

CARE OF THE BODY, THE. F. Cavanagh.

CARE OF THE TEETH, THE. A. T. Pitts.

EYES OF OUR CHILDREN, THE. N. Bishop Harman.

HEALTH FOR THE MIDDLE-AGED. Seymour Taylor. *Third Edition.*

HEALTH OF A WOMAN, THE. R. Murray Leslie.

HEALTH OF THE SKIN, THE. George Pernet.

HOW TO LIVE LONG. J. Walter Carr.

PREVENTION OF THE COMMON COLD, THE. O. K. Williamson.

STAYING THE PLAGUE. N. Bishop Harman.

THROAT AND EAR TROUBLES. Macleod Yearsley. *Third Edition.*

TUBERCULOSIS. Clive Riviere.

HEALTH OF THE CHILD, THE. O. Hilton. *Second Edition. 2s. net.*

The 'Home Life' Series

Illustrated. Demy 8vo.

HOME LIFE IN AMERICA. Katherine G. Busbey. *Second Edition. 12s. 6d. net.*

HOME LIFE IN CHINA. I. Taylor Headland. *12s. 6d. net.*

HOME LIFE IN FRANCE. Miss Betham Edwards. *Sixth Edition. 7s. 6d. net.*

HOME LIFE IN GERMANY. Mrs. A. Sidgwick. *Third Edition. 12s. 6d. net.*

HOME LIFE IN HOLLAND. D. S. Meldrum. *Second Edition. 12s. 6d. net.*

HOME LIFE IN ITALY. Lina Duff Gordon. *Third Edition. 12s. 6d. net.*

HOME LIFE IN NORWAY. H. K. Daniels. *Second Edition. 12s. 6d. net.*

HOME LIFE IN SPAIN. S. L. Bensusan. *Second Edition. 12s. 6d. net.*

BALKAN HOME LIFE. Lucy M. J. Garnett. *12s. 6d. net.*

Leaders of Religion

Edited by H. C. BEECHING. *With Portraits*

Crown 8vo. 3s. net each volume

AUGUSTINE OF CANTERBURY. E. L. Cutts.

BISHOP BUTLER. W. A. Spooner.

BISHOP WILBERFORCE. G. W. Daniell.

CARDINAL MANNING. A. W. Hutton, *Second Edition.*

CARDINAL NEWMAN. R. H. Hutton.

CHARLES SIMEON. H. C. G. Moule.

GEORGE FOX, THE QUAKER. T. Hodgkin. *Third Edition.*

JOHN DONNE. Augustus Jessop.

JOHN HOWE. R. F. Horton.

JOHN KEBLE. Walter Lock. *Seventh Edition.*

JOHN KNOX. F. MacCunn. *Second Edition.*

JOHN WESLEY. J. H. Overton.

LANCELOT ANDREWES. R. L. Ottley. *Second Edition.*

LATIMER. R. M. and A. J. Carlyle.

THOMAS CHALMERS. Mrs. Oliphant. *Second Edition.*

THOMAS CRANMER. A. J. Mason.

THOMAS KEN. F. A. Clarke.

WILLIAM LAUD. W. H. Hutton. *Fourth Edition.*

The Library of Devotion

With Introductions and (where necessary) Notes

Small Pott 8vo, cloth, 3s. net; also some volumes in leather, 3s. 6d. net each volume

BISHOP WILSON'S SACRA PRIVATA.

BOOK OF DEVOTIONS, A. *Second Edition.*

CHRISTIAN YEAR, THE. *Fifth Edition.*

CONFESSIONS OF ST. AUGUSTINE, THE. *Ninth Edition. 3s. 6d. net.*

DAY BOOK FROM THE SAINTS AND FATHERS, A.

DEATH AND IMMORTALITY.

DEVOTIONS FROM THE APOCRYPHA.

DEVOTIONS OF ST. ANSELM, THE.

DEVOTIONS FOR EVERY DAY IN THE WEEK AND THE GREAT FESTIVALS.

GRACE ABOUNDING TO THE CHIEF OF SINNERS.

GUIDE TO ETERNITY, A.

HORAE MYSTICAE. A Day Book from the Writings of Mystics of Many Nations.

IMITATION OF CHRIST, THE. *Eighth Edition.*

INNER WAY, THE. *Third Edition.*

INTRODUCTION TO THE DEVOUT LIFE, AN.

LIGHT, LIFE, and LOVE. A Selection from the German Mystics.

LITTLE BOOK OF HEAVENLY WISDOM, A. A Selection from the English Mystics.

LYRA APOSTOLICA.

LYRA INNOCENTIUM. *Third Edition.*

LYRA SACRA. A Book of Sacred Verse. *Second Edition.*

MANUAL OF CONSOLATION FROM THE SAINTS AND FATHERS, A.

ON THE LOVE OF GOD.

PRECES PRIVATAE.

PSALMS OF DAVID, THE.

SERIOUS CALL TO A DEVOUT AND HOLY LIFE, A. *Fifth Edition.*

SONG OF SONGS, THE.

SPIRITUAL COMBAT, THE.

SPIRITUAL GUIDE, THE. *Third Edition.*

TEMPLE, THE. *Second Edition.*

THOUGHTS OF PASCAL, THE. *Second Edition.*

Little Books on Art

With many Illustrations. Demy 16mo. 5s. net each volume

Each volume consists of about 200 pages, and contains from 30 to 40 Illustrations, including a Frontispiece in Photogravure

ALBRECHT DÜRER. L. J Allen.
ARTS OF JAPAN, THE. E. Dillon. *Third Edition.*
BOOKPLATES. E. Almack.
BOTTICELLI. Mary L. Bonnor.
BURNE-JONES. F. de Lisle. *Third Edition.*
CELLINI. R. H. H. Cust.
CHRISTIAN SYMBOLISM. Mrs. H. Jenner.
CHRIST IN ART. Mrs. H. Jenner.
CLAUDE. E. Dillon.
CONSTABLE. H. W. Tompkins. *Second Edition.*
COROT. A. Pollard and E. Birnstingl.
EARLY ENGLISH WATER-COLOUR. C. E. Hughes.
ENAMELS. Mrs. N. Dawson. *Second Edition.*
FREDERIC LEIGHTON. A. Corkran.
GEORGE ROMNEY. G. Paston.

GREEK ART. H. B. Walters. *Fifth Edition.*
GREUZE AND BOUCHER. E. F. Pollard.
HOLBEIN. Mrs. G. Fortescue.
JEWELLERY. C. Davenport. *Second Edition.*
JOHN HOPPNER. H. P. K. Skipton.
SIR JOSHUA REYNOLDS. J. Sime. *Second Edition.*
MILLET. N. Peacock. *Second Edition.*
MINIATURES. C. Davenport, V.D., F.S.A. *Second Edition.*
OUR LADY IN ART. Mrs. H. Jenner.
RAPHAEL. A. R. Dryhurst. *Second Edition*
RODIN. Muriel Ciolkowska.
TURNER. F. Tyrrell-Gill.
VANDYCK. M. G. Smallwood.
VELAZQUEZ. W. Wilberforce and A. R. Gilbert.
WATTS. R. E. D. Sketchley. *Second Edition.*

The Little Guides

With many Illustrations by E. H. NEW and other artists, and from photographs

Small Pott 8vo. 4s. net each volume

The main features of these Guides are (1) a handy and charming form ; (2) illustrations from photographs and by well-known artists ; (3) good plans and maps ; (4) an adequate but compact presentation of everything that is interesting in the natural features, history, archæology, and architecture of the town or district treated.

CAMBRIDGE AND ITS COLLEGES. A. H. Thompson. *Fourth Edition, Revised.*
CHANNEL ISLANDS, THE. E. E. Bicknell.
ENGLISH LAKES, THE. F. G. Brabant.
ISLE OF WIGHT, THE. G. Clinch.
LONDON. G. Clinch.
MALVERN COUNTRY, THE. Sir B.C.A.Windle. *Second Edition.*
NORTH WALES. A. T. Story.

OXFORD AND ITS COLLEGES. J. Wells. *Tenth Edition.*
ST. PAUL'S CATHEDRAL. G. Clinch.
SHAKESPEARE'S COUNTRY. Sir B. C. A. Windle. *Fifth Edition.*
SOUTH WALES. G. W. and J. H. Wade.
TEMPLE, THE. H. H. L. Bellot.
WESTMINSTER ABBEY. G. E. Troutbeck. *Second Edition.*

The Little Guides—continued

BEDFORDSHIRE AND HUNTINGDONSHIRE. H. W. Macklin.

BERKSHIRE. F. G. Brabant.

BUCKINGHAMSHIRE. E. S. Roscoe. *Second Edition, Revised.*

CAMBRIDGESHIRE. J. C. Cox.

CHESHIRE. W. M. Gallichan.

CORNWALL. A. L. Salmon. *Second Edition.*

DERBYSHIRE. J. C. Cox. *Second Edition.*

DEVON. S. Baring-Gould. *Fourth Edition.*

DORSET. F. R. Heath. *Fourth Edition.*

DURHAM. J. E. Hodgkin.

ESSEX. J. C. Cox. *Second Edition.*

GLOUCESTERSHIRE. J. C. Cox. *Second Edition.*

HAMPSHIRE. J. C. Cox. *Third Edition.*

HEREFORDSHIRE. G. W. and J. H. Wade.

HERTFORDSHIRE. H. W. Tompkins.

KENT. J. C. Cox. *Second Edition, Re-written.*

KERRY. C. P. Crane. *Second Edition.*

LEICESTERSHIRE AND RUTLAND. A. Harvey and V. B. Crowther-Beynon.

LINCOLNSHIRE. J. C. Cox.

MIDDLESEX. J. B. Firth.

MONMOUTHSHIRE. G. W. and J. H. Wade.

NORFOLK. W. A. Dutt. *Fourth Edition, Revised.*

NORTHAMPTONSHIRE. W. Dry. *Second Edition, Revised.*

NORTHUMBERLAND. J. E. Morris. 5*s. net.*

NOTTINGHAMSHIRE. L. Guilford.

OXFORDSHIRE. F. G. Brabant. *Second Edition.*

SHROPSHIRE. J. E. Auden. *Second Edition.*

SOMERSET. G. W. and J. H. Wade. *Fourth Edition.*

STAFFORDSHIRE. C. Masefield. *Second Edition.*

SUFFOLK. W. A. Dutt. *Second Edition.*

SURREY. J. C. Cox. *Third Edition, Re-written.*

SUSSEX. F. G. Brabant. *Fifth Edition.*

WARWICKSHIRE. J. C. Cox.

WILTSHIRE. F. R. Heath. *Third Edition.*

YORKSHIRE, THE EAST RIDING. J. E. Morris.

YORKSHIRE, THE NORTH RIDING. J. E. Morris.

YORKSHIRE, THE WEST RIDING. J. E. Morris. 5*s. net.*

BRITTANY. S. Baring-Gould. *Second Edition.*

NORMANDY. C. Scudamore. *Second Edition.*

ROME. C. G. Ellaby.

SICILY. F. H. Jackson.

The Little Library

With Introduction, Notes, and Photogravure Frontispieces

Small Pott 8vo. Each Volume, cloth, 2s. 6d. net; also some volumes in leather at 3s. 6d. net

Anon. A LITTLE BOOK OF ENGLISH LYRICS. *Second Edition.* 3*s. 6d. net.*

Austen (Jane). PRIDE AND PREJUDICE. *Two Volumes.* NORTHANGER ABBEY.

Bacon (Francis). THE ESSAYS OF LORD BACON.

Barnett (Annie). A LITTLE BOOK OF ENGLISH PROSE. *Third Edition.*

Beckford (William). THE HISTORY OF THE CALIPH VATHEK.

Blake (William). SELECTIONS FROM THE WORKS OF WILLIAM BLAKE.

Browning (Robert). SELECTIONS FROM THE EARLY POEMS OF ROBERT BROWNING.

Canning (George). SELECTIONS FROM THE ANTI-JACOBIN: With some later Poems by GEORGE CANNING.

Cowley (Abraham). THE ESSAYS OF ABRAHAM COWLEY.

The Little Library—continued

Crabbe (George). SELECTIONS FROM THE POEMS OF GEORGE CRABBE.

Crashaw (Richard). THE ENGLISH POEMS OF RICHARD CRASHAW.

Dante Alighieri. PURGATORY. PARADISE.

Darley (George). SELECTIONS FROM THE POEMS OF GEORGE DARLEY.

Kinglake (A. W.). EOTHEN. Second Edition. 2s. 6d. net

Locker (F.). LONDON LYRICS.

Marvell (Andrew). THE POEMS OF ANDREW MARVELL.

Milton (John). THE MINOR POEMS OF JOHN MILTON.

Moir (D. M.). MANSIE WAUCH.

Nichols (Bowyer). A LITTLE BOOK OF ENGLISH SONNETS.

Smith (Horace and James). REJECTED ADDRESSES.

Sterne (Laurence). A SENTIMENTAL JOURNEY.

Tennyson (Alfred, Lord). THE EARLY POEMS OF ALFRED, LORD TENNYSON.
IN MEMORIAM.
THE PRINCESS.
MAUD.

Vaughan (Henry). THE POEMS OF HENRY VAUGHAN.

Waterhouse (Elizabeth). A LITTLE BOOK OF LIFE AND DEATH. Nineteenth Edition.

Wordsworth (W.). SELECTIONS FROM THE POEMS OF WILLIAM WORDSWORTH.

Wordsworth (W.) and Coleridge (S. T.). LYRICAL BALLADS. Third Edition.

The Little Quarto Shakespeare

Edited by W. J. CRAIG. With Introductions and Notes

Pott 16mo. 40 Volumes. Leather, price 1s. 9d. net each volume

Miniature Library

Demy 32mo. Leather, 3s. 6d. net each volume

EUPHRANOR: A Dialogue on Youth. Edward FitzGerald.

THE RUBÁIYÁT OF OMAR KHAYYÁM. Edward FitzGerald. Fifth Edition. Cloth, 1s. net.

POLONIUS; or, Wise Saws and Modern Instances. Edward FitzGerald.

The New Library of Medicine

Edited by C. W. SALEEBY. *Demy 8vo*

AIR AND HEALTH. Ronald C. Macfie. Second Edition. 10s. 6d. net.

CARE OF THE BODY, THE. F. Cavanagh. Second Edition. 10s. 6d. net.

CHILDREN OF THE NATION, THE. The Right Hon. Sir John Gorst. Second Edition. 10s. 6d. net.

DRUGS AND THE DRUG HABIT. H. Sainsbury. 10s. 6d. net.

FUNCTIONAL NERVE DISEASES. A. T. Schofield. 10s. 6d. net.

HYGIENE OF MIND, THE. Sir T. S. Clouston. Sixth Edition. 10s. 6d. net.

INFANT MORTALITY. Sir George Newman. 10s. 6d. net.

PREVENTION OF TUBERCULOSIS (CONSUMPTION), THE. Arthur Newsholme. Second Edition. 12s. 6d. net.

The New Library of Music

Edited by ERNEST NEWMAN. *Illustrated. Demy 8vo.* 10s. 6d. net

BRAHMS. J. A. Fuller-Maitland. *Second Edition.*

HANDEL. R. A. Streatfeild. *Second Edition.*

HUGO WOLF. Ernest Newman.

Oxford Biographies

*Illustrated. Fcap. 8vo. Each volume, cloth, 4s. net ;
also some in leather, 5s. net*

DANTE ALIGHIERI. Paget Toynbee. *Fifth Edition.*

GIROLAMO SAVONAROLA. E. L. S. Horsburgh. *Sixth Edition.*

JOHN HOWARD. E. C. S. Gibson.

SIR WALTER RALEIGH. I. A. Taylor.

CHATHAM. A. S. McDowall.

CANNING. W. Alison Phillips.

Nine Plays

Fcap. 8vo. 3s. 6d. net

ACROSS THE BORDER. Beulah Marie Dix.

HONEYMOON, THE. A Comedy in Three Acts. Arnold Bennett. *Third Edition.*

GREAT ADVENTURE, THE. A Play of Fancy in Four Acts. Arnold Bennett. *Fourth Edition.*

MILESTONES. Arnold Bennett and Edward Knoblock. *Eighth Edition.*

IDEAL HUSBAND, AN. Oscar Wilde. *Acting Edition.*

KISMET. Edward Knoblock. *Third Edition.*

TYPHOON. A Play in Four Acts. Melchior Lengyel. English Version by Laurence Irving. *Second Edition.*

WARE CASE, THE. George Pleydell.

GENERAL POST. J. E. Harold Terry. *Second Edition.*

Sport Series

Illustrated. Fcap. 8vo. 2s. net

FLYING, ALL ABOUT. Gertrude Bacon.

GOLF DO'S AND DONT'S. 'Stancliffe.' *Sixth Edition.*

GOLFING SWING, THE. Burnham Hare. *Fourth Edition.*

HOW TO SWIM. H. R. Austin.

WRESTLING. P. Longhurst.

The States of Italy

Edited by E. ARMSTRONG and R. LANGTON DOUGLAS
Illustrated. Demy 8vo

MILAN UNDER THE SFORZA, A HISTORY OF. Cecilia M. Ady. 12s. net.

VERONA, A HISTORY OF. A. M. Allen. 15s. net.

PERUGIA, A HISTORY OF. W. Heywood. 15s. net.

The Westminster Commentaries

General Editor, WALTER LOCK
Demy 8vo

ACTS OF THE APOSTLES, THE. R. B. Rackham. *Seventh Edition.* 16s. net.

AMOS. E. A. Edghill. 8s. 6d. net.

CORINTHIANS, I. H. L. Goudge. *Fourth Edition.* 8s. 6d. net.

EXODUS. A. H. M'Neile. *Second Edition.* 15s. net.

EZEKIEL. H. A. Redpath. 12s. 6d. net.

GENESIS. S. R. Driver. *Tenth Edition.* 16s. net.

HEBREWS. E. C. Wickham. 8s. 6d. net.

ISAIAH. G. W. Wade. 16s. net.

JEREMIAH. L. E. Binns. 16s. net.

JOB. E. C. S. Gibson. *Second Edition.* 8s. 6d. net.

PASTORAL EPISTLES, THE. E. F. Brown. 8s. 6d. net.

PHILIPPIANS, THE. Maurice Jones. 8s. 6d. net.

ST. JAMES. R. J. Knowling. *Second Edition.* 8s. 6d. net.

ST. MATTHEW. P. A. Micklem. 15s. net.

The 'Young' Series

Illustrated. Crown 8vo

YOUNG BOTANIST, THE. W. P. Westell and C. S. Cooper. 6s. net.

YOUNG CARPENTER, THE. Cyril Hall. 6s. net.

YOUNG ELECTRICIAN, THE. Hammond Hall. Second Edition. 6s. net.

YOUNG ENGINEER, THE. Hammond Hall. Third Edition. 6s. net.

YOUNG NATURALIST, THE. W. P. Westell. 7s. 6d. net.

YOUNG ORNITHOLOGIST, THE. W. P. Westell. 6s. net.

Methuen's Cheap Library

Fcap. 8vo. 2s. net

ALL THINGS CONSIDERED. G. K. Chesterton.

BEST OF LAMB, THE. Edited by E. V. Lucas.

BLUE BIRD, THE. Maurice Maeterlinck.

CHARLES DICKENS. G. K. Chesterton.

CHARMIDES, AND OTHER POEMS. Oscar Wilde.

CHITRAL: The Story of a Minor Siege. Sir G. S. Robertson.

CUSTOMS OF OLD ENGLAND, THE. F. J. Snell.

DE PROFUNDIS. Oscar Wilde.

FAMOUS WITS, A BOOK OF. W. Jerrold.

FROM MIDSHIPMAN TO FIELD-MARSHAL. Sir Evelyn Wood, F.M., V.C.

HARVEST HOME. E. V. Lucas.

HILLS AND THE SEA. Hilaire Belloc.

IDEAL HUSBAND, AN. Oscar Wilde.

IMPORTANCE OF BEING EARNEST, THE. Oscar Wilde.

INTENTIONS. Oscar Wilde.

JANE AUSTEN AND HER TIMES. G.' E. Mitton.

JOHN BOYES, KING OF THE WA-KIKUYU. John Boyes.

LADY WINDERMERE'S FAN. Oscar Wilde.

LETTERS FROM A SELF-MADE MERCHANT TO HIS SON. George Horace Lorimer.

LIFE OF JOHN RUSKIN, THE. W. G. Collingwood.

LIFE OF ROBERT LOUIS STEVENSON, THE. Graham Balfour.

LITTLE OF EVERYTHING, A. E. V. Lucas.

LORD ARTHUR SAVILE'S CRIME. Oscar Wilde.

LORE OF THE HONEY-BEE, THE. Tickner Edwardes.

MAN AND THE UNIVERSE. Sir Oliver Lodge.

MARY MAGDALENE. Maurice Maeterlinck.

MIRROR OF THE SEA, THE. J. Conrad.

MIXED VINTAGES. E. V. Lucas.

MODERN PROBLEMS. Sir Oliver Lodge.

MY CHILDHOOD AND BOYHOOD. Leo Tolstoy.

MY YOUTH. Leo Tolstoy.

OLD COUNTRY LIFE. S. Baring-Gould.

OLD TIME PARSON, THE. P. H. Ditchfield.

ON EVERYTHING. Hilaire Belloc.

ON NOTHING. Hilaire Belloc.

OSCAR WILDE: A Critical Study. Arthur Ransome.

PICKED COMPANY, A. Hilaire Belloc.

REASON AND BELIEF. Sir Oliver Lodge.

R. L. S. Francis Watt.

SCIENCE FROM AN EASY CHAIR. Sir Ray Lankester.

SELECTED POEMS. Oscar Wilde.

SELECTED PROSE. Oscar Wilde.

SHEPHERD'S LIFE, A. W. H. Hudson.

SHILLING FOR MY THOUGHTS, A. G. K. Chesterton.

SOCIAL EVILS AND THEIR REMEDY. Leo Tolstoy.

SOME LETTERS OF R. L. STEVENSON. Selected by Lloyd Osbourne.

SUBSTANCE OF FAITH, THE. Sir Oliver Lodge.

SURVIVAL OF MAN, THE. Sir Oliver Lodge.

TOWER OF LONDON, THE. R. Davey.

TWO ADMIRALS. Admiral John Moresby.

VAILIMA LETTERS. Robert Louis Stevenson.

VARIETY LANE. E. V. Lucas.

VICAR OF MORWENSTOW, THE. S. Baring-Gould.

WOMAN OF NO IMPORTANCE, A. Oscar Wilde.

A Selection only

Books for Travellers

Crown 8vo.   8s. 6d. net each

Each volume contains a number of Illustrations in Colour

AVON AND SHAKESPEARE'S COUNTRY, THE. A. G. Bradley. *Second Edition.*

BLACK FOREST, A BOOK OF THE. C. E. Hughes.

CITIES OF LOMBARDY, THE. Edward Hutton.

CITIES OF ROMAGNA AND THE MARCHES, THE. Edward Hutton.

CITIES OF SPAIN, THE. Edward Hutton. *Fifth Edition.*

CITIES OF UMBRIA, THE. Edward Hutton. *Fifth Edition.*

FLORENCE AND NORTHERN TUSCANY, WITH GENOA. Edward Hutton. *Third Edition.*

LAND OF PARDONS, THE (Brittany). Anatole Le Braz. *Fourth Edition.*

LONDON REVISITED. E. V. Lucas. *Third Edition. 8s. 6d. net.*

NAPLES. Arthur H. Norway. *Fourth Edition. 8s. 6d. net.*

NAPLES AND SOUTHERN ITALY. Edward Hutton.

NAPLES RIVIERA, THE. H. M. Vaughan. *Second Edition.*

NEW FOREST, THE. Horace G. Hutchinson. *Fourth Edition.*

NORWAY AND ITS FJORDS. M. A. Wyllie.

ROME. Edward Hutton. *Third Edition.*

ROUND ABOUT WILTSHIRE. A. G. Bradley. *Third Edition.*

SIENA AND SOUTHERN TUSCANY. Edward Hutton. *Second Edition.*

SKIRTS OF THE GREAT CITY, THE. Mrs. A. G. Bell. *Second Edition.*

VENICE AND VENETIA. Edward Hutton.

WANDERER IN FLORENCE, A. E. V. Lucas. *Sixth Edition.*

WANDERER IN PARIS, A. E. V. Lucas. *Thirteenth Edition.*

WANDERER IN HOLLAND, A. E. V. Lucas. *Sixteenth Edition.*

WANDERER IN LONDON, A. E. V. Lucas. *Eighteenth Edition.*

WANDERER IN VENICE, A. E. V. Lucas. *Second Edition.*

Some Books on Art

ART, ANCIENT AND MEDIEVAL. M. H. Bulley. Illustrated. *Crown 8vo. 7s. 6d. net.*

BRITISH SCHOOL, THE. An Anecdotal Guide to the British Painters and Paintings in the National Gallery. E. V. Lucas. Illustrated. *Fcap. 8vo. 6s. net.*

DECORATIVE IRON WORK. From the XIth to the XVIIIth Century. Charles ffoulkes. *Royal 4to. £2 2s. net.*

FRANCESCO GUARDI, 1712-1793. G. A. Simonson. Illustrated. *Imperial 4to. £2 2s. net.*

ILLUSTRATIONS OF THE BOOK OF JOB. William Blake. *Quarto. £1 1s. net.*

ITALIAN SCULPTORS. W. G. Waters. Illustrated. *Crown 8vo. 7s. 6d. net.*

OLD PASTE. A. Beresford Ryley. Illustrated. *Royal 4to. £2 2s. net.*

ONE HUNDRED MASTERPIECES OF SCULPTURE. With an Introduction by G. F. Hill. Illustrated. *Demy 8vo. 12s. 6d. net.*

ROYAL ACADEMY LECTURES ON PAINTING. George Clausen. Illustrated. *Crown 8vo. 7s. 6d. net.*

SAINTS IN ART, THE. Margaret E. Tabor. Illustrated. *Third Edition. Fcap. 8vo. 5s. net.*

SCHOOLS OF PAINTING. Mary Innes. Illustrated. *Second Edition. Cr. 8vo. 8s. net.*

CELTIC ART IN PAGAN AND CHRISTIAN TIMES. J. R. Allen. Illustrated. *Second Edition. Demy 8vo. 10s. 6d. net.*

Some Books on Italy

FLORENCE AND HER TREASURES. H. M. Vaughan. Illustrated. *Fcap. 8vo. 6s. net.*

FLORENCE AND THE CITIES OF NORTHERN TUSCANY, WITH GENOA. Edward Hutton. Illustrated. *Third Edition. Cr. 8vo. 8s. 6d. net.*

LOMBARDY, THE CITIES OF. Edward Hutton. Illustrated. *Cr. 8vo. 8s. 6d. net.*

MILAN UNDER THE SFORZA, A HISTORY OF. Cecilia M. Ady. Illustrated. *Demy 8vo. 12s. 6d. net.*

NAPLES : Past and Present. A. H. Norway. Illustrated. *Fourth Edition. Cr. 8vo. 8s. 6d. net.*

NAPLES RIVIERA, THE. H. M. Vaughan. Illustrated. *Second Edition. Cr. 8vo. 8s. 6d. net.*

NAPLES AND SOUTHERN ITALY. E. Hutton. Illustrated. *Cr. 8vo. 8s. 6d. net.*

PERUGIA, A HISTORY OF. William Heywood. Illustrated. *Demy 8vo. 15s. net.*

ROME. Edward Hutton. Illustrated. *Third Edition. Cr. 8vo. 8s. 6d. net.*

ROMAGNA AND THE MARCHES, THE CITIES OF. Edward Hutton. *Cr. 8vo. 8s. 6d. net.*

ROME. C. G. Ellaby. Illustrated. *Small Pott 8vo. 4s. net.*

SICILY. F. H. Jackson. Illustrated. *Small Pott 8vo. 4s. net.*

SICILY : The New Winter Resort. Douglas Sladen. Illustrated. *Second Edition. Cr. 8vo. 7s. 6d. net.*

SIENA AND SOUTHERN TUSCANY. Edward Hutton. Illustrated. *Second Edition. Cr. 8vo. 8s. 6d. net.*

UMBRIA, THE CITIES OF. Edward Hutton. Illustrated. *Fifth Edition. Cr. 8vo. 8s. 6d. net.*

VENICE AND VENETIA. Edward Hutton. Illustrated. *Cr. 8vo. 8s. 6d. net.*

VENICE ON FOOT. H. A. Douglas. Illustrated. *Second Edition. Fcap. 8vo. 6s. net.*

VENICE AND HER TREASURES. H. A. Douglas. Illustrated. *Fcap. 8vo. 6s. net.*

VERONA, A HISTORY OF. A. M. Allen. Illustrated. *Demy 8vo. 15s. net.*

DANTE ALIGHIERI : His Life and Works. Paget Toynbee. Illustrated. *Fourth Edition. Cr. 8vo. 6s. net.*

LAKES OF NORTHERN ITALY, THE. Richard Bagot. Illustrated. *Second Edition. Fcap. 8vo. 6s. net.*

SAVONAROLA, GIROLAMO. E. L. S. Horsburgh. Illustrated. *Fourth Edition. Cr. 8vo. 6s. net.*

SKIES ITALIAN : A Little Breviary for Travellers in Italy. Ruth S. Phelps. *Fcap. 8vo. 5s. net.*

PART III.—A SELECTION OF WORKS OF FICTION

Albanesi (E. Maria). I KNOW A MAIDEN. *Third Edition. Cr. 8vo. 7s. net.*

THE GLAD HEART. *Fifth Edition. Cr. 8vo. 7s. net.*

Aumonier (Stacy). OLGA BARDEL. *Cr. 8vo. 7s. net.*

Bagot (Richard). THE HOUSE OF SERRAVALLE. *Third Edition. Cr. 8vo. 7s. net.*

Bailey (H. C.). THE SEA CAPTAIN. *Third Edition. Cr. 8vo. 7s. net.*

THE HIGHWAYMAN. *Third Edition. Cr. 8vo. 7s. net.*

THE GAMESTERS. *Second Edition. Cr. 8vo. 7s. net.*

THE YOUNG LOVERS. *Second Edition. Cr. 8vo. 7s. net.*

Baring - Gould (S.). THE BROOM-SQUIRE. Illustrated. *Fifth Edition. Cr. 8vo. 7s. net.*

Barr (Robert). IN THE MIDST OF ALARMS. *Third Edition. Cr. 8vo. 7s. net.*

THE COUNTESS TEKLA. *Fifth Edition. Cr. 8vo. 7s. net.*

THE MUTABLE MANY. *Third Edition. Cr. 8vo. 7s. net.*

Begbie (Harold). THE CURIOUS AND DIVERTING ADVENTURES OF SIR JOHN SPARROW, BART.; OR, THE PROGRESS OF AN OPEN MIND. *Second Edition. Cr. 8vo. 7s. net.*

Belloc (H.). EMMANUEL BURDEN, MERCHANT. Illustrated. *Second Edition. Cr. 8vo. 7s. net.*

Bennett (Arnold). CLAYHANGER. *Twelfth Edition. Cr. 8vo. 8s. net.*

HILDA LESSWAYS. *Eighth Edition. Cr. 8vo. 7s. net.*

THESE TWAIN. *Fourth Edition. Cr. 8vo. 7s. net.*

THE CARD. *Thirteenth Edition. Cr. 8vo. 7s. net.*

THE REGENT: A FIVE TOWNS STORY OF ADVENTURE IN LONDON. *Fifth Edition. Cr. 8vo. 7s. net.*

THE PRICE OF LOVE. *Fourth Edition. Cr. 8vo. 7s. net.*

BURIED ALIVE. *Ninth Edition. Cr. 8vo. 7s. net.*

A MAN FROM THE NORTH. *Third Edition. Cr. 8vo. 7s. net.*

THE MATADOR OF THE FIVE TOWNS. *Second Edition. Cr. 8vo. 7s. net.*

WHOM GOD HATH JOINED. *A New Edition. Cr. 8vo. 7s. net.*

A GREAT MAN: A FROLIC. *Seventh Edition. Cr. 8vo. 7s. net.*

Benson (E. F.). DODO: A DETAIL OF THE DAY. *Seventeenth Edition. Cr. 8vo. 7s. net.*

Birmingham (George A.). SPANISH GOLD. *Seventeenth Edition. Cr. 8vo. 7s. net.*

THE SEARCH PARTY. *Tenth Edition. Cr. 8vo. 7s. net.*

LALAGE'S LOVERS. *Third Edition. Cr. 8vo. 7s. net.*

GOSSAMER. *Fourth Edition. Cr. 8vo. 7s. net.*

THE ISLAND MYSTERY. *Second Edition. Cr. 8vo. 7s. net.*

THE BAD TIMES. *Second Edition. Cr. 8vo. 7s. net.*

Bowen (Marjorie). I WILL MAINTAIN. *Ninth Edition. Cr. 8vo. 7s. net.*

DEFENDER OF THE FAITH. *Seventh Edition. Cr. 8vo. 7s. net.*

WILLIAM, BY THE GRACE OF GOD. *Second Edition. Cr. 8vo. 7s. net.*

GOD AND THE KING. *Sixth Edition.*
Cr. 8vo. 7s. net.

PRINCE AND HERETIC. *Third Edition.*
Cr. 8vo. 7s. net.

A KNIGHT OF SPAIN. *Third Edition.*
Cr. 8vo. 7s. net.

THE QUEST OF GLORY. *Third Edition.*
Cr. 8vo. 7s. net.

THE GOVERNOR OF ENGLAND. *Third
Edition.* Cr. 8vo. 7s. net.

THE CARNIVAL OF FLORENCE. *Fifth
Edition.* Cr. 8vo. 7s. net.

MR. WASHINGTON. *Third Edition.* Cr.
8vo. 7s. net.

"BECAUSE OF THESE THINGS. . . ."
Third Edition. Cr. 8vo. 7s. net.

THE THIRD ESTATE. *Second Edition.*
Cr. 8vo. 7s. net.

Burroughs (Edgar Rice). THE RETURN
OF TARZAN. *Fcap. 8vo. 2s. net.*

THE BEASTS OF TARZAN. *Second
Edition.* Cr. 8vo. 6s. net.

THE SON OF TARZAN. Cr. 8vo. 7s. net.

A PRINCESS OF MARS. Cr. 8vo. 5s. net.

Castle (Agnes and Egerton). THE
GOLDEN BARRIER. *Third Edition.*
Cr. 8vo. 7s. net.

Conrad (Joseph). A SET OF SIX. *Fourth
Edition.* Cr. 8vo. 7s. net.

VICTORY: AN ISLAND TALE. *Sixth
Edition.* Cr. 8vo. 9s. net.

Conyers (Dorothea). SANDY MARRIED.
Fifth Edition. Cr. 8vo. 7s. net.

OLD ANDY. *Fourth Edition.* Cr. 8vo. 7s.
net.

THE BLIGHTING OF BARTRAM. *Third
Edition.* Cr. 8vo. 7s. net.

B. E. N. Cr. 8vo. 7s. net.

Corelli (Marie). A ROMANCE OF TWO
WORLDS. *Thirty-fifth Edition.* Cr. 8vo.
7s. 6d. net.

VENDETTA; OR, THE STORY OF ONE FOR-
GOTTEN. *Thirty-fifth Edition.* Cr. 8vo.
8s. net.

THELMA: A NORWEGIAN PRINCESS.
Fifty-ninth Edition. Cr. 8vo. 8s. 6d. net.

ARDATH: THE STORY OF A DEAD SELF.
Twenty-fourth Edition. Cr. 8vo. 7s. 6d.
net.

THE SOUL OF LILITH. *Twentieth
Edition.* Cr. 8vo. 7s. net.

WORMWOOD: A DRAMA OF PARIS.
Twenty-second Edition. Cr. 8vo. 8s. net.

BARABBAS: A DREAM OF THE WORLD'S
TRAGEDY. *Fiftieth Edition.* Cr. 8vo. 8s.
net.

THE SORROWS OF SATAN. *Sixty-third
Edition.* Cr. 8vo. 7s. net.

THE MASTER-CHRISTIAN. *Eighteenth
Edition.* 184th Thousand. Cr. 8vo.
8s. 6d. net.

TEMPORAL POWER: A STUDY IN
SUPREMACY. *Second Edition.* 150th
Thousand. Cr. 8vo. 6s. net.

GOD'S GOOD MAN: A SIMPLE LOVE
STORY. *Twentieth Edition.* 159th Thousand. Cr. 8vo. 8s. 6d. net.

HOLY ORDERS: THE TRAGEDY OF A
QUIET LIFE. *Third Edition.* 121st
Thousand. Cr. 8vo. 8s. 6d. net.

THE MIGHTY ATOM. *Thirty-sixth
Edition.* Cr. 8vo. 7s. 6d. net.

BOY: A SKETCH. *Twentieth Edition.* Cr.
8vo. 6s. net.

CAMEOS. *Fifteenth Edition.* Cr. 8vo.
6s. net.

THE LIFE EVERLASTING. *Eighth Edition.* Cr. 8vo. 8s. 6d. net.

Crockett (S. R.). LOCHINVAR. Illustrated. *Fifth Edition.* Cr. 8vo. 7s. net.

THE STANDARD BEARER. *Second
Edition.* Cr. 8vo. 7s. net.

Doyle (Sir A. Conan). ROUND THE RED
LAMP. *Twelfth Edition.* Cr. 8vo. 7s.
net.

Dudeney (Mrs. H.). THIS WAY OUT.
Cr. 8vo. 7s. net.

Fry (B. and C. B.). A MOTHER'S SON.
Fifth Edition. Cr. 8vo. 7s. net.

Harraden (Beatrice). THE GUIDING
THREAD. *Second Edition.* Cr. 8vo.
7s. net.

Hichens (Robert). THE PROPHET OF
BERKELEY SQUARE. *Second Edition.*
Cr. 8vo. 7s. net.

TONGUES OF CONSCIENCE. *Fourth
Edition.* Cr. 8vo. 7s. net.

FELIX: THREE YEARS IN A LIFE. *Seventh Edition.* Cr. 8vo. 7s. net.

THE WOMAN WITH THE FAN. *Eighth Edition.* Cr. 8vo. 7s. net.

BYEWAYS. Cr. 8vo. 7s. net.

THE GARDEN OF ALLAH. *Twenty-sixth Edition.* Illustrated. Cr. 8vo. 8s. 6d. net.

THE CALL OF THE BLOOD. *Ninth Edition.* Cr. 8vo. 8s. 6d. net.

BARBARY SHEEP. *Second Edition.* Cr. 8vo. 6s. net.

THE DWELLER ON THE THRESHOLD. Cr. 8vo. 7s. net.

THE WAY OF AMBITION. *Fifth Edition.* Cr. 8vo. 7s. net.

IN THE WILDERNESS. *Third Edition.* Cr. 8vo. 7s. net.

Hope (Anthony). A CHANGE OF AIR. *Sixth Edition.* Cr. 8vo. 7s. net.

A MAN OF MARK. *Seventh Edition.* Cr. 8vo. 7s. net.

THE CHRONICLES OF COUNT AN-TONIO. *Sixth Edition.* Cr. 8vo. 7s. net.

PHROSO. Illustrated. *Ninth Edition.* Cr. 8vo. 7s. net.

SIMON DALE. Illustrated. *Ninth Edition.* Cr. 8vo. 7s. net.

THE KING'S MIRROR. *Fifth Edition.* Cr. 8vo. 7s. net.

QUISANTÉ. *Fourth Edition.* Cr. 8vo. 7s. net.

THE DOLLY DIALOGUES. Cr. 8vo. 7s. net.

TALES OF TWO PEOPLE. *Third Edition.* Cr. 8vo. 7s. net.

A SERVANT OF THE PUBLIC. Illustrated. *Fourth Edition.* Cr. 8vo. 7s. net.

MRS. MAXON PROTESTS. *Third Edition.* Cr. 8vo. 7s. net.

A YOUNG MAN'S YEAR. *Second Edition.* Cr. 8vo. 7s. net.

Hyne (C. J. Cutcliffe). MR. HORROCKS, PURSER. *Fifth Edition.* Cr. 8vo. 7s. net.

FIREMEN HOT. *Fourth Edition.* Cr. 8vo. 7s. net.

CAPTAIN KETTLE ON THE WAR-PATH. *Third Edition.* Cr. 8vo. 7s. net.

RED HERRINGS. Cr. 8vo. 6s. net.

Jacobs (W. W.). MANY CARGOES. *Thirty-third Edition.* Cr. 8vo. 5s. net. Also Cr. 8vo. 2s. 6d. net.

SEA URCHINS. *Nineteenth Edition.* Cr. 8vo. 5s. net. Also Cr. 8vo. 3s. 6d. net.

A MASTER OF CRAFT. Illustrated. *Eleventh Edition.* Cr. 8vo. 5s. net.

LIGHT FREIGHTS. Illustrated. *Fifteenth Edition.* Cr. 8vo. 5s. net.

THE SKIPPER'S WOOING. *Twelfth Edition.* Cr. 8vo. 5s. net.

AT SUNWICH PORT. Illustrated. *Eleventh Edition.* Cr. 8vo. 5s. net.

DIALSTONE LANE. Illustrated. *Eighth Edition.* Cr. 8vo. 5s. net.

ODD CRAFT. Illustrated. *Fifth Edition.* Cr. 8vo. 5s. net.

THE LADY OF THE BARGE. Illustrated. *Tenth Edition.* Cr. 8vo. 5s. net.

SALTHAVEN. Illustrated. *Fourth Edition.* Cr. 8vo. 5s. net.

SAILORS' KNOTS. Illustrated. *Sixth Edition.* Cr. 8vo. 5s. net.

SHORT CRUISES. *Third Edition.* Cr. 8vo. 5s. net.

King (Basil). THE LIFTED VEIL. Cr. 8vo. 7s. net.

Lethbridge (Sybil C.). ONE WOMAN'S HERO. Cr. 8vo. 7s. net.

London (Jack). WHITE FANG. *Ninth Edition.* Cr. 8vo. 7s. net.

Lowndes (Mrs. Belloc). THE LODGER. *Third Edition.* Cr. 8vo. 7s. net.

Lucas (E. V.). LISTENER'S LURE: AN OBLIQUE NARRATION. *Twelfth Edition.* Fcap. 8vo. 6s. net.

OVER BEMERTON'S: AN EASY-GOING CHRONICLE. *Sixteenth Edition.* Fcap. 8vo. 6s. net.

MR. INGLESIDE. *Thirteenth Edition.* Fcap. 8vo. 6s. net.

LONDON LAVENDER. *Twelfth Edition.* Fcap. 8vo. 6s. net.

LANDMARKS. *Fifth Edition.* Cr. 8vo. 7s. net.

THE VERMILION BOX. *Fifth Edition.* Cr. 8vo. 7s. net.

Lyall (Edna). DERRICK VAUGHAN, NOVELIST. *44th Thousand.* Cr. 8vo. 5s. net.

McKenna (Stephen). SONIA: BETWEEN
TWO WORLDS. *Sixteenth Edition. Cr. 8vo.*
8s. net.
NINETY-SIX HOURS' LEAVE. *Fifth
Edition. Cr. 8vo. 7s. net.*
THE SIXTH SENSE. *Cr. 8vo. 6s. net.*
MIDAS & SON. *Cr. 8vo. 8s. net.*

Macnaughtan (S.). PETER AND JANE.
Fourth Edition. Cr. 8vo. 7s. net.

Malet (Lucas). THE HISTORY OF SIR
RICHARD CALMADY: A ROMANCE.
Seventh Edition. Cr. 8vo. 7s. net.
THE WAGES OF SIN. *Sixteenth Edition.
Cr. 8vo. 7s. net.*
THE CARISSIMA. *Fifth Edition. Cr
8vo. 7s. net.*
THE GATELESS BARRIER. *Fifth Edi-
tion. Cr. 8vo. 7s. net.*

Mason (A. E. W.). CLEMENTINA.
Illustrated. *Ninth Edition. Cr. 8vo. 7s.
net.*

Maxwell (W. B.). VIVIEN. *Thirteenth
Edition. Cr. 8vo. 7s. net.*
THE GUARDED FLAME. *Seventh Edi-
tion. Cr. 8vo. 7s. net.*
ODD LENGTHS. *Second Edition. Cr. 8vo.
7s. net.*
HILL RISE. *Fourth Edition. Cr. 8vo. 7s.
net.*
THE REST CURE. *Fourth Edition. Cr.
8vo. 7s. net.*

Milne (A. A.). THE DAY'S PLAY. *Sixth
Edition. Cr. 8vo. 7s. net.*
ONCE A WEEK. *Cr. 8vo. 7s. net.*

Morrison (Arthur). TALES OF MEAN
STREETS. *Seventh Edition. Cr. 8vo. 7s.
net.*
A CHILD OF THE JAGO. *Sixth Edition.
Cr. 8vo. 7s. net.*
THE HOLE IN THE WALL. *Fourth
Edition. Cr. 8vo. 7s. net.*
DIVERS VANITIES. *Cr. 8vo. 7s. net.*

Oppenheim (E. Phillips). MASTER OF
MEN. *Fifth Edition. Cr. 8vo. 6s. net.*
THE MISSING DELORA. Illustrated.
Fourth Edition. Cr. 8vo. 7s. net.
THE DOUBLE LIFE OF MR. ALFRED
BURTON. *Second Edition. Cr. 8vo. 7s.
net.*
A PEOPLE'S MAN. *Third Edition. Cr.
8vo. 7s. net.*
MR. GREX OF MONTE CARLO. *Third
Edition. Cr. 8vo. 7s. net.*

THE VANISHED MESSENGER. *Second
Edition. Cr. 8vo. 7s. net.*
THE HILLMAN. *Cr. 8vo. 7s. net.*

Oxenham (John). A WEAVER OF
WEBS. Illustrated. *Fifth Edition. Cr.
8vo. 7s. net.*
PROFIT AND LOSS. *Sixth Edition.
Cr. 8vo. 7s. net.*
THE SONG OF HYACINTH, AND OTHER
STORIES. *Second Edition. Cr. 8vo. 7s.
net.*
LAURISTONS. *Fourth Edition. Cr. 8vo.
7s. net.*
THE COIL OF CARNE. *Sixth Edition.
Cr. 8vo. 7s. net.*
THE QUEST OF THE GOLDEN ROSE.
Fourth Edition. Cr. 8vo. 7s. net.
MARY ALL-ALONE. *Third Edition. Cr.
8vo. 7s. net.*
BROKEN SHACKLES. *Fourth Edition.
Cr. 8vo. 7s. net.*
"1914." *Third Edition. Cr. 8vo. 7s. net.*

Parker (Gilbert). PIERRE AND HIS
PEOPLE. *Seventh Edition. Cr. 8vo. 7s.
net.*
MRS. FALCHION. *Fifth Edition. Cr.
8vo. 7s. net.*
THE TRANSLATION OF A SAVAGE.
Fourth Edition. Cr. 8vo. 7s. net.
THE TRAIL OF THE SWORD. Illus-
trated. *Tenth Edition. Cr. 8vo. 7s. net.*
WHEN VALMOND CAME TO PONTIAC:
THE STORY OF A LOST NAPOLEON. *Seventh
Edition. Cr. 8vo. 7s. net.*
AN ADVENTURER OF THE NORTH:
THE LAST ADVENTURES OF 'PRETTY
PIERRE.' *Fifth Edition. Cr. 8vo. 7s. net.*
THE SEATS OF THE MIGHTY. Illus-
trated. *Twentieth Edition. Cr. 8vo. 7s.
net.*
THE BATTLE OF THE STRONG: A
ROMANCE OF TWO KINGDOMS. Illustrated.
Seventh Edition. Cr. 8vo. 7s. net.
THE POMP OF THE LAVILETTES.
Third Edition. Cr. 8vo. 6s. net.
NORTHERN LIGHTS. *Fourth Edition.
Cr. 8vo. 7s. net.*

Perrin (Alice). THE CHARM. *Fifth
Edition. Cr. 8vo. 7s. net.*

Phillpotts (Eden). CHILDREN OF THE
MIST. *Sixth Edition. Cr. 8vo. 7s. net.*

THE HUMAN BOY. With a Frontispiece.
Seventh Edition. Cr. 8vo. 7s. net.

SONS OF THE MORNING. *Second Edition.* Cr. 8vo. 7s. net.

THE RIVER. *Fourth Edition.* Cr. 8vo. 7s. net.

THE AMERICAN PRISONER. *Fourth Edition.* Cr. 8vo. 7s. net.

DEMETER'S DAUGHTER. *Third Edition.* Cr. 8vo. 7s. net.

THE HUMAN BOY AND THE WAR. *Third Edition.* Cr. 8vo. 7s. net.

Ridge (W. Pett). A SON OF THE STATE. *Third Edition.* Cr. 8vo. 7s. net.

THE REMINGTON SENTENCE. *Third Edition.* Cr. 8vo. 7s. net.

MADAME PRINCE. *Second Edition.* Cr. 8vo. 7s. net.

TOP SPEED. *Second Edition.* Cr. 8vo. 7s. net.

SPECIAL PERFORMANCES. Cr. 8vo. 6s. net.

THE BUSTLING HOURS. Cr. 8vo. 7s. net.

Rohmer (Sax). THE DEVIL DOCTOR. *Third Edition.* Cr. 8vo. 7s. net.

THE SI-FAN MYSTERIES. *Second Edition.* Cr. 8vo. 7s. net.

TALES OF SECRET EGYPT. Cr. 8vo. 6s. net.

THE ORCHARD OF TEARS. Cr. 8vo. 6s. net.

Swinnerton (F.). SHOPS AND HOUSES. Cr. 8vo. 7s. net.

Wells (H. G.). BEALBY. *Fifth Edition.* Cr. 8vo. 7s. net.

Williamson (C. N. and A. M.). THE LIGHTNING CONDUCTOR: The Strange Adventures of a Motor Car. Illustrated. *Twenty-second Edition.* Cr. 8vo. 7s. net.

THE PRINCESS PASSES: A Romance of a Motor. Illustrated. *Ninth Edition.* Cr. 8vo. 7s. net.

LADY BETTY ACROSS THE WATER. *Nineteenth Edition.* Cr. 8vo. 7s. net.

SCARLET RUNNER. Illustrated. *Fourth Edition.* Cr. 8vo. 7s. net.

LORD LOVELAND DISCOVERS AMERICA. Illustrated. *Second Edition.* Cr. 8vo. 7s. net.

THE GOLDEN SILENCE. Illustrated. *Eighth Edition.* Cr. 8vo. 7s. net.

THE GUESTS OF HERCULES. Illustrated. *Fourth Edition.* Cr. 8vo. 7s. net.

IT HAPPENED IN EGYPT. Illustrated. *Seventh Edition.* Cr. 8vo. 7s. net.

A SOLDIER OF THE LEGION. *Second Edition.* Cr. 8vo. 7s. net.

THE SHOP GIRL. Cr. 8vo. 7s. net.

THE LIGHTNING CONDUCTRESS. *Third Edition.* Cr. 8vo. 7s. net.

SECRET HISTORY. Cr. 8vo. 7s. net.

THE LOVE PIRATE. Illustrated. *Third Edition.* Cr. 8vo. 7s. net. *Also* Cr. 8vo. 3s. 6d. net.

CRUCIFIX CORNER. Cr. 8vo. 6s. net.

Wilson (Romer). MARTIN SCHULER. Cr. 8vo. 7s. net.

Books for Boys and Girls

Illustrated. Crown 8vo. 5s. net.

Getting Well of Dorothy, The. Mrs. W. K. Clifford. 6s. net.

Girl of the People, A. L. T. Meade.

Honourable Miss, The. L. T. Meade.

Master Rockafellar's Voyage. W. Clark Russell.

Red Grange, The. Mrs. Molesworth.

There was once a Prince. Mrs. M. E. Mann.

Methuen's Cheap Novels

Fcap. 8vo. 2s. net.

ABANDONED. W. Clark Russell.

ADVENTURES OF DR. WHITTY, THE. George A. Birmingham.

ANGLO-INDIANS, THE. Alice Perrin.

ANNA OF THE FIVE TOWNS. Arnold Bennett.

ANTHONY CUTHBERT. Richard Bagot.

BABES IN THE WOOD. B. M. Croker.

BAD TIMES, THE. George A. Birmingham.

BARBARY SHEEP. Robert Hichens.

BECAUSE OF THESE THINGS. . . . Marjorie Bowen.

BELOVED ENEMY, THE. E. Maria Albanesi.

BELOW STAIRS. Mrs. Alfred Sidgwick.

BOTOR CHAPERON, THE. C. N. and A. M. Williamson.

BOY. Marie Corelli.

BRANDED PRINCE, THE. Weatherby Chesney.

BROKEN SHACKLES. John Oxenham.

BROOM SQUIRE, THE. S. Baring-Gould.

BURIED ALIVE. Arnold Bennett.

BYEWAYS. Robert Hichens.

CALL OF THE BLOOD, THE. Robert Hichens.

CAMEOS. Marie Corelli.

CARD, THE. Arnold Bennett.

CARISSIMA, THE. Lucas Malet.

CEASE FIRE. J. M. Cobban.

CHANCE. Joseph Conrad.

CHANGE IN THE CABINET, A. Hilaire Belloc.

CHINK IN THE ARMOUR, THE. Mrs. Belloc Lowndes.

CHRONICLES OF A GERMAN TOWN. The Author of "Mercia in Germany."

COIL OF CARNE, THE. John Oxenham.

CONVERT, THE. Elizabeth Robins.

COUNSEL OF PERFECTION, A. Lucas Malet.

CROOKED WAY, THE. William Le Queux.

DAN RUSSEL THE FOX. E. Œ. Somerville and Martin Ross.

DARNELEY PLACE. Richard Bagot.

DEAD MEN TELL NO TALES. E. W. Hornung.

DEMETER'S DAUGHTER. Eden Phillpotts.

DEMON, THE. C. N. and A. M. Williamson.

DESERT TRAIL, THE. Dane Coolidge.

DEVIL DOCTOR, THE. Sax Rohmer.

DOUBLE LIFE OF MR. ALFRED BURTON, THE. E. Phillips Oppenheim.

DUKE'S MOTTO, THE. J. H. McCarthy.

EMMANUEL BURDEN. Hilaire Belloc.

END OF HER HONEYMOON, THE. Mrs. Belloc Lowndes.

FAMILY, THE. Elinor Mordaunt.

FIRE IN STUBBLE. Baroness Orczy.

FIREMEN HOT. C. J. Cutcliffe Hyne.

FLOWER OF THE DUSK. Myrtle Reed.

GATE OF THE DESERT, THE. John Oxenham.

GATES OF WRATH, THE. Arnold Bennett.

GENTLEMAN ADVENTURER, THE. H. C. Bailey.

GOLDEN CENTIPEDE, THE. Louise Gerard.

GOLDEN SILENCE, THE. C. N. and A. M. Williamson.

GOSSAMER. George A. Birmingham.

GOVERNOR OF ENGLAND, THE. Marjorie Bowen.

GREAT LADY, A. Adeline Sergeant.

GREAT MAN, A. Arnold Bennett.

GUARDED FLAME, THE. W. B. Maxwell.

GUIDING THREAD, THE. Beatrice Harraden.

HALO, THE. Baroness von Hutten.

HAPPY HUNTING GROUND, THE. Alice Perrin.

HAPPY VALLEY, THE. B. M. Croker.

HEART OF HIS HEART. E. Maria Albanesi.

HEART OF THE ANCIENT WOOD, THE. Charles G. D. Roberts.

HEATHER MOON, THE. C. N. and A. M. Williamson.

HERITAGE OF PERIL, A. A. W. Marchmont.

HIGHWAYMAN, The. H. C. Bailey.

HILLMAN, THE. E. Phillips Oppenheim.

HILL RISE. W. B. Maxwell.

HOUSE OF SERRAVALLE, THE. Richard Bagot.

HYENA OF KALLU, THE. Louise Gerard.

ISLAND PRINCESS, HIS. W. Clark Russell.

Methuen's Cheap Novels—continued.

JANE. Marie Corelli.

JOHANNA. B. M. Croker.

JOSEPH. Frank Danby.

JOSHUA DAVIDSON, COMMUNIST. E. Lynn Linton.

JOSS, THE. Richard Marsh.

KINSMAN, THE. Mrs. Alfred Sidgwick.

KNIGHT OF SPAIN, A. Marjorie Bowen.

LADY BETTY ACROSS THE WATER. C. N. and A. M. Williamson.

LALAGE'S LOVERS. George A. Birmingham.

LANTERN BEARERS, THE. Mrs. Alfred Sidgwick.

LAURISTONS. John Oxenham.

LAVENDER AND OLD LACE. Myrtle Reed.

LIGHT FREIGHTS. W. W. Jacobs.

LODGER, THE. Mrs. Belloc Lowndes.

LONG ROAD, THE. John Oxenham.

LOVE AND LOUISA. E. Maria Albanesi.

LOVE PIRATE, THE. C. N. and A. M. Williamson.

MARY ALL-ALONE. John Oxenham.

MASTER OF THE VINEYARD. Myrtle Reed.

MASTER'S VIOLIN, THE. Myrtle Reed.

MAX CARRADOS. Ernest Bramah.

MAYOR OF TROY, THE. "Q."

MESS DECK, THE. W. F. Shannon.

MIGHTY ATOM, THE. Marie Corelli.

MIRAGE. E. Temple Thurston.

MISSING DELORA, THE. E. Phillips Oppenheim.

MR. GREX OF MONTE CARLO. E. Phillips Oppenheim.

MR. WASHINGTON. Marjorie Bowen.

MRS. MAXON PROTESTS. Anthony Hope.

MRS. PETER HOWARD. Mary E. Mann.

MY DANISH SWEETHEART. W. Clark Russell.

MY FRIEND THE CHAUFFEUR. C. N. and A. M. Williamson.

MY HUSBAND AND I. Leo Tolstoy.

MY LADY OF SHADOWS. John Oxenham.

MYSTERY OF DR. FU-MANCHU, THE. Sax Rohmer.

MYSTERY OF THE GREEN HEART, THE. Max Pemberton.

NINE DAYS' WONDER, A. B. M. Croker.

NINE TO SIX-THIRTY. W. Pett Ridge.

OCEAN SLEUTH, THE. Maurice Drake.

OLD ROSE AND SILVER. Myrtle Reed.

PATHS OF THE PRUDENT, THE. J. S. Fletcher.

PATHWAY OF THE PIONEER, THE. Dolf Wyllarde.

PEGGY OF THE BARTONS. B. M. Croker.

PEOPLE'S MAN, A. E. Phillips Oppenheim.

PETER AND JANE. S. Macnaughtan.

POMP OF THE LAVILETTES, THE. Sir Gilbert Parker.

QUEST OF GLORY, THE. Marjorie Bowen.

QUEST OF THE GOLDEN ROSE, THE. John Oxenham.

REGENT, THE. Arnold Bennett.

REMINGTON SENTENCE, THE. W. Pett Ridge.

REST CURE, THE. W. B. Maxwell.

RETURN OF TARZAN, THE. Edgar Rice Burroughs.

ROUND THE RED LAMP. Sir A. Conan Doyle.

ROYAL GEORGIE. S. Baring-Gould.

SAÏD, THE FISHERMAN. Marmaduke Pickthall.

SALLY. Dorothea Conyers.

SALVING OF A DERELICT, THE. Maurice Drake.

SANDY MARRIED. Dorothea Conyers.

SEA CAPTAIN, THE. H. C. Bailey.

SEA LADY, THE. H. G. Wells.

SEARCH PARTY, THE. George A. Birmingham.

SECRET AGENT, THE. Joseph Conrad.

SECRET HISTORY. C. N. and A. M. Williamson.

SECRET WOMAN, THE. Eden Phillpotts.

SET IN SILVER. C. N. and A. M. Williamson.

SEVASTOPOL, AND OTHER STORIES. Leo Tolstoy.

SEVERINS, THE. Mrs. Alfred Sidgwick.

SHORT CRUISES. W. W. Jacobs.

SI-FAN MYSTERIES, THE. Sax Rohmer.

SPANISH GOLD. George A. Birmingham.

SPINNER IN THE SUN, A. Myrtle Reed.

STREET CALLED STRAIGHT, THE. Basil King.

SUPREME CRIME, THE. Dorothea Gerard.

TALES OF MEAN STREETS. Arthur Morrison.

TARZAN OF THE APES. Edgar Rice Burroughs.

Methuen's Cheap Novels—continued.

TERESA OF WATLING STREET. Arnold Bennett.

THERE WAS A CROOKED MAN. Dolf Wyllarde.

TYRANT, THE. Mrs. Henry de la Pasture.

UNDER WESTERN EYES. Joseph Conrad.

UNOFFICIAL HONEYMOON, THE. Dolf Wyllarde.

VALLEY OF THE SHADOW, THE. William Le Queux.

VIRGINIA PERFECT. Peggy Webling.

WALLET OF KAI LUNG. Ernest Bramah.

WAR WEDDING, THE. C. N. and A. M. Williamson.

WARE CASE, THE. George Pleydell.

WAY HOME, THE. Basil King.

WAY OF THESE WOMEN, THE. E. Phillips Oppenheim.

WEAVER OF DREAMS, A. Myrtle Reed.

WEAVER OF WEBS, A. John Oxenham.

WEDDING DAY, THE. C. N. and A. M. Williamson.

WHITE FANG. Jack London.

WILD OLIVE, THE. Basil King.

WILLIAM, BY THE GRACE OF GOD. Marjorie Bowen.

WOMAN WITH THE FAN, THE. Robert Hichens.

WO₂. Maurice Drake.

WONDER OF LOVE, THE. E. Maria Albanesi.

YELLOW CLAW, THE. Sax Rohmer.

YELLOW DIAMOND, THE. Adeline Sergeant.

Methuen's One and Threepenny Novels

Fcap. 8vo. 1s. 3d. net

BARBARA REBELL. Mrs. Belloc Lowndes.

BY STROKE OF SWORD. Andrew Balfour.

DERRICK VAUGHAN, NOVELIST. Edna Lyall.

HOUSE OF WHISPERS, THE. William Le Queux.

INCA'S TREASURE, THE. E. Glanville.

KATHERINE THE ARROGANT. Mrs. B. M. Croker.

MOTHER'S SON, A. B. and C. B. Fry.

PROFIT AND LOSS. John Oxenham.

RED DERELICT, THE. Bertram Mitford.

SIGN OF THE SPIDER, THE. Bertram Mitford.

PRINTED BY MORRISON AND GIBB LIMITED, EDINBURGH

27/6/19.

CPSIA information can be obtained at www.ICGtesting.com
Printed in the USA
LVOW13*1443301013

359302LV00016B/164/P